# Online Dating For

BESTSELLING BOOK SERIES

## Internet Terms and Acronyms

AAMOF: As A Matter Of Fact

AFK: Away From Keyboard

ASAP: As Soon As Possible

ASCII: American Standard Code for Information Interchange

ASL: Age/Sex/Location

ATM: At The Moment

AWGTHTGTTA: Are We Going To Have To Go Through This Again?

AWYR: Awaiting Your Reply

AYOR: At Your Own Risk

AYPI: And Your Point Is

B4N: Bye For Now

BAB: Build A Bridge

BAK: Back At Keyboard

BBFN: Bye Bye For Now

BBL: Be Back Later

BBW: Big Beautiful Woman

BCNU: Be Seeing You

BEG: Big Evil Grin

BF: Boy Friend

BFFL: Best Friends For Life

BSOD: Blue Screen Of Death

BTAIM: Be That As It May

BTU: Back To You

BTW: By The Way

BTWBO: Be There With Bells On

BWK: Big Wet Kiss

C4N: Ciao For Now

CBL: Come Back Later

CU: See You

CUL: Catch You Later

CUL8R: See You Later

CYA: Cover Your A_ _

DLN: Don't Leave Now

DLTBBB: Don't Let The Bed Bugs Bite

EG: Evil Grin

F2F: Face to face

FAQ: Frequently Asked Question(s)

FOTCL: Falling Off The Chair Laughing

FTF: Face To Face

GFAK: Go Fly A Kite

GIGO: Garbage In Garbage Out

GL: Good Luck

GMAB: Give Me A Break

GOI: Get Over It

GTG: Got To Go

GTSY: Glad To See You

H&K: Hug and Kiss

HAK: Hugs and kisses

HHOK: Ha Ha, Only Kidding

HHO 1/2 K: Ha Ha, Only Half Kidding

HIG: How's It Going?

## For Dummies: Bestselling Book Series for Beginners

# Online Dating For Dummies®

Cheat Sheet

BESTSELLING BOOK SERIES

| | |
|---|---|
| HIH: Hope It Helps | PDQ: Pretty Darn(ed) Quick(ly) |
| ICBW: I Could Be Wrong | PITA: Pain In The A_ _ |
| IGP: I Gotta Pee | PMP: Peeing My Pants |
| IGTP: I Get The Point | ROFL: Rolling On The Floor Laughing |
| IMO: In My Opinion | ROTFL: Rolling On The Floor Laughing |
| ISO: In Search Of | ROTFLMHO: Rolling On The Floor Laughing My Head Off |
| J/K: Just Kidding | |
| JAM: Just A Minute | ROTFLSTC: Rolling On The Floor Scaring The Cat |
| JAS: Just A Second | RUOK: Are You OK? |
| KISS: Keep It Simple, Stupid | SFLA: Stupid Four Letter Acronym |
| KIT: Keep In Touch | SWF/SBM/SJF/etc: Single [insert ethnicity or religion here] Male/ Female |
| L8R: Later | |
| LOL: Laughing Out Loud | |
| LOL: Lots Of Love | SYT: See You Tonight |
| LOL: Lots Of Luck | TAFN: That's All For Now |
| LOLA: Laughing Out Loud Again | TBDL: To Be Discussed Later |
| LTIP: Laughing Till I Puke | TNTC: Too Numerous To Count |
| N1: Nice One | TTFN: Ta Ta For Now |
| N2S: Needless 2 Say | TTYL: Talk To You Later |
| NRN: No Reply Necessary | TTYS: Talk To You Soon |
| NTTAWWT: Not That There's Anything Wrong With That | TYCLO: Turn Your CAPS LOCK Off! |
| | TYVM: Thank You Very Much |
| OAO: Over And Out | TX: Thanks |
| OATUS: On A Totally Unrelated Subject | WGTG: Well, Got To Go |
| | WRU: Who Are You |
| OBTW: Oh, By The Way | YW: You're Welcome |
| PDA: Public Display of Affection | |

Copyright © 2004 Wiley Publishing, Inc.
All rights reserved.
Item 3815-2.
For more information about Wiley Publishing, call 1-800-762-2974.

## For Dummies: Bestselling Book Series for Beginners

# Online Dating FOR DUMMIES®

## by Judith Silverstein, MD, and Michael Lasky, JD

WILEY

Wiley Publishing, Inc.

**Online Dating For Dummies**®

Published by
**Wiley Publishing, Inc.**
111 River St.
Hoboken, NJ 07030-5774
www.wiley.com

For general information on our other products and services or to obtain technical support, please contact our Customer Care Department within the U.S. at 800-762-2974, outside the U.S. at 317-572-3993, or fax 317-572-4002.

Wiley also publishes its books in a variety of electronic formats. Some content that appears in print may not be available in electronic books.

Library of Congress Control Number: 2003114373

ISBN: 0-7645-3815-2

10 9 8 7 6 5 4 3 2 1

1B/QV/RR/QT/IN

**WILEY** is a trademark of Wiley Publishing, Inc.

# About the Authors

Most Dummies book authors have advanced degrees and have written scholarly dissertations in the subject matter of their book. Our authors don't but are nonetheless highly qualified. The concept of online dating is relatively new. We know of no university giving PhDs in online dating, but if there were, the authors would probably deserve an honorary one, due to their acquired depth of knowledge.

Their experience comes from the trenches. For 18 months, this was no research project for them. Both authors were engaged in a real life effort of scouring the online-dating universe for the *right* one. After much trial and much more error, they found each other, and then the *Dummies* people found them. They weren't only successful in their online-dating quest, but also in the most treacherous type of online dating: the long-distance relationship, because they don't yet live in the same city.

In researching this book, they have interviewed and gotten to know thousands of online daters and studied hundreds of online sites.

They're still very much happy together, the book is done, and they were able to keep their day jobs. This is what they do when they aren't writing:

**Judith Silverstein, MD** (or "Judy" in the book), always wanted to become a ballerina, or the Queen of France, but as often happens in life, things didn't work out as planned. She wound up as a Board certified dermatologist in private practice, who has been published in many accredited medical journals. In explaining the relationship between dermatology and online dating, she has been often quoted as saying, "You can get burned on a date, even if you are wearing sunscreen."

**Michael Lasky, JD,** spends his waking hours as a patent/trademark attorney and brand strategy consultant, and cofounder of Altera Law Group, in Minneapolis. He is a world recognized speaker and sort-of playwright, having written, amongst other things, *Nightmare on Namestreet,* a parody (licensed by Warner Bros.) about the dire consequences of choosing the wrong brand name for your product. He says that he coauthored *Online Dating For Dummies* to avoid being typecast as a Perry Mason type, but we think he did it for fun.

# Dedication

We dedicate this book to those who discovered the magic of online dating and by which their lives were made forever better.

# Authors' Acknowledgments

We wish to acknowledge the following people for their help:

To our families, for allowing us a year in front of a PC to write this book.

To our editors (Norm Crampton, Tim Gallan, and Chad Sievers), for giving us free reign to say what needed to be said, good or bad about this subject and for their enthusiasm about the subject matter. To our publisher and marketing specialist (in the persons of Diane Steele and Melisa Duffy), for trusting us to know what we were doing, even when we went out of the bookstore box and into the world of Internet marketing.

We'd also like to thank Sandy Blackthorn for trying to teach us how to write like dummies. It's not as easy as it looks, and they sure didn't teach this stuff where we went to college. Sandy made us look, well, not too dumb, and we owe her much thanks for that.

Finally, we want to thank the hundreds of people we met and interviewed. For those of you who are worried, just as no dolphins were injured in the writing of this book, so too are your identities safe.

—Judy and Michael

## Publisher's Acknowledgments

We're proud of this book; please send us your comments through our Dummies online registration form located at www.dummies.com/register/.

Some of the people who helped bring this book to market include the following:

*Acquisitions, Editorial, and Media Development*

**Senior Project Editor:** Tim Gallan

**Acquisitions Editor:** Norman Crampton

**Copy Editor:** Chad R. Sievers

**Editorial Program Assistant:** Holly Gastineau-Grimes

**Technical Editor:** Allen Wyatt, Discovery Computing

**Editorial Manager:** Christine Meloy Beck

**Editorial Assistants:** Melissa S. Bennett, Elizabeth Rea

**Cover Photos:** © Cocoon/ImageState/PictureQuest

**Cartoons:** Rich Tennant, www.the5thwave.com

*Production*

**Project Coordinator:** Courtney MacIntyre

**Layout and Graphics:** Joyce Haughey, Stephanie D. Jumper, Michael Kruzil, Barry Offringa, Heather Ryan, Scott Tullis, Shae Wilson

**Proofreaders:** Laura Albert, TECHBOOKS Production Services

**Indexer:** TECHBOOKS Production Services

**Publishing and Editorial for Consumer Dummies**

    **Diane Graves Steele,** Vice President and Publisher, Consumer Dummies

    **Joyce Pepple,** Acquisitions Director, Consumer Dummies

    **Kristin A. Cocks,** Product Development Director, Consumer Dummies

    **Michael Spring,** Vice President and Publisher, Travel

    **Brice Gosnell,** Associate Publisher, Travel

    **Kelly Regan,** Editorial Director, Travel

**Publishing for Technology Dummies**

    **Andy Cummings,** Vice President and Publisher, Dummies Technology/General User

**Composition Services**

    **Gerry Fahey,** Vice President of Production Services

    **Debbie Stailey,** Director of Composition Services

# Contents at a Glance

# Table of Contents

# Introduction

*T*he fact that you even have this book in your hands means that you're giving Internet dating at least passing consideration. Chances are you've heard about Internet dating from a friend, or an online banner ad caught your eye. And still you're skeptical. We were. Perhaps you have some fears from all those sensationalized horror stories, or you think that Internet dating is only for the disenfranchised or socially unskilled. But you're wrong. Approximately 20 million people can tell you otherwise. And if you survey your options (as we do in Chapter 2), you can realize what an amazing tool online dating is.

This book can get you off the fence and on the Internet-dating path, but with the skill of a seasoned pro. Figuring out Internet dating, like anything else, can be a process of trial and error. We want you to do the trial part, because, frankly, it's fun. The error part is another matter. We tell you our errors, and those of many others we talked to so you can avoid them. Figuring out how to attract the right prospects and understanding how to gravitate toward your compatible prospects is the key to Internet dating, and this book can help.

We, Judy and Michael, your authors, are regular people with day jobs, not professional writers. And this book wasn't some scientific research project for us. We lived it. Long before we wrote this book, we independently decided that Internet dating was right for us, and, in fact, we met each other online. We're proof that Internet dating works. As a result, we offer our advice based on our own experiences as well as the help of many other Internet daters.

Jumping into online dating with no preparation at all is possible. We see a lot of such *newbies* (Internet-dating rookies) meandering about the dating sites, spending the first few months frustrated and disappointed and believing that "no good matches are out there." Many people give up before they acquire the tools to make this great method of dating work. If you follow the techniques in this book, your odds of meeting great potential matches will greatly improve, and you'll have more fun in the process.

# *About This Book*

If you have no Internet-dating experience, you may want to read from beginning to end. We even include some basic computer technical how-to information for people who are lacking in computer skills. But we've written the book so that you can jump in any place and get what you want quickly.

As you read, keep in mind that Internet-dating services change their software constantly, and new dating sites come online weekly, so some information and screen displays may have changed by the time you read about them. Don't be concerned. Most of the tips and techniques in this book don't depend on the Internet site you choose.

# *Conventions Used in This Book*

When you come across lingo or jargon that requires a definition, we *italicize* the term. E-mail addresses and Web sites appear in monofont. And you're probably wondering what's the deal with the text in gray boxes? Those are sidebars. Sometimes we get a little sidetracked and want to relay an anecdote or discuss something that's a little off topic. In those cases, we use a sidebar.

# *Foolish Assumptions*

Actually, we don't assume all that much. You're probably interested in online dating, but we don't even assume that you have a computer. In fact, Chapter 3 talks about the kinds of hardware and software you need to get online. We do assume that you have a little bit of computer knowledge — enough to turn on your computer, connect to the Internet, send and receive e-mail, and surf the Web. If you haven't mastered these skills, check out the latest versions of *Windows For Dummies* by Andy Rathbone (or *Macs For Dummies* by David Pogue, if you use a Mac) and *The Internet For Dummies,* by John R. Levine, Margaret Levine Young, and Carol Baroudi. Wiley Publishing, Inc. publishes all three books.

This book is about enhancing your dating experience using the Internet *effectively* as a tool. For some people that means simply getting dates with suitable people, and for others, it means finding the love of their life. What we won't help you achieve is finding an e-mail order bride or helping you find porno sites masquerading as online-dating sites.

# How This Book Is Organized

Like all *For Dummies* books, the topics are organized by chapter, and related chapters are grouped together in parts. This book is a reference, not a tutorial, so the chapters are self-contained and can stand on their own. You don't have to read Chapter 4 to understand Chapter 5. We'd be glad if you read the book from cover to cover, but you don't have to. Feel free to skip around. Flip through the book and read what stands out for you.

The following is a brief summary of what each part of the book covers

## Part 1: Making Online Dating Work for You

Long before imagining that we would write this book (and obviously, before we met each other) we each independently ventured online with much enthusiasm, some trepidation, and quite frankly, absolutely no idea of what we were doing. What we came to realize was that online dating is an incredibly powerful tool for meeting great people. The possibilities for success are far greater than we imagined, but there are many blind alleys and wrong turns lying in wait, which can take you off the path to success. We discovered better ways to date online. We want to help you get your head in the right place by getting psyched up for the experience that awaits you, give you a fair comparison of the alternatives, and make you hardware savvy so that you don't get distracted from your goal.

## Part 1I: So Many Online Dating Sites, So Little Time

The hardest part of online dating may be choosing a site. Most people make the choice based on someone else's recommendation (whose interests and objectives may be different), an Internet review site's analysis (most are sponsored sites and not objective), or just the luck of the draw (the site that they've seen on a banner ad). A lot is riding on your choice and no site is right for everyone. If you choose the wrong site, you stand a good chance of becoming quickly disillusioned and dropping out before appreciating the power before you. In this part, we give you tips to help you find the right site for you before you pay your money so your chances of a good experience and outcome are vastly greater.

# Part III: Jumping Aboard for the Online Time of Your Life

This part is the nitty-gritty section. After you sign up for a site, you soon realize that you have to put forth some effort for it to work. We walk you through each step of the process from the Q&A, which seems entirely innocuous but isn't, to the essay questions, with which you will form a love-hate relationship. The information in Part III can show you how to project an accurate and powerful image of yourself that makes you stand out from the masses of competitors and draw good matches to your posted profile.

# Part IV: Initiating Contact: You've Got Mail

Don't assume that just because you get incoming e-mail that you can turn these initial messages into dates (or that you will want to). Initiating a relationship through anonymous e-mail is very different from meeting someone face to face. In this part, we provide some helpful guidelines that make it work. We help you know how to make those initial e-mails blossom into budding connections. More importantly, we show you other ways to improve your odds beyond sitting by the screen and waiting for your e-mail box to fill up and overcome that dreaded rejection, which you can't avoid, but you can manage. Finally, you want to meet some of the prospects that sound good. Who calls whom? Where do you meet? What next? This part covers it all.

# Part V: Skirting the Hazards of Online Dating

Some people are surprised to hear that Internet dating is safe, and if done properly, much safer than meeting a complete stranger face to face. But Internet dating, like with all dating, has risks. This part shows you how online dating gives you defenses you never had with in-person dating and powerful clues to watch for to minimize the chance of being deceived by people who aren't all they said they were.

Finally, one of the "hazards" of online dating that most people don't typically consider is becoming involved in a long-distance relationship, which is infinitely more likely online than in person.

Because so many people, including your authors, find themselves drawn to online prospects out of their locale, this part gives you a reality checklist of what to expect if you go down that long-distance path.

## Part VI: The Part of Tens

This part contains lists of two key issues including ten ways to succeed at online dating, and its evil twin, ten ways to screw up at online dating. After you read this book, coming back to the part of tens once and while makes a great three-minute refresher course.

# Icons Used in This Book

We use little pictures, called icons, to flag different kinds of info throughout the book. These icons appear in the book's margins. The icons and their meanings include

This icon covers practical how-to advice that can make your life easier. Here's a tip we thought we'd start with: If you're in a public place, such as a cafeteria eating lunch, or at an airport waiting area, bring this book with you and place it face up on the seat or table next to you. In a few minutes, you'll find singles coming over to you asking you about Internet dating. You'll see that everyone is curious about Internet dating, and the presence of this book is the perfect icebreaker to ask an innocent question (and perhaps see if you're datable)! Reading this book in public is much more convenient than renting a cute puppy (and you'll never need a pooper scooper).

This icon warns you so you can avoid hassles, headaches, embarrassment, and other unpleasantness.

This icon gives some conceptual information to keep in mind.

The Secret Sauce icon provides some really great insider info.

This icon includes words of wisdom or experiences straight from Michael's mouth, usually a male point of view, which is sometimes very different from his coauthor, Judy.

The She Said icon precedes words of wisdom and experiences from Judy, which is sometimes a counterpoint to Michael's.

# Where to Go from Here

If you have no clue what online dating is all about, head to Chapter 1. If you already have a clue or two, use the handy table of contents or index to find a topic that interests you. Jumping around (in the book, not in a public place) is okay.

# Tell Us What You Think

We want to hear about your online-dating experiences. After you've been online for a while, you may have some words of wisdom to tell us for future edition of this book. Let us know at

- ✔ mail@datingauthors.com
- ✔ www.datingauthors.com

# Part I
# Making Online Dating Work for You

The 5th Wave    By Rich Tennant

©RICHTENNANT

"It's really an entertaining piece of software.
There's non-stop action, plenty of surprises,
and it takes strategy and good reflexes to
win. Whoever thought online dating would
be this much fun?"

## In this part . . .

The key to success in many endeavors is having the right state of mind *and* the right tools! This is so true of online dating. In writing this book, and indeed in our own online experiences, we saw some people having lots of fun and success, while a few seemed to be running into only the wrong kind of people. We know that this is statistically impossible, so it seems to boil down to this: If you're psyched for success, and you don't get frustrated by computer glitches, your chances of being among the ones having fun are much greater. This part gets you psyched about online dating and gives you a fair comparison of the alternatives. Then we get you hardware-ready to hit the net so you will be ready *to go forth and meet.*

# Chapter 1

# The Magic of Online Dating

*C*lose your eyes and imagine you're walking down a crowded street in Manhattan during the lunchtime rush on a pleasant summer day. Assume you're a single woman, divorced six months ago, in your late 30s or early 40s, and finally ready to start dating again.

You scan the crowd. Half are women. Of the men, some are way too young, too old, or too unattractive, but among the 200 or so people in your field of vision, 15 or so, may be age and gender appropriate. And within that 15, you see three that strike you as datable. What do you do? Do you go up to each of them and ask them if they're single, straight, and interested in a date this Saturday? And even if you had the courage to do just that, would you really want to date a complete stranger? By the time you had the courage to walk over to him, he may have already headed back to work, and you just missed him and the two other prospects across the street. This is the dilemma of modern urban adult singles. Dates (and maybe even mates) are out there, but where? And in any case, how many dates can you go on before randomly stumbling into a match?

Now imagine this alternate reality: You log on XYZ-onlinedating.com. You run a search of the database of prospects that sound suitable to you: a man, divorced, living within 25 miles (40km) from your home, about 5-feet-10-inches (180cm) tall, weight 160 to180 lbs (70–80 kg), with a master's degree and children. The search returns 75 prospects, of which 55 have photos.

Scanning the photos, you find five who are extremely attractive, 15 more whose looks appeal to you, five more who give you a so-so chemical response, and the rest, you couldn't imagine dating. Of the 20 or so that pique your interest, you read their personal essays and preferences in women. Half of the essays are pretty lame, but a few show signs of life. In fact, after reading the essays of some of the guys you didn't think were visually interesting, you find a couple more who seem to have enough upstairs to make up for their apparent visual weakness. You write to a few, and a few respond. You've done this all in about two hours from your kitchen and in your pajamas, late at night.

Both scenarios are completely realistic. In each case, appropriate singles are out there but in the first case, you simply don't know who they are. Even if they held up signs saying "I'm available," you wouldn't know anything about them. So making contact is a double crapshoot. What are the odds that you will pick out a good, single one before you confidence goes below sea level?

# Adding a Little Order to Your Dating

Traditional dating is fundamentally random. Consider this:

By sheer luck, you're invited to a party. By chance, you meet a friend there. The friend is talking to someone who is single. You find the person physically interesting. He or she also shows signs of interest. You start a conversation that goes well. The party ends. One of you has the courage to propose exchanging phone numbers. You have a second date. You find out more about this person. You like what you see. So does he or she. And so on and so on.

Notice that if, at any step along the way, you realize you're not a match, you quit and wait until another random event (like the party) occurs and you try again.

Considering the advantages of online dating, especially when compared to finding a mate in the nonvirtual world, we are amazed that the human race has managed to propagate without the benefit of computers up to this point in time.

Internet dating offers these benefits:

> ✔ You know that (almost) every person posted online is available and looking for some kind of companionship, so that embarrassing question "are you in a relationship" is assumed to be "no".

✔ You know with a reasonable degree of accuracy, a great deal of data about each prospect (age, height, location, education, vocation, children, religion, and so on) before you exchange word one. (Dating sites that use personality profiles provide even more advanced data.)

✔ You know something about how he or she thinks and writes (depending on the dating site).

✔ You know roughly what he or she looks like.

✔ You know how to contact him or her.

✔ You have the chance to exchange e-mail and talk on the phone without ever revealing your identify, until you're comfortable doing so.

✔ You can move on to the next prospect quickly if there seems to be little interest after initial contacts.

✔ You can do all this for less than what it costs you to go out to dinner at a moderate-priced restaurant.

No other form of dating compares in its ability to bring so many available singles together with tons of information about each, and it provides a quick and efficient way to ferret out matches.

# Why Online Dating Is a Good Idea

You're reading this book, so you're at least intrigued by the concept of online dating. If you're not sure if this mode of dating is right for you, the next few sections offer some selling points, and if you need more convincing, check out the rest of Part I.

## An almost limitless supply of people are online

Remember the earlier example about meeting someone at a party? Never mind how random that whole event is. How *frequent* is it that you find yourself in a situation where you're surrounded by age-appropriate singles? Online, you're surrounded by age-appropriate singles every time you log on. And if you don't find enough people at one site, you can go to any of hundreds of other sites, or you can simply wait a while and a new crop of singles will have signed on.

In effect the number of potential matches is essentially limitless and perpetually changing. Compare that to your current social circles. In addition to college, when was the last time you were exposed to a few hundred age-appropriate matches?

## Internet dating is way more convenient than traditional dating

When was the last time you prospected for dates in your pajamas at 3 a.m.? The whole concept of virtual dating is that the community of single prospects is available to you whenever you want to meet them. For people with day jobs, children, and other social obligations, prospecting online at odd hours is the only way to go.

Not only can you log on at odd hours, but you also can log on for short amounts of time. In our example of the party, you have to dress up and commit to several hours of socializing with the possibility of not even meeting one age-appropriate single. You know who is age appropriate online, and you can initiate contact in ten minutes and log off. Then log on again later or the next day and see if you got a response.

## You can parallel-date at warp speed

In our party example, your odds of striking up a conversation with *one* potential prospect is relatively small, but the chances of meeting two or three? Well, your chances are right up there with being hit by a meteorite.

Online, you can certainly initiate contact with multiple prospects at the same time because the process of initiating contact is so simple. Then you can engage them in e-mail and phone exchanges until you can determine which, if any, are worth dating. If none, you just go back to the trough.

Some "brilliant" mastermind once said dating is a "numbers game." As you meet more people, your odds of meeting a "good one" improve. Internet dating is entirely designed around fast and efficient initial contacts. After you see potential, you can then slow down the normal dating speed and concentrate on determining if you have a true match — just like in traditional dating.

## Internet dating eliminates the awkwardness of first introductions

Are you good at walking up to a stranger and saying hello? Not too many people are and we weren't either. In online dating, the effort of making first contact is so slight that the fear of rejection simply melts away. After you initiate an e-mail exchange, a reply arrives and the ice thaws. For many people, just getting past the initial encounter successfully makes the rest of dating easier.

# Unlocking Internet Dating's Secrets

If you're going to succeed at online dating, you have to recognize that it's different from traditional dating. So, what's the secret to Internet dating? In order to succeed, remember to use the Internet as a way to gain insight into the available and appropriate singles. Remember that a dating site is much more than a directory of available singles; it's a means to get into the prospect's character and personality by virtue of an ongoing exchange that takes place before you meet! And that's why Internet dating is traditional dating turned on its head. When you finally do meet your prospect in person, you aren't strangers. The date is with someone who is a suitable match with respect to age, values, and future goals. The date feels like a reunion and proceeds at a much more advanced level. The date is like getting "together again. . . . for the first time" (thanks Yogi Berra).

Therefore, to succeed at Internet dating, you must

- ✔ Have a good sense of who you are

- ✔ Have a good sense of what you're looking for in a date/mate

- ✔ Have a reliable way to get online, surf the Web, send and receive e-mail, and maybe even take part in online chats

- ✔ Read the prospects' profiles carefully (for example, looking past the photos) and try to find nuggets of information about the prospects that make them suitable

- ✔ Engage in e-mail exchanges with prospects to ferret out additional information that can tell you if your prospects are a reasonable match

- ✔ If you discover you're not a match, you can disengage quickly, and move on with minimal discomfort.

If you follow this plan, which we explain thoroughly in this book, you can vastly improve your odds of de-randomizing the dating process.

# Overcoming Preconceived Notions of Who Is Online

If we have convinced you that online dating makes perfect sense as an efficient and effective way to meet appropriate people, make sure you head into the process in the right state of mind.

Every new invention ever developed has had its naysayers. Internet dating is just one more example that has its detractors. The press loves to run stories of nightmare experiences of online daters, but in fact these stories are rare, and certainly more likely with encounters at a bar. We also suspect that these nightmarish online encounters are far more likely to occur in the many available free chat rooms, rather than a reputable online dating service with its requisite essay and cost commitments.

The fact is that Internet dating is *very* mainstream today. The numbers of people reported dating online in North America ranges from 10 to 30 million! And Internet dating includes more than just 20-somethings. The fastest-growing segment of online daters is older than 40, and it makes perfect sense, because that group is the least likely to have access to more traditional avenues for dating (see Chapter 2).

Furthermore, dating sites indicate that their members tend to be more highly educated and financially well off than the general public. Part of that may be due to the fact that Internet dating requires some knowledge and access to computers, as well as the ability to pay the subscription fee.

So if you're thinking that Internet dating is for computer geeks or desperate people who can't get a date, you need only spend a few minutes perusing any national dating site to change your mind in a hurry.

# Chapter 2

# Considering the Alternatives to Online Dating

*In This Chapter*

▶ Exploring some traditional ways of meeting people

▶ Checking out some newer, creative ways to meet people

*D*ating methods have been around since before the pyramids. In fact, except for Adam and Eve, who had very limited choices, people have been struggling for eons to find the perfect mate.

Many societies employed matchmakers to arrange every aspect of mating. (Some still do.) Fortunately, though, after writing and printing were invented, other means of finding a mate became available. Still, few new methods of meeting people showed up until just a few decades ago. At that time, plenty of options appeared, and many are still plausible alternatives to Internet dating.

In this chapter, we share some alternatives to Internet dating. And the reason we've included it in a book *about* Internet dating? We think that for perspective, you need to be aware of the various options available.

However, remember that Internet dating is growing at double-digit rates every year while other forms of finding a date are flat or falling off. Internet dating, although far from perfect, is clearly the most effective and efficient method of getting introduced to a large number of available singles. After you check out these alternatives (and compare them with the benefits of online dating, which we tell you about in this book), we think you'll agree with our assessment.

# Traditional Ways to Find a Date without a Computer

Some dating and mating methods have remained unchanged for decades, if not centuries. This section takes a look at some of those traditional methods and sorts out the pros and (mostly) cons of each.

## Fishing off the company pier: Meeting people at work

You might think the office is a reasonable place to meet people. It's a shame, but using the office to find a potential date is a bad idea (and completely taboo).

At your workplace, you see how a person interacts with other people. You get to see him or her under stress, at lunch, in meetings, and especially at office parties. Where else can you find that many opportunities to observe and consider a potential date?

But, alas, instead of becoming the great dating/mating ground, the office has become a virtual dating desert because of the risk of sexual harassment and lawsuits. The few who venture into that demilitarized zone do so at extreme peril. The reason? Usually, secret affairs are the only office romances that survive because secrecy is the common denominator that makes them work in the present legal environment. In other words, office lovers usually keep their romances secret or one person finds a new job.

And if by chance the latter doesn't happen, you have another downside to consider: In the event that the romance is unsuccessful, you can't escape the painful fact that you must frequently interact with the very person you once shared intimacy and love with.

So, in short, even though the office is the best place to meet people and watch them interact in a variety of eye-opening situations, it's the worst place to find a potential date due to a variety of, well, eye-opening situations. Our advice? Scratch workplace romance.

# *Meeting people at bars and other smoky places*

Trust us, bars are really inefficient places to meet people. Why? For the following reasons:

- Your *hit rate* (odds of leaving the bar with a phone number or e-mail address) is very low for the time invested.

- You need to dress up to look attractive, which takes time.

- You lose out on much-needed sleep. The best bar hopping occurs late at night, which limits the number of consecutive days you can bar hop without cutting into minimum sleeping requirements and childcare needs (the latter, mind you, already incurring expenses before you have your first drink).

- The atmosphere of bars is loud, dark, and smoky — rarely the best atmosphere for getting to know someone.

- Intoxication may skew your judgment in terms of who you meet (and may endanger your life on the drive home).

- Walking up to a complete stranger takes great courage.

- Standing in a bar alone takes almost as much courage.

- Everyone in the bar witnesses your rejection.

- The women's restroom always has a line!

So why do people go to bars anyway? In some places, a local bar is *the* social hall, especially in small towns where very few appropriate venues are available for singles.

To lessen the intimidation factor of the bar scene — primarily, to avoid feeling uncomfortable alone — many people go to bars in a group. Women, who find safety in numbers, particularly go to bars in groups. However, being in a group actually makes it harder for an individual to approach you.

Because of the noise, smoke, and general lack of illumination, bars are very tough places to get to know someone. Of course, if you find an interesting person at a bar, we suggest that you both *leave* and go to a 24-hour restaurant or some other public place that you can talk. But in the world of bar-hopping etiquette, doing so is rarely possible on the first meeting, lest your new interest misinterpret your suggestion to depart as an overt sexual suggestion.

Furthermore, not everyone at a bar wants to find a date. The reality is that many people go to bars to socialize with friends — not necessarily with the expectation of meeting new people.

## Meeting people at your church or religiously sponsored singles event

Many people use church- or synagogue-sponsored functions as a way to meet singles. Although we certainly see nothing wrong with that approach, we can think of some disadvantages:

- ✔ You may already know everyone.
- ✔ The group rarely has a reasonable balance between men and women.
- ✔ Even if a balance exists between the genders, they may be decades apart in age.
- ✔ Just like dating at the office, if you end a relationship with someone you met at church, you have to see that person regularly at church in the future. (However, changing churches is easier than changing jobs.)
- ✔ If you break up, your relationship may be a source of lively gossip for the rest of the congregation.
- ✔ If you've been affiliated with your church a long time, odds are you've already dated everyone in the church that you remotely tolerate.

## Meeting people at social or special-interest clubs

Any club or organization you're a member of is a legitimate venue for date hunting. However, that doesn't make it a *good* place for such an endeavor. Here are some reasons why you may not want to find a potential date at a social or special-interest club:

- ✔ If group members can see through your purpose for joining the organization — to get a date — they may toss you out, or at least no longer consider you a serious member.

> ✔ If you date a member of the organization and then break up, how do you feel about running into him/her at every organizational meeting thereafter? It can get pretty uncomfortable.
>
> ✔ If you fail with one club member, finding another person to date within the group may be tough after the group has had a chance to watch your past intra-club dating activities.

If an organization is designed for any purpose other than dating, such as a gardening club or an antiques club, then the group may only have a few available, willing singles.

## Meeting people on cruise ships and singles vacations

If you believe the ads, cruises are the hottest way to vacation and an even hotter way to meet singles. In truth, very few cruises are specifically designated for singles, not even the *Love Boat.*

Some tour operators book a portion of the ship for singles. If you're considering this option, ask the tour operators how many singles they expect on each ship. Asking them the expected age distribution is even more important. And remember that *buyer beware* applies to whatever they say. For example, if you're 50-something and you end up on a 30-something cruise, you're guaranteed an uphill struggle to meet an age-appropriate date/mate.

Don't forget the price tag, either. You have to pay a hefty singles-supplement for a private room. (And you'll probably want one unless you're okay with having your roommate pace the decks all night while you have some private time with a new-found friend.)

For those of you seeking an age-*in*appropriate date (someone more than 10 years younger than you), a cruise ship is the worst place to be. The reality is that in person, your maturity and accomplishments won't match up to a 20- or 30-something. Yeah, we know — sometimes the truth hurts.

You can also choose from a few singles-only vacation spots (mostly in the Caribbean), like Club Med. However, even Club Med, which grew up on the singles crowd, has become family friendly (encouraging families with very young children) just to stay afloat. These vacations are usually pricey and carry no guarantees of meeting anyone. But at least you'll get a tan.

## Come sail away with me

When I became single again, I didn't have a clue how to reintegrate myself into the singles' scene. Naturally, I sought the advice of a married friend, who, in retrospect, was probably the last person I should've asked.

My friend said that joining a sailing club was a great way to meet singles. Although she was married, she knew several people who had found mates, or at least dates, in her club. So I figured, "Why not?" and checked into it.

I found that because I didn't own a sailboat, I had to wait until a crew needed an extra hand, which could be this season or next (the season where I live is only four months long). I also discovered that I could be assigned to a crew of six or eight — after I shelled out many thousands of dollars to be in the club and to help pay for the cost of boat rental and maintenance. And, of course, I would have additional expenses, such as for the proper attire to make a landlubber look like an up-and-coming mariner and for the many apres-sail drinkathons.

I found that because sailing involves a lot of setup, I had to start at 6 a.m. at the dock (5 a.m. from my house) and end at 9 p.m. every Saturday or Sunday, weather permitting. And I found that failure to attend every week was considered a mutiny, so I would have to cancel most of my weekend activities throughout the sailing season.

Now all that stuff was essentially okay. But the clincher: I discovered that even after following all those rules and guidelines, my crew of three men and three women may all be married (usually to each other). At best, I could hope for one single person (hopefully a woman) on each boat. Considering the odds, I never hoisted anchor.

Any dating between people from different geographic locations increases the chance of becoming involved in a long-distance relationship (LDR); we definitely have nothing against LDRs. (Judy and Michael live in different cities.) Nonetheless, we know how difficult sustaining an LDR is, and it's certainly not for everyone. The best way to avoid an LDR is the same as the best way to avoid smoking: Don't ever start.

# Relying on luck: Meeting people in random places

You don't need a statistics degree to realize that finding a dating match is frighteningly random. So why not just let nature take its course? After all, if you were married previously, you probably did it that way before.

We know a couple of good reasons why meeting people in random places may not work again:

- ✔ The last time you met your mate — or significant other or whatever your term of choice is — you were probably in a social environment with a high concentration of singles (such as college) and mating was the name of the game (with occasional studying thrown in to keep your parents happy). But odds are that nowadays you're in a full-time job somewhere in the suburbs, you may have children, and your access to other singles is limited. Furthermore, your time is seriously limited. You have few waking hours to be out there, and you need to use those hours more productively.

- ✔ You're not as young as you used to be, and your pool of single friends is vastly smaller than it used to be (many are married).

In short, you can't leave matters to chance any longer.

## Meeting people through personal ads

Until recently, newspapers were the main non-face-to-face option for connecting singles. Granted, even though some people used personal ads in the past, many people didn't consider them a viable choice to meet other singles because of their brevity. (Try sharing all the information you need to share in a 30-word ad.) Now with the Internet, personal ads have lost most of the appeal they had. In order to hold their ground, many newspaper publishers have combined 21st-century technology with their paper and ink format. Typically nowadays, you can have one of these options added to your print personal ad:

- ✔ **A voicemail box:** You and your prospects can listen to each other and leave a voice message.

  We think the voicemail box is a great addition. It makes the major problems with print ads (they're very short, full of cryptic acronyms, and completely unstructured) more tolerable. However, this voice feature doesn't come cheap. Some newspapers give you the ad for free, but require respondants to reply by voice only at $2.99/minute or so. (They also charge you to listen to the responses.) That cost may discourage prospects from responding to several ads. Anyway, we still think personal ads are likely to go the way of rotary phones and eight-track players.

✔ **A posting on your newspaper's Web site:** People can access your personal ad online.

We think the Web-site posting of the print ad simply begs the question "Why not a real Internet dating site?"

## Meeting people through your friends

Doesn't meeting people through your friends sound so simple and harmless? Trust us, it's not. Meeting love interests is a real pain in the keister for your amigos.

Using this option, you need to enlist your friends' help to ferret out those hidden singles, like buried treasure, who live among you but rarely appear in your social circles. You're hypothetically supposed to:

1. **Call every one of your friends — and even casual acquaintances — and demand that they search their souls for names of any singles.**

2. **Warn your friends that you'll call back in a week, ready to receive this list.**

3. **Repeat as needed until you achieve satisfaction, or until your friends no longer talk to you.**

Extracting contacts from your friends is like a dental procedure. And just as with a dental procedure, you may require an anesthetic before you have the nerve to call your friends again.

This method may result in a (meager) harvest, but in any event, we think the price may be too great.

## Getting desperate: Meeting people on blind dates

"I've been on so many blind dates, I should get a free dog."

*Wendy Leibman, comedienne*

Everyone hates them. Need we say more?

# Newer Ways to Find a Date (Mostly) without a Computer

The advent of the computer and Internet certainly livened up the dating world, but some technology-free (or at least technology-lean) methods have also emerged that try to match singles. Some started before the Internet, so we're not sure whether they'll survive. Others are like halfway houses between traditional means (like personal ads) and online methods. Perhaps some singles perceive these methods as a bit less challenging than diving deep into cyberspace.

## Joining an arranged lunch club

If you live in a large city, a luncheon club organizer may be available to you. Essentially, these clubs are artificially created lunch encounters. Prior to the lunch, you may only know the time, place, cost, and that the meal will have an equal number of males and females who are roughly age appropriate. Some are lunches of eight or more singles at one table, and others are just for two at a time, much like an arranged blind date (yikes!).

With lunch clubs, the two-for-lunch arrangements are much less competitive, but if the date isn't going well, you're in for a *long* lunch. Try to find a lunch club that gives you a chance to look over the selection of prospects instead of requiring you to accept the blind assignment.

Some lunch-club arrangers run background checks on their participants. If this matters to you, be sure to ask before you sign up. (Note that the quality of the background checks varies greatly. Some are worthless. See Chapter 18 for the details.)

Arranged lunches do have advantages:

- ✔ **The lunches are live, not virtual.** You have face-to-face contact with your dates.

- ✔ **Unlike other social settings, the lunches are managed encounters.** You always find age-appropriate, gender-appropriate singles around the table.

- ✔ **The participants or lunch organizers don't hold it against you if you're a computer neophyte.** You don't have to worry about accidentally closing the window and logging off.

- ✔ **You can eat, which can be a great consolation if all else fails.** Just drown yourself in the French onion soup if you're totally bored.

And they have some disadvantages:

- ✔ **The lunches are essentially blind dates arranged by people you don't know.** Usually, the arrangers only have your bio to work with and the stable of available lunch dates for the day. At best, you may manage one lunch a week (more likely one per month, according to your contract).

- ✔ **The lunches take time — and a lot of it.** You have to show up and stay for a meal lasting one to two hours.

- ✔ **The lunches are very expensive.** Although your price may vary, we've heard of organizations that charge upwards of $200 to $300 per meeting (and that doesn't even include lunch). On top of that, if you're trying to meet royalty or titans of industry, expect to pay a lot more for the exclusivity. Marrying into money doesn't come cheap.

People who are shy or you don't stand out in a crowd may feel uncomfortable competing with a group of people at a table. The two-for-lunch arrangements may suit you better. But remember that then you have only one prospect to meet per lunch and the cost is still comparable to being situated with eight others.

In an eight-at-a-time lunch, the seating arrangement at the table is critical, but you almost certainly won't know whom you should sit next to until it's too late. When in doubt, sit in the middle rather than the end of the table.

## Guess who's coming to lunch?

Who's the person you'd least like to be paired with on a two-for-lunch date? How about your ex? Well, a friend told us of such an experience, and really it's not that far-fetched. All the lunch arranger has to work with are some very tangible requirements (like height, weight, hair color, and common interests). Obviously people who lived together for a long time probably have similar activities and tastes. We're actually surprised that it doesn't happen more often.

# Video dating

This form of dating is actually relatively old. Cheap videotaping machines were available about 30 years ago.

The concept is this: You pay a hefty sum to have the video-dating company make a short video of you talking about yourself. You also fill out a questionnaire about your likes and dislikes. The dating company then assembles your profile and some photos into a book and invites others to come to the office to review prospects. You're allowed a certain number of dates for a fixed fee, but the prospect date must approve before you receive his or her phone number. To do that, your prospect must come to the office to view your photos and video.

The process is rather arcane and particularly expensive, but it does have one advantage: The dating company has the ability to screen its members. (The reason the company can afford to screen is that you pay quite a lot for the service. It's pre-included in that particularly expensive fee.) Just so you know, the screening is usually for a criminal record in your local community *only*. If you're wondering about the company's screening procedures, you need to ask explicitly. You also need to sign a waiver to be screened yourself.

Keep in mind that all the viewings take a great amount of time, so you'll find yourself hanging around the dating company's office a lot.

# Speed (or turbo) dating

We're amazed that it took so many millennia for people to think up speed dating. It's so clever and simple. And speed dating requires no hardware.

Imagine combining the speed of Internet dating with the face-to-face contact of a bar. Then throw in the fact that everyone is present trying to meet each other. Speed dating works like this:

1. **You find a speed/turbo dating venue in your town and sign up.**

2. **You meet at the designated place and time and take a seat at one of eight or ten tables for two.**

   A person of the opposite sex is also seated at each table.

3. When the *starter* (person in charge) launches you off, you then have seven minutes to converse, engage, cajole, or just plain stare at your table mate.

4. When the time is up, you switch to a new table with a new partner.

5. After you commune with all eight to ten turbo daters, you vote for those you want to see again and turn your score card in to the organizer.

6. You go home.

7. If — and only if — both of you voted for each other do you get the person's contact info.

   Consequently, you may get a chance to talk again with all ten people, or you may end up not getting to communicate again with any of them.

If you don't mind winding up with a lot of phone calls, you may want to vote for all ten prospects after a speed-dating session. At least you have a chance to follow up further with some of them.

Speed dating favors people who are fast on their feet. If you're a good interviewer or a stand-up comic, you'll do well. On the flip side, speed dating presents you with the possibility for some pretty strong rejection — especially painful if the rejection comes from people you thought were sure bets for future contact.

## Going to chat rooms

A *public chat room* is an electronic version of Hyde Park Corner in London. In a chat room, anyone can get on a soapbox and say anything they like to whoever is willing to listen . . . or no one at all.

---

### It's just like mixing peanut butter with chocolate

If you don't find speed dating frenzied enough, you may want to try adding a touch of suspense (and humiliation) by joining a speed-dating *cruise*. It works just like regular speed dating except that you and all the other people — yep, those you reject and those who reject *you* — are all confined on board for the duration of the cruise.

After a few rounds, you'll be climbing the mast, desperately looking for signs of land or a passing Russian submarine to seek asylum.

A public chat room is an electronically formed *instant* community. Kind of like a rowdy bar, with plenty of drunks, no rules, no order, and no bouncer.

Some chat rooms have no specific purpose, and others are founded around a topic. Of course, dating is the focus in some chat rooms.

What are chat rooms good for? After much unscientific and painfully dull research, we conclude that they have no purpose whatsoever.

So why do they exist?

- ✔ They came into existance as the first true online-dating sites (before dating software was developed).

- ✔ They can be at least as entertaining as Jerry Springer and of similar quality.

- ✔ Anyone can join, and they usually don't have fees. They're often made up of potty-mouthed anarchists and teenagers.

Can you find the love of your life there? Sure, but it's a heck of a random walk. You may as well try bobbing in the ocean.

 Next time you want to spend quality time hanging out in a public chat room, consider equally effective and entertaining alternatives, like looking for dust bunnies under the bed or changing your motor oil in the winter.

# Chapter 3

# Maximizing Your Ability to Connect Online

*In This Chapter*

▶ Knowing what hardware is essential for online dating

▶ Figuring out what kind of Internet Service Provider (ISP) and e-mail account you need

▶ Familiarizing yourself with Internet lingo

*Everything should be made as simple as possible.*
*But not simpler.*

Albert Einstein

*I*f your fear of online dating has anything to do with an inner fear of computers and the Internet, this chapter should alleviate it. Although this chapter provides some techie information, we want to give you the necessary information to gnaw on and digest for successful online dating — and not one byte more.

## Gearing Up with the Hard Stuff (Hardware Needs)

Computers, connection lines, and printers — all three items fall into a category called *hardware,* and you need access to one of each for Internet dating. This section gives you cut-to-the chase explanations about the essentials.

## Get thee to a computer, any computer

Obviously if you want to date online, you need access to a computer. But what kind? And with how much horsepower? Well, if your present computer is fewer than 3 years old, it's probably more than adequate. The type of computer doesn't matter. PC or Mac is fine.

Note that you don't actually have to own a computer to date online. You can use a computer at a library (if you don't mind pesky librarians looking over your shoulder to conduct a routine porn-check) or at a friend's house (if you don't mind your friend reading your e-mail). A cyber cafe works fine, too. Keep in mind, though, that non-home use of a computer puts you at risk for loss of privacy. A criminal-minded but tech-smart individual can steal your password and view your Internet activities because you leave a trail long after you leave the computer. For this reason, we suggest changing your password frequently, like washing your hands after you use the restroom.

Change your e-mail password every time you visit an Internet cafe — especially overseas, where your risks of password piracy are significantly increased.

One of the places you don't want to date online is your office (unless you're the boss). Many companies monitor employee use of the computer, either directly or by logging Web sites visited. Regardless of how you retrieve your mail, such as with Yahoo or Hotmail, your company can fully monitor your activities. And even if your company doesn't mind whether you date online from work, do you really want the geeks in the information systems department monitoring your dating traffic?

## Select thine link to the Internet

To connect to the Internet, you need an *Internet Service Provider (ISP)*, a company that connects your computer to the Internet. And you can choose from several. An easy way to find ISPs is to ask about them at your local computer store.

An ISP uses hardware to connect your computer to the Internet, and the difference between the various types of connections is speed.

If you have a dial-up connection (one that uses your regular phone line), you spend a lot of time waiting for graphics, particularly photos, to download. Because Internet dating has lots of photos, dial-up systems can be very frustrating.

If you can hook up to a high-speed connection — DSL (digital subscriber line), cable modem, or satellite — you'll immediately notice the improvement in your surfing and dating experience because Web pages appear much faster. However, high-speed connections cost more than dial-up services.

If you can't get high-speed access in your area (or don't want to bother), don't sign up for a dating site that's full of unnecessary (but eye-catching) graphics. You'll also appreciate sites that have small, thumbnail-sized photos of prospects because the photos download quickly. However, you have to squint to see them. (If you want a close-up look, you can still click on the picture for the full-size version, but you'll have to wait while it downloads.)

## Buyeth a printer

Benjamin Franklin may have said the only two things in life you can count on are death and taxes. If he were still alive today, he probably would add computer crashes to that list. Trust us, we know all about computer crashes. Therefore, if you value some of your e-mail correspondence, save it by printing it, which means you need to own a printer. (If you're using a library PC for your online dating, you can just use the library's printer, but you usually have to pay 10 cents per page.)

If you decide you absolutely must print a really juicy e-mail when you're at the library or public place, conduct a test print of something less titillating before you print the spicy stuff. Very often the printer next to your computer isn't attached to your computer. (Why do they do that?) Your computer may print to the network printer at the desk of Ms. Nofunnystuff, the head librarian.

# Acquiring the Soft Goods (Software Needs)

The online-dating site provides most of the software you'll need, so you're practically all set. You just need to consider one specific piece of software: an e-mail account for online dating.

## Examining the two types of e-mail accounts

You can choose from two major kinds of e-mail accounts, and they're *very* different:

### Web mail accounts

Web mail accounts are e-mail accounts, like `Yahoo.com` and `Hotmail.com`, that you can only read while you're connected to the Web. As soon as your Web connection ends, your messages disappear from the screen. They're not lost, but the messages aren't saved on your computer.

Web mail is nice because you can easily use it at a Web cafe, library, or on a friend's computer. It leaves no e-mail traces behind on any computer you use. But, if you want to see your messages when you're offline (on the computer but not on the Internet), you must print them or download them (see the section "Buyeth a printer" for the challenging details).

### POP mail accounts

You see POP mail accounts, also known as POP3, which stands for Post Office Protocol mostly at the office, using programs like Outlook and Eudora. They're very slick in that they enable you to save, store, and categorize e-mail. They also enable you to keep all your mail on your own PC in case you want to read it when you're offline. If your PC crashes, however, your mail is lost (unless you opted to save a copy at the e-mail provider's simultaneously).

The best e-mail choice for a determined Internet dater is Web mail. A few sites offer you both options, but if not, go with the Web type. Web mail gives you more flexibility, and usually it's free. It also enables you to stay in touch even when you're on vacation, and in the world of online-dating etiquette, dropping out of sight — even for a few days — is the equivalent of being dumped. (We talk about online-dating etiquette in Chapter 15.)

## Creating a special e-mail account for dating only

You'll want to set up a special e-mail account exclusively for Internet dating. Even if your dating site includes its own e-mail service, as soon as you meet someone you like, you'll probably want to *go private,* that is, — communicate outside of the dating service's system so that the site can't monitor your communications. (Besides, prospects often ask for your private e-mail address so that you can send photos to each other.)

Set up a special e-mail account exclusively for dating to keep your dating e-mails separate from your real-life e-mails. Be careful; you don't want to give the person your "wrong" e-mail address. He or she may be a psycho and continue to harass you in some way. (Psychos aren't overly common, but just like in face-to-face dating, you do meet your occasional freak.) If you have a free account established just for dating, you can eliminate the problem by simply closing the account and opening a new one if someone stalks you online. But if you commingle your dating mail with your regular mail on your permanent e-mail account (like AOL), you'd be reluctant to close it, even if you're getting harassed or *spammed* (getting flooded with unsolicited junk email) by a dater. Best choice? Channel all your dating mail into a free, disposable account. We like Yahoo because it is quite easy to set up and has less razzmatazz to deal with than many others. If you are an AOL user, you may be able to use one of your spare e-mail accounts. These can be easily disposed of if you run into undesirable and persistent individuals.

## Using instant messaging

Instant messaging is best known as IM or IRC (Internet Relay Chat). In short, it enables you to send and receive short messages quickly — almost instantly. Presently, AOL's IM system is the most commonly used, but you don't have to subscribe to AOL to use it. In fact, almost all pay online-dating sites provide their own IM services.

# Talking the Talk: Internet Lingo

If you've been around computer types long enough, you realize that many people believe the way to make others think they're highly knowledgeable is to use as many computer acronyms as possible. Online dating is pretty much the same, but we warn you not to fall into that trap.

# Internet dating-specific terms and acronyms

So that you're armed and prepared to field the most common acronyms, even if you don't use them, here are the most common of them:

- **LOL:** Laughing out loud. This all too common and truly annoying acronym is the e-mail equivalent of the sit-com laugh track. It means "I am laughing now" or "This is funny, ha ha." We guess there's a point to LOL because e-mail lacks facial gestures. However, if what you're writing is funny enough for your recipient to get the joke, don't tack on LOL. A poor joke or weak sarcastic remark isn't made funny because you follow it with this acronym.

- **ISO:** In search of. This one is a throwback from the days of newspaper personal ads, where each word cost a dollar. ISO equals "in search of two dollars saved."

- **SWF/SBM/SJF/and so on:** Single (insert ethnicity or religion here) male/female. For example, SWF stands for single white female; SBM, single black male; and SJF, single Jewish female. The problem is that you can't always guess what the middle initial means. Like with SCF. Is that single *Christian* female? Single *Catholic* female?

There are literally thousands of acronyms, and if you want to spend a few days gazing at them, set your search engine to *Internet Acronyms* and read on, dude.

# Emoticons: Keyboard smileys and such

As if acronyms weren't enough, someone somewhere figured out the keyboard equivalent of the smiley face . . . and many more faces. These keyboard-created faces are called *emoticons,* and like acronyms, they often look stupid to the recipient.

Regardless, you need to know what they are so you can at least recognize one when you see it. Here are some of the more common emoticons:

:)      Happy person

:(      Sad person

:-)     Happy person with a nose

:-(     Sad person with a nose

:——( Person who is sad because he or she has a large nose

Again, there are thousands, perhaps millions more and more ridiculous. Set your search engine to *Internet emoticon* for an eyeful.

# Part II
# So Many Online Dating Sites, So Little Time

The 5th Wave          By Rich Tennant

"I'm looking for someone who will love me for who I think I am."

## In this part . . .

The hardest part of online dating may be the step of choosing a site. A lot is riding on your choice. If you choose a site that caters to the wrong age group, lacks the features you will ultimately want, or just doesn't have enough subscribers, it may sour your experience. As a beginner, you're likely to be drawn to flashy Web pages, but the true value of a site is its ability to deliver to you people with whom you would be comfortable. That means no site is right for everyone.

In this part, we make you a savvy user *before* you make your first purchase. You'll know the questions to ask and features to seek out so that your chances of finding a good fit from the start will be vastly improved.

# Chapter 4

# Wheeling and Dealing: Dating Site Cost Options

*H*ow much is the perfect mate worth to you? Personally, we think that's an absurd question because no one ever really knows whether they're getting the *perfect* anything, let alone mate. Furthermore, you can't measure a perfect mate in dollars. But because dollars are indeed what you have to spend to get on the better online-dating sites, we figure a bit of a comparison can give you some perspective of their value.

So in this chapter, we look at the costs involved with Internet-dating sites, and this chapter highlights the benefits and drawbacks of free versus pay sites.

## Talk About a Bargain!

An online-dating site does two fundamental things that you can't do yourself:

✔ It introduces you to a large population of people who are visiting the site for only one reason: to meet singles.

✔ It provides you with a system (profile postings and e-mail exchanges) to narrow down the field to a manageable number of potentially appropriate matches.

Believe it or not, through Internet dating you can improve your chances of meeting the person of your dreams by 500 times (assuming that you'll have access to 500 more potentially appropriate people than you have now). And you can do it for the equivalent sum that you'd spend on any one of the following:

- A dinner for one, with wine, at a four-star restaurant (about $85 plus tip)
- A large sackful of hammers
- 250 pounds of kitty litter (for a really heavy kitty)

Each of those items costs $75 to $125, which is about the cost of six months on an Internet-dating pay site. Hardly a significant sum, especially if the outcome changes your life. On the flip side, imagining that any of the preceding items could ever have such a lasting effect is difficult (although we have to admit we have our favorites in the list).

The cost of Internet dating is actually an incredible bargain if you succeed. And even if you don't succeed at first and are still in the quest phase, it still saves you much time, money, and aggravation over the alternatives.

## Comparing the cost of the competition

Comparing the cost of the competition to Internet dating is useful:

- A typical personal ad in a large city newspaper costs $20 per week. For six months, the cost is more than $400.
- A video-dating service (where you make a tape of yourself and others view it at the dating-service office) offers 10 to 20 dates in six months at a cost of at least $1,000.
- A speed-dating session (where you meet people in person for 7 to 10 minutes in serial order) costs about $50 per session. You chat with 10 and 15 people each time but usually get the names of only one or two (they have to agree to give you their names). At the rate of one session per month, six months cost $300.

## Comparing the cost of a real date

Now consider the cost of a *real* date (where you actually meet in person) to the cost of online dating. A real date can easily cost at least $50 if you're paying for two. And even if you're not the one paying, you have to dress and coif for the occasion, which can easily cost the same.

You're probably thinking that Internet dating ultimately turns into real dating, so the costs are only *delayed,* not avoided. Yes and no. Yes, a successful Internet romance will turn into a real (in-person) romance, but, no, the costs aren't just delayed. The difference is that you'll have fewer *real* dates that are more successful because they're better screened. Fewer and better-screened dates equal a bargain.

In addition, with Internet dating, your first encounter with each other is always by e-mail (free), and the first time you get together in person usually isn't for dinner but for coffee. (Even in the most extravagant of coffee shops, the cost doesn't exceed $15.)

To boot, you have much more at stake than money when you go on a real date:

- ✔ **Your time is at stake.** And your time is worth more than you think. You quickly discover this how valuable your time is when you find yourself dating too many unsuitable prospects.

- ✔ **Your ego is at stake.** And your ego is very fragile. Even if you're tough as nails, rejection is hard to take. Online rejection is so much easier to handle (see Chapter 16 for the details). Better screening means fewer face-to-face rejections.

- ✔ **Your mental health is at stake.** Getting "up" for a date takes a lot of energy. Traditional dating, especially, makes the first meeting like an interrogation or job interview because you know so little about your date in advance.

- ✔ **Your judgment is at stake.** If your mission is to find a mate, clarity of judgment is important. If you've had too many bad dates and they've beaten you down, you may lose the ability to know good from bad.

# Facing the Consequences of Using Free Sites

You've probably heard the saying "There's no free lunch." Then along came the Internet, and it seemed — for a while — that some things in life were indeed free.

Contrary to popular belief, however, even during the Internet's infancy, not everything online was free. Because so much stuff was — and still is — free, many people think that *everything* on the Internet should be. That's why some people gravitate to free Internet-dating sites.

For the most part, though, free sites aren't good sites. They come with certain consequences, which is what this section's all about.

## Weeding through the Internet advertisements

Free (nondenominational) dating sites usually include advertising. The consequence of receiving lots of ads isn't limited to their nuisance value.

✔ If you're not on a high-speed Internet connection, you spend a good deal of your life downloading the advertising. Worse yet, the advertising has priority over any other data.

✔ Advertising includes *JavaScripts* (the stuff that makes banner advertising jitter, shake and probably causes blindness in laboratory mice), which make your screen come alive with junk.

✔ The ultimate annoyance is the latest invention of Internet advertising: pop-up boxes. They're like roaches. No matter how many you smash, you can never get rid of them.

✔ Most advertisers try to track your online behavior with *cookies,* which are little data files left on your computer to track your activities on their site. If you set your browser to block them, the site may not work at all.

✔ Some advertisers attempt to capture your *IP address* ( the electronic location of your computer on the Web and indirectly, your mailbox address) and then direct masses of dating-oriented junk mail to you. (As we wrote this book, both our Yahoo and POP e-mail accounts received massive dosages of ads related to dating and, more particularly, sex.) That's why we suggest that you set up a separate e-mail address for Internet dating and that you *never* use your office e-mail account.

## Limited scope of coverage

Free sites are generally geographically limited because their sponsors usually have some local affiliation and because most people want to date in their local area anyway.

However, if the local affiliation has a specific religious, ethnic, or philosophical orientation that doesn't match your own, you may feel uncomfortable using the site.

If a religious organization runs the site, make sure that you agree to limit your choice of dates to persons of the same religious persuasion. The only reason the site exists is to match such people.

## Lack of sophisticated features

The most obvious difference between free and pay sites is their level of software sophistication (features). Free sites tend to be *freeform* sites instead of *structured* sites. Freeform sites tend to give you very little useful information about your prospects. And without structure, you can't conduct a thorough and meaningful word search on your important preferences. (Turn to Chapter 5 for the nitty-gritty details about freeform and structured sites.)

Moreover, other fun features, such as audio files (sound files of prospect's voice), instant messaging, and auto-matching (machine-generated matches) are almost always lacking. What you get at free sites is pretty bare bones.

## Lack of supervision

Be prepared. Occasionally some messed-up people invade Internet-dating sites. Commercial operators try to tame (evict) this crowd through solid supervision.

On free sites, the Internet-Dating Police Force simply isn't as available as on pay sites. Such vigilance costs money, and they need to be on duty 24/7.

Granted, free sites usually have a sys-op (system operator) who can be roused in a few days with a few e-mails, but that may be too late to stop a lunatic e-mailer from harassing many people.

## No barriers to entry

Internet dating is so easy that nearly anyone can sign up and play. Unfortunately, this ease can be a problem on free sites. Most of us are serious about our dating, and we don't want to be distracted by people who aren't equally serious. But if people don't have to pay anything, signing up doesn't require any form of committed participation.

Likewise, serious conventional daters don't want to be distracted by people who don't belong on the site at all, (like married people). In this case, a terrific barrier to entry is the almighty dollar (well, in the Internet world, the almighty credit card). Married people have a hard time explaining Internet-dating service fees on their credit cards, so they rarely get past the free trial.

# The Way to Go: Pay Sites

You get what you pay for in life, Internet-dating sites included. Unlike free sites, with pay sites you don't have the headache of endless advertising messages screaming in your face. In addition, the scope of coverage and available features are broad and robust. Solid supervision is provided (to weed out the wackos), and appropriate barriers to entry are in place.

To emphasize that last point, consider how easy it is to be an Internet-dating fraud, the more hurdles to entry there are, the safer a site is likely to be. The problem is finding balance. A site that keeps everyone out is completely free of fraud but also of available dates!

The most effective way to find balance is to combine fees and other barriers to entry. A site doesn't need much of a barrier to keep out the undesirables or at least make them easy to detect.

Pay sites provide effective barriers against bad folks by

- ✔ **Requiring long essays.** Some systems require a minimum length for answers to essay questions. If you see a profile in which the person makes no serious attempt to complete the essay, you may as well give that one a pass. Although the person may not be very articulate, he or she could also be a *gamer* or *player* (a person on a site for amusement and not really dating).

- ✔ **Requiring a photo.** Very few sites make this requirement because they fear having fewer participants. However, if you limit yourself to people who post a photo, even though you may eliminate many perfectly good matches, you also eliminate a larger percentage of problem postings that hide behind the anonymity of a no-photo posting. Sorry to say, but if you don't post a photo, you're separating yourself from the class of serious daters.

Of course, a posted photo may be fake, so somewhere in your correspondence thread, ask for a second photo. Few frauds have a series of related fake photos.

✔ **Requiring a payment only by credit card.** Credit-card payments are highly traceable. After a payment is made, law enforcement can easily access the records. Even if a card is stolen, repeated charges to the card will eventually be cut off when the owner reports the lost card or bogus charges.

✔ **Requiring approval of all postings.** Like a bouncer checking IDs at a bar, most pay sites read your posting and almost all look at your photo. They read your essays electronically to spot those seven dirty words that comedian George Carlin used to do a shtick about — the ones that could never be uttered on TV — as well as a few thousand more that can't be used on vanity license plates. A few sites actually have humans read your essays word for word. All look for embedded e-mail addresses, like "You can reach me at my house dot com if you get my drift," because they don't want you to circumvent their fee system.

Having the sites read your essays is good for the most part, because they ferret out some seriously inappropriate types who can't hold their tongue (well, fingers).

You find that some pay sites put great emphasis on barriers to entry. For example, some sites charge relatively high fees in an attempt to create an aura of exclusivity. And some sites add other criteria, such as allowing only Ivy League graduates, *plus* fees to create greater selectivity.

## Determining how much you have to pay

Assuming that you're convinced that you get what you pay for, how much should you pay? Most sites are pretty close in their fees for the initial month — usually $20 to $30.

Dating-site fees have risen a lot. Just a few years ago, many sites charged about 50 percent less. But the fact that people are still willing to pay means they feel the value is sufficient to justify the cost.

Most sites now use a monthly payment plan. Basically, you get unlimited use of the features for a fixed fee per month (see the following section for typical fees). In general, this system is better because you don't feel inhibited about making contact unlike a token system where you weigh each contact you make very carefully.

In a token system, you buy a certain number of tokens and you use one every time you write. Token systems are nice if you're a dabbler in the online-dating scene or if you travel a lot and wouldn't benefit from a time-limited engagement. However, the disadvantage of this method is that you become very judicious about using your eTokens and may become annoyed when you don't get a reply from someone (consequently, a wasted token).

## Getting the best deal

Online-dating sites aren't bashful about trying to get you to stay for long-term commitments. Are they a good idea? Yes, usually. For example, see the pricing plan of one major site:

- 1 month: $24.95
- 3 months: $54.95 (or $19 per month)
- 6 months: $99.95 (or $17 per month)
- 12 months: $149.95 ($13 per month)

Our advice is

- Never sign up for a long-term plan unless you've taken a fully functional test drive (see Chapter 7 for a full explanation).
- Sign up for a one-month plan, which is more expensive but a cheap mistake if you don't like the site. You can try another site and then come back, if necessary.
- After paying for one month, either move on to a new site or spring for "not less than **six months**." Yup, we meant six months, but we don't expect you to work searches for dates 24/7 of those 180 days. Take days, weeks, and some months off in the process. Online dating could have a life-altering outcome (such as meeting your mate). If you take your time, and don't feel rushed, you'll have a better and more thoughtful experience.

## Paying the piper

If you want to venture into the online-dating world, know that you need to remain patient. For you instant-gratification types, you probably won't find your life partner after paying for one month on an Internet dating site. Remember that online dating takes time.

Even paying for less than six months is probably too short of a time, and it'll rush you into being an urgent dater, which isn't a good dater to be. If you pay for six months (or even a year) and find your dream mate on Day 2, consider yourself the luckiest person on earth and money very well spent. Think of all the bad dates you missed.

Even if you pay for an entire year, don't expect to use the site every week or every month. You'll hopefully get into a relationship or two along the way and need to suspend (not cancel!) your account. Or you may just need a rest from time to time. (Check out the section "Suspending or removing your posting" for more information.)

Beware the auto-debit monster! When you give a credit-card authorization for payment for your first subscription period, you'll probably be authorizing the site to automatically renew your subscription in perpetuity, possibly well beyond your eventual marriage and death. So if you sign up for six months, at some point you may be debited another six-month charge without warning. This feature is nasty, it's legal, it's stated in the small print, and all sites do it.

If you pay by credit card, after you sign up for a long-term contact (three months to one year) on most systems, you may immediately resign. Doing so doesn't mean you lose your contract term. It just means that you've squashed the auto-debit monster. (If by chance you accidentally cancel your subscription, just send the site an e-mail to explain the problem.)

## *Maintaining your privacy*

People rarely use the terms *Internet* and *privacy* together in a positive way. A lot of snooping goes on there. Most of it is benign, but you never know for sure.

What you probably encounter most isn't snooping but another form of invasion of privacy: When you pay for your subscription by e-mail, you may later find your e-mail box getting full of junk mail (related — sometimes loosely — to things a single person may want). We think the rewards of Internet dating outweigh the hassle of the alternatives, but if you're really concerned about maximizing your privacy, take these steps:

✔ **Install a privacy checker on your computer.** The checker reviews most dating sites' privacy policies for you and reports the results to you (and they aren't pretty). A good free one, from AT&T, is at www.privacybird.com. If the site doesn't meet your standards for privacy, which you set yourself, a crow caws and warns you to read the policy or waive your objections.

✔ **Pay by check.** Yes, the old paper kind sent by mail. Cross out your driver's license number and social security number before mailing it. Paying by check is the best way to protect your privacy short of sending small bills in an envelope or getting a traveler's check. Although sending a check is the safest way to pay, it's completely impractical for most people who want instant gratification. Some sites have abolished such payments anyway.

✔ **Read the small print.** Yes, those long, boring contracts that you must agree to when you sign up for almost everything on the Web. If you don't like what you read, don't sign up. I (Michael here) must admit that even though I'm a lawyer, I can rarely bring myself to read them. Most contracts are horrible, and no one would ever sign them if they could stand to read them.

## Suspending or removing your posting

You may suspend your posting for several reasons:

✔ You're tired, frustrated, or exhausted by the mania of Internet dating.

✔ You've met someone, and as a sign of commitment, you want to take down your billboard, so to speak.

✔ You're on vacation and don't want the mail to pile up.

At other times, you may want to permanently cancel your posting:

✔ You've *really* met someone. The right one.

✔ You've given up for good.

✔ You've joined a religious order that doesn't permit dating.

Whatever the reason, you need to know that the site will remove your posting.

Every site has a method for suspension and closure of an account, but that doesn't necessarily mean the account will actually disappear. For example, one of our postings was intentionally removed, but six months later it reopened like magic. Why? Well, sometimes it's a mistake. For example, the site may have a crash, the data may get reloaded from a prior tape, and you may reappear. Sometimes, though, it's not a mistake. The site may need more "faces," and yours may be sufficiently available to help out the (company's) cause, in which case you may get restored. You may or may not get mail, but your photo remains posted and you don't know it.

You can effectively ensure that you're really deleted: Before you suspend or resign, delete your photo and essay answers. Wait a few days and then resign. The company won't likely restore a posting that has no photo or essay, and your privacy will be secure.

If you're only suspending, remember to print your profile before deleting it because you don't want to recreate it from memory.

# Chapter 5

# Spotting the Differences from Site to Site

*Y*ou can select an Internet-dating site in one of two ways. The most common way is to take a friend's advice. Now, granted, that's not a bad method, but keep in mind that your friend may also give stock tips like "Buy Enron."

We recommend the second way to select an online-dating site using good old-fashioned hands-on research. In other words, become familiar with the important features of online-dating sites, which vary from site to site, know how the differences in features can affect your dating experience, and then choose a site based on your assessment and particular needs.

In this chapter, we help you know what to look for when selecting a site. Armed with this information and a tour of some of the best sites (see Chapter 6), you can quickly narrow the field to one or two sites that suit your preferences.

Your tastes may change as you get more sophisti-cated at online dating, so you may want to look back at this chapter for a fresh perspective after you gain some experience.

# Picking a Dating Site with the Right Personality

At first blush, you may think that all Internet-dating sites are pretty much the same: lists of prospects and a way to contact them. But subtle differences exist, and they make the online-dating experience more fun and productive. Developing an eye for the subtle but important differences takes some time.

Internet-dating sites are a lot like theme parks at first. The more sophisticated ones have tons of goodies (like lots of lands to visit — with great dating prospects in each one). When you first arrive, you don't know where to begin, and everything seems overwhelming. But after you get your bearings, you soon realize that getting around is fairly easy (and fun), and you begin navigating with ease and confidence.

Internet-dating sites comprise a collection of features that together give the site its personality. Some of the features are mere conveniences, but some really make a difference in your online experiences. For example, the way a site handles e-mail messaging can make a big difference in how engaging (or manic) the site is and how much effort is required to keep track of the many e-mails you'll receive from prospects.

Although different sites have literally dozens of features, familiarize yourself with a handful of really important feature differences. After you get to know them, you can select the features that best fit your preferences and choose the features that aid your chances for success.

Be aware of some of these key feature differences:

- Sites have either *structured* profiles (they ask questions, you answer them) or *freeform* profiles (they ramble, you ramble).

  *Note:* Sites really distinguish themselves in the number of detailed questions they pose of all prospects and hence what juicy stuff you can find out about someone before making contact. In addition, some sites *require* answers, and others let you leave them blank, thus defeating the purpose of the questions. Don't assume that the sites that require little information about you are better. There is a price to pay. If you don't have to say much about yourself, neither do your *prospects,* and your search will ultimately become a mere photo contest.

✔ Sites either use your own private (preexisting) e-mail box for messages or provide you (at signup) with one specifically for online-dating purposes.

✔ Sites may or may not provide other information goodies that give you clues about your prospects' online activities (like the last time they signed on, how actively they're looking, who they've looked at, and more).

HE SAID

# Guy talk

Everybody seems to have an interesting story about how they started Internet dating. My introduction was less than perfect. A guy friend who knew I was recently divorced told me that I *had to* try this Internet dating. He said he was dating three women per week — sometimes two per day.

I asked him which site he was using, but in typical guy fashion, he couldn't remember any of the names. He said, "Just put the words *Internet dating* into your search engine, and you'll find lots of them." Because it's a guy thing not to ask for help — especially for any type of driving directions, Internet driving included — I decided not to press the issue with him. I just drove in as he suggested.

Well, he was right about it being easy to find dating *hits* online (a hit is a site which contains the words that matched what you searched for). A quick search of the phrase *Internet dating* on google.com produced 1,750,000 hits. By the time I investigated all those sites, I figured I'd probably get around to my first date from the old age home.

Of course, I soon figured out that several sites calling themselves "dating" sites sure weren't. Many sites, for example, were offering women from distant lands ready for *immediate* marriage. But because I was just getting out of a marriage, the last thing I wanted was an immediate new one, especially with a woman, albeit beautiful, from a country that started with "a former People's Republic of . . . ." (See what we have to say about e-mail order brides later in this chapter.)

After much distraction, I found some legitimate, domestically based Internet-dating sites. They all seemed to have a lot in common. Their front pages all featured photos of great looking 30-somethings ogling each other, anxiously awaiting an opportunity to live happily ever after, but aside from that, they were indistinguishable.

Bottom line? I spent several months and experimented a lot before "hitting on" some really great sites. What I discovered from the experience was this: Even the better sites have big differences, and success comes from matching your tastes and personality with the site's personality and features.

## Structure: Do ya love it or hate it?

Every Internet-dating site has a place for you to present your information. The place is usually called your *personal profile,* and it's your presentation of your cyber self. How you fill out this profile is vitally important, so we devote several chapters to it (see Chapters 8 through12), but for purposes of this discussion, the question is this: How do sites get that information out of you?

Sites approach the task of getting your profile in very different ways:

✔ At one end of the spectrum are *freeform* sites, which merely present vast expanses of blank screen, like the great plains of Siberia (or, in this case, Cyberia). The sites offer no specific questions to answer. The basics, like height, weight, eye color, children, ideals in a mate — the most basic of profile information — are omitted, and you're left to your own imagination to write something interesting, attractive, and useful. No one tells you what to write or how much to say, or even to say anything at all.

✔ At the other end of the spectrum are *structured* sites, which ask you numerous questions, some multiple choice, and some essay. The multiple-choice questions include the "basics" (like height, weight, eye color, children, and so on), but also some rather obtuse questions, such as "do you have any body art?" and give you a chance to inject some humor because at least one of the choices is often "off the wall." The essay questions, almost always ask you to describe your *perfect* match, questions about your personality, likes and dislikes, and so on. The site may also ask less specific questions, which allow you to say more about yourself and your goals, such as "how do you see yourself in five years."

Take heed, lest ye fall for some common misconceptions:

The freeform method may seem like the simplest way to present your profile, but in fact, it's the most difficult. You have to figure out what's appropriate to write, how much to say, and how to organize it. If you're very creative, this task is heaven, but for the rest us, it's no fun.

You may be thinking, "Yeah, but regardless, isn't freeform still the best type? I mean, with freeform I technically don't have to say anything about myself, but everyone else has to tell all." Sorry, it just doesn't work that way. If you can remain secretive, so can your prospects, and your online-dating experience will be much like an electronic dartboard. Random.

### *Freeform: Where less is less*

For the most part, freeform systems are a disaster. Because the form doesn't force answers, many postings contain virtually nothing useful. If you want to embark on a serious, significant relationship, expect a site to provide the bare basics of every prospect — like height, weight, age, education, children, and religious preference.

On a freeform site, extracting the basic information from your prospect is a major challenge. If you try, you may be accused of resurrecting the Spanish Inquisition (which no one appreciates and, of course, no one expects). And even if you succeed, you end up spending so much e-mail capital just getting the basics that you never get to the more important character issues.

To see what we're talking about, look at this pretty lame but entirely typical example of a freeform essay:

> "Hi!! Valentine's Day is approaching, and I still don't have a sweetheart. If you're like me, you're looking to spend this special day with someone. Let me know. I'd love to meet you." Jane, Madison, WI

To add insult to injury, Jane felt no compulsion to provide a photo (say, for example, that it *was* an available feature); Jane listed in a grouping of women aged 20 to 30. That's all we know of her. What would entice you to write to her?

The problem is, without structure, people tend not to write much at all, and so from a reader's point of view, you often don't have much to work with. In the online-dating world, you can find so many better available postings. If you came across a profile like the preceding Jane example, you'd probably just click the "Next" button. Freeform systems are really the next generation after personal want ads in the newspaper. The sites want their users to be brief and succinct, but for what real reason? The problem is, however, that without structure, people have a natural tendency to say very little, so as a reader you don't have much to work with.

That said, we want to share a tidbit in defense of freeform systems. They do have one advantage: You usually don't have a limit to how much you can write. If you have a lot to say, and someone's willing to read it, a freeform system may be perfect.

So why do freeform sites exist if they're so ineffective? Part of the reason is that freeform software is easy to write (read: cheap) and many freeform sites are free (no charge). The other part is that everyone resists filling out questionnaires (even though they love to read others'), so freeform sites provide the lowest resistance to signing up. Because dating-site operators want the maximum number of postings, low resistance can be an attractive, albeit short-term, advantage.

### The structured sites: Try 'em, you'll like 'em

Most serious Internet-dating sites are structured. They ask for answers to specific questions, although they vary greatly in how structured they are and in whether they actually require answers (so as not to scare off novice prospects). The various questions on such sites provide two ways of answering, depending on the question at hand: Pick and choose your answer from a predetermined selection of answers (we call this flavor Q&A) and the other type of question, where you answer an open-ended question with no suggestions (we call this flavor Essay).

Focus on these questions you routinely see on the more structured dating sites:

- ✔ **Age:** Well, technically, some sites never actually ask your age but somehow know it. So how do they guess so accurately? When you give them your birth date when registering your credit-card information, it's a no-brainer calculation (and you lose the opportunity to lie). Note too that some systems don't display your actual age but put you in 10-year age band.

    Age banding can work for you or against you. If the site puts you in the upper part of an age band, consider using a different site.

- ✔ **Body type (that is, weight):** The choices offered are somewhat abstract. Terms like *slim* and *fat* are replaced by words like *toned, chiseled, rubenesque,* and *height/weight proportional.* We strongly suggest you try to answer with what you are, not what you wish you could be. It's the only body you have, and you'll be bringing it with you when you finally meet your prospect in person.

- ✔ **Children:** Got 'em? Most sites ask only whether you have any children, not how old they are or whom they're living with. We think this is a pretty big oversight of many sites.

- ✔ **Drinking habits:** All drinking styles are covered, from "alcohol makes my engine race" to "I drink like a fish."

- ✔ **Education:** You see options for high school, college, advanced degree, or degree names themselves (BA, MA, PhD). Beware: some people think they qualify for "some college" if they've attended a frat party.

✓ **Eye color:** You have no set rules here, so if you have two different-colored eyes, or you have colored contacts, choose whichever color suits your fancy.

✓ **Hair color:** Note that this item is usually word-searchable, so if you select the *dark* blonde option from the available list of choices, you won't be found in a search of *blondes* because blonde and dark blonde are totally separate options. And remember that the question is what color your hair *is,* not how it got that color. By the way, if you're bald, wearing a baseball cap in your photos is the international signal that you're folically-challenged. Don't hide it. Lots of women like it and say so in their profiles. Besides, unless you're on a truly blind date, they're going to discover it soon enough.

✓ **Height:** Your answer is supposed to be your height from tip to toe, not counting phone books, orange crates, or stiletto heels.

✓ **Income:** Sites offer income bands along with several polite, humorous, and downright snarky choices, like "only the IRS knows," "I subsist on nuts and berries," and "none of your darn business!"

✓ **Location:** The site may derive your location from your zip code (in which case the city name may not be right) or by simply asking you.

You may not want to be listed in your home city. Supplying a different zip code usually fixes the problem, but it may also cause your credit card to be rejected. So change the zip/postal code after you've completed the signup. Consider a listing a zip code in a geographic area that is a reasonably easy drive for a casual coffee date.

✓ **Marital status:** Every option is covered (divorced, single, and so on), including, believe it or not, married. Turn to Chapter 9 for more about this issue.

✓ **Occupation:** You have to choose from the options offered, so you don't have much latitude. If you're a certified public PhD ornithologist, you may have to go with *exterminator.* Of course, you always have the proverbial choice of "Tell You Later."

✓ **Religion:** Aside from the usual choices, you find options like "Just Christian," "Pagan," "Religion isn't a part of my life," and "I'm religious only on airplanes and roller coasters."

✓ **Sexual orientation:** Some sites ask about your open-mindedness with respect to gays, lesbians, and bisexuals. Other sites may ask whether you're gay, lesbian, or bisexual and provide matching services for this choice. Exclusively alternative sexual-orientation–specific sites are available, if you're interested. See the tour of sites in Chapter 6.

✔ **Smoking/drug habits:** If you're a strident nonsmoker and don't want to associate with anyone who has a more relaxed opinion, most sites make it easy for you to make your opinion known.

Typically, sites ask even more types of Q&A questions — some more useful than others — but the preceding list gives you a good feel for what to expect. In all cases, more questions are definitely better.

That said, you need to know that some select sites contain specific questions you may find important or interesting. If the answers to any of these questions are very important to you, you may want to select a site that requires answers to them.

✔ **Description of your ideal mate:** You can often draw out personality preferences with this question.

✔ **Expectations for a first date:** Although you may think this question is silly, it sometimes does reveal interesting and telling information.

✔ **How you characterize your sense of humor:** You can't rely on the answer to this one, but at least you can use it as a reality check on the other answers.

✔ **Specifics on children:** Want 'em? Want more of 'em? The answer to this question is a deal breaker for many people. You may want to know the answer upfront. And other more specifics on children include with whom do they reside, and how old are they? Many people want this answer upfront, but few sites are willing to ask it. We don't know why they don't.

✔ **Your spending habits:** This question is only helpful in the extreme. People often make a joke of it, so don't take it too seriously.

✔ **Your usual safer-sex practices:** Most sites are still reluctant to ask this one, except the more sexually provocative ones, so you may have to ask these questions yourself in your e-mail exchanges.

If you have certain criteria that your prospects must meet (such as religion, age of children, or education), be sure that the site you choose has this essential information in its profile questionnaire. If not, pick another site, or you may find the search process very frustrating.

If you want deeper insight into your prospect, go with a structured system. The combination of the Q&A and essay questions really works. Add a photo and you've got some solid stuff about your prospects.

# E-mail boxes: Yours or theirs?

Internet dating involves an exchange of plenty of e-mails. In fact, e-mail is the heart of the *virtual* phase of Internet dating. Through e-mail, you get to know enough about your prospect to make that critical decision about whether to continue on to phone contact.

 If you don't have e-mail now, you're gonna have to get it. You must have an e-mail account before signing up for a dating site. All dating sites ask for your e-mail address even if you won't be using it for communication with prospects.

 And need we remind you that a private e-mail address (not one provided by your employer) is best if you opt for a dating site that doesn't provide an internal, on-site mailbox? Internet dating on company time/dime is unethical, doesn't assure privacy, and may threaten your livelihood if your boss catches you.

 If you don't know how to type, work on your typing skills because longer, more engaging e-mails draw similarly engaging e-mails from prospects. Using the excuse "I hate to type" on the Internet is the equivalent of saying, "The cat ate my homework" in high school.

## Squinting for a better look: Photo size matters

When comparing dating sites, you'll quickly find that some sites use tiny, almost microscopic photos. They do so to speed the screen display for people who have slower dial-up modem connections. Usually, you can click on a photo to enlarge it, but not always. And if you can't, you find that squinting at a photo and still having no idea what a person looks like is extremely frustrating.

Moral of the story? We can't overemphasize how important photos are. When choosing a site, thoroughly check out the clarity of its photo display system. (Photos are so important that we devote an entire chapter to the subject. Check out Chapter 12 for the whole scoop.)

Depending on the site you choose, you'll receive e-mail in one of two places:

- ✔ Your personal e-mail account (like AOL, Yahoo, or Hotmail). We call this type of site a *BYOE* (bring your own e-mail) site.

- ✔ Your e-mail account inside the dating site. We call this type of site an *all-in-one site.*

So does it really matter which type of site you use? Well, yes, because the type determines the activity level of your Internet-dating experience.

### All-in-one sites: Party on, dude

When you go to a party, you expect to meet new people, and you hope people will walk up to you and introduce themselves. All-in-one sites are like that. You often get mail *while* you're perusing other people's profiles. These sites are exciting, and sometimes the frenzy of e-mail coming and going is nonstop.

On an all-in-one site, you can check whether your e-mail was ignored or read, or whether it got the dreaded *deleted* treatment. If you get deleted, that's a sure bet the prospect doesn't want to continue the e-mail exchange. Don't worry about it. Instead, be thankful you were spared a useless exchange of further e-mails.

Now that you're all hyped up about all-in-one sites, we have some bad news: Most all-in-one sites don't save your messages beyond a certain number of days or beyond a maximum number of messages. Your only option is to print them, punch them, and put them in a binder. If you don't save them on paper, they're lost forever. In short, managing the flood of e-mail you're likely to get can be a major pain with all-in-one sites.

Use these tips on the strengths and weaknesses of all-in-one sites (you're welcome):

- ✔ You don't need to have a personal e-mail account.

- ✔ Keeping dating mail separate from other personal mail is easy.

- ✔ You get instant hyperlinking to writers' profiles. (You can jump from their mail messages directly to their full profiles by clicking on their screen names or photos.)

- ✔ You're more likely to get e-mail when you're online.

- ✔ The online experience feels livelier — sometimes frenetic and less virtual.

✔ Some of your e-mail interaction is nearly live because both parties are online.

✔ These sites combine the advantages of chat with the advantages of e-mail.

✔ Saving and printing e-mails isn't easy. You need to know how to print a screen shot.

### BYOE sites: Uh, less frenzy, please

Really the difference between the BYOE and all-in-one site is the ease of e-mail organization in BYOE versus the beehive-like frenetic pace of the all-in-one. The e-mail organization in BYOE has the ability to archive your e-mails in perpetuity and put them in neat folders to keep prospects straight.

Okay, here's a cheat sheet on the strengths and weaknesses of BYOE sites (you're welcome):

✔ You can easily organize e-mail by creating folders in your personal e-mail system.

✔ You can keep an unlimited number of e-mails (within the limits allowed by your personal e-mail provider).

✔ You can keep e-mails forever in electronic form.

✔ If you're prone to cyber addiction, the less-frenetic pace of these sites is less likely to suck you in.

✔ Printing e-mail is easy. Just click Print.

# How would you like to break the ice?

Sites offer various ways to help you break the ice with prospects, from chat rooms to features that tell you who's currently online to a rather scary Big Brother–type of feature.

### Wanna chat?

Some sites offer a *chat* feature, which is an online version of live conversation. Many Internet users like chat because it's a half step between exchanging regular e-mail and going directly to telephone contact. Chat has the immediacy of a phone conversation but maintains your anonymity — that may be sacrificed after you enter the phone zone.

Another attraction is that you don't have to write long, involved e-mails. With chat, you can write short bursts. In addition, chat provides more immediate gratification. You don't have to wait for the next e-mail response, which may take minutes, hours, or days. And you have the opportunity to observe your prospective date thinking on his or her feet (or, rather, fingers) without the safety net of the time and reflection afforded by regular e-mail.

Chat comes in two flavors: *public chat,* which is a group free-for-all experience with everyone participating, and *private chat,* which is strictly limited to live e-mail conversations between t wo people privately.

### Public chatting

Public chat is a bit like the floor of the stock exchange, with people yelling across the room to others you can't identify. Public chat is a party you're guaranteed admission to, but with no certainty that you'll connect with anyone.

Some online-dating sites have specialized chat rooms that make a minimal attempt at creating an affinity between chatters. Most are groups defined by age. Remember these tips about public chat:

- ✔ Peeking in on an age group outside your own may be interesting. This experience may help you understand the virtue of dating *within* your age group (if you find that you can't relate to the ongoing chat in the other age group).

- ✔ Most chat systems allow you to *lurk,* that is, observe without participating — but typically you won't be invisible.

### Private chatting

Private chat is a one-on-one real-time e-mail exchange — kind of an e-mail version of a two-way radio.

Like in two-way radio exchanges, only one person can talk at a time. If you're familiar with any flavor of instant messaging, you know what we mean. The important difference between public and private chat is that you and your contact are off in a private room together and are completely anonymous.

## Finding out who else is online

Some Internet-dating sites offer a "who's online" feature that tells you what members are browsing the system right now. Usually, you know this info by an attention-getting icon, like a light bulb or flashing symbol.

Why do you care that someone is "live?" Because it's your chance to connect with someone immediately — someone you know is *active* on the system. If the "live" folks don't reply to your e-mail quickly, they may already be engaged in another chat, or not interested in your overtures. In any case, it won't be because they didn't see your message.

## Having R2D2 pick your date: Letting the dating site suggest a match

When "computer" dating first started, many people assumed that the computer did the matching and all they had to do was put their stats into the box and out popped a slip of paper with his/her name (and perhaps a Chinese proverb or two). In theory, finding a match is possible, and indeed, Match.com has introduced an interesting personality profile to try to give you enough data to know what kind of person you should be looking for. Practically speaking, the science of mating isn't even as good as the science of weather forecasting, but it's far more entertaining.

Almost all pay sites provide some system for the computer to take your stats (for example, answers to your Q&A multiple-choice questions) and match you to others. We call this *auto-match*. This service is always optional and you need to activate it. You often have a fair amount of control over how the computer does the matching. Some systems match characteristics head to head (if you prefer blondes, you'll only be matched to blondes), but others will ask: even if you prefer blondes, is it an important characteristic in your matches? If not, your computer matches list blondes first, but not exclusively. Of course, the matching goes well beyond physical traits to personality traits, but the degree of sophistication depends on the number and type of questions you answered when signing up. Online sites don't use the essay questions when computing a match because no software is capable of reading between the lines . . . yet.

## Comparing e-mail systems

Most sites are now of the all-in-one site type. Anytime you're logged onto the site, other users can see that you're "live" and contact you. You receive instant notification of waiting mail. In fact, many people seek prospects from the *Who's On* because they know that their message will be seen (and hopefully responded to) immediately. This benefit generally isn't possible on BYOE sites because e-mail messages are sent to your outside e-mail box (like Yahoo) and you don't get any notification of incoming mail.

In some sites, you can have a list of computer matches sent to your private e-mail box once a week or once a day. This delivery can be a real nice distraction to a slow day. The delivery usually includes a thumbnail-sized photo and a teaser portion of the profile. The photos are hyperlinked back to the dating site so all you have to do is click on the photo and you can read the full profile.

As personality matches, this auto-match feature is a disappointment, in our opinion, but might be fun to try, especially when you are new to online dating. Although the feature simply doesn't provide enough data on you or your prospects and not enough computing power to provide useful data, but the matches do make great icebreakers!

Turn your auto-match in to a great icebreaker:

- ✔ Run the auto-match feature on your site.

- ✔ Scan your results and write a brief e-mail to the matches that interest you.

- ✔ Write a non-intrusive message because it reduces the chance of rejection. Write a message like:

    "Hey, the computer running this dating site insisted that we'd be a great match. Who am I to argue with a guy like Bill Gates? Do you think there might be something worth exploring here, or should we report this to Microsoft as a bug?"

You don't have to rely on your dating site to provide you with icebreakers like winks and auto-matching; you can create your own opportunity or give people something to write to you about. Many people who have taken the Meyers-Briggs Personality Inventory sometime in their lives have posted their results in their profiles (Michael's is a Meyers Briggs INTJ and Judy's is INTJ too). If you see a Meyers-Briggs score, and you want to make contact, you can reply with yours or use a bit of humor:

> Your profile mentioned that you're an INTJ. I frankly have no idea what that means, but if you're no longer dating that Meyers-Briggs guy, would you be willing to tell me a bit about yourself?

# *I always feel like somebody's watching me*

A new phenomenon we've noticed is what we not so affectionately call the Big Brother feature. In most systems, you can view and peruse postings in complete anonymity, and no one knows who you've looked at or how often you've visited a posting to fantasize over his or her great looks. But with the Big Brother feature operating, every time you peruse a profile, the site reports it to that user. Yikes!

Why would any site add such a feature? Because it works as an icebreaker. For example, if someone looks at your profile and you know it, you may feel more comfortable writing the person: "Hi, I noticed you gave me a look. I think you look pretty interesting, too. Why don't we chat?"

If you prefer to do your scouting cloaked in darkness, the site usually offers a way to turn off the Big Brother feature, but you have to dig for it. Look at the bottom of the opening pages; there may be some small and inconspicuous list of underlined words that are hyperlinks you can click on.

Sites have plenty of poorly documented features, some of which are pretty important (like the Big Brother feature). Snoop around your site's home page to ferret out all the goodies. Remember, unlike grandma's fine china, you can't break anything by doing this.

# Avoiding the Deadwood

You may be surprised to know that a large number of postings on an Internet-dating site are deadwood. These listings are people who've moved on, given up, or found a mate and are living happily every after — but forgot to remove their posting. Or they're people who didn't pay for the service but are nevertheless posted. Regardless, you need to know that they can't exchange e-mail with you.

To understand about deadwood, you need to look at the three main objectives of Internet-dating sites:

- ✔ To attract new members
- ✔ To have the largest possible number of users
- ✔ To get those users to pay the monthly fee

All sites need to maximize their user numbers, and one enticement they use is to allow you to post without payment. These kinds of postings look just like regular postings, but in fact the people are limited visitors and can't send e-mails to you, although they can receive them.

One consequence is that if you're just waiting for e-mails to be sent to you (you're not proactively sending your own), many people won't contact you. But you won't have any way of knowing which ones.

You may unknowingly send a message to a limited visitor (a person not authorized to send e-mails) and think you're being rejected when you don't hear back from the person. All the more reason not to be discouraged by what appears to be rejection.

Be aware that some sites don't have a deadwood problem because they don't allow unpaid postings except during the trial period — and those users have full rights to send and receive mail.

# Protecting Your Anonymity

Internet-dating sites recognize your need to remain anonymous until you decide to reveal your identity. You can write to anyone without identifying yourself (except for the screen name you choose on your profile page). However, if you ever reply to anyone directly from your private e-mail account to his or her private e-mail account, you need to confirm that your identity isn't revealed by your e-mail system.

When you initially signed up for your e-mail service (like Yahoo or AOL), the service provider probably asked for your name. What you may not know is that some systems automatically put your name in your return e-mail address.

For example, if your e-mail address is dummiesbook@yahoo.com, you may not realize that your return e-mail address (the one sent with each of your messages) may have your *real* name embedded as, say, <JaneSmith>dummiesbook@yahoo.com. Unless you want to reveal your true identity, you need to remove it.

Each e-mail system has a unique way of editing this feature, but here's how you can change it in Yahoo: Go to "Mail Options" and then "General Preferences." Then edit your "From" name and "Reply To" name. Leaving them blank is just fine too.

# "Um, This Is Not What I Bargained For" (The Sex Sites)

Because sex is the No. 1 use of the Internet (come on, you knew that), are you really shocked that sex-related sites have found ways to hide within other services, including Internet-dating sites? You'll almost certainly encounter these slippery operators, so you may as well be on guard for them.

## Online sexual solicitations

Say you're a male and you just signed up for an Internet-dating site. You're very likely to receive this message within minutes of signing up, before you have any sense of what the service is like:

> Hi, John337. I'm Laura and I think you're really cute! I know I'm a bit young for you, but age doesn't matter to me. What I really want is someone who excites me. I don't reply to messages on this dating site, but I have my own Web page where you can see some more "revealing" photos of me. Looking forward to hearing from you soon... Love, Laura

I got several of these, from Laura and her friends. You may think today is your lucky day. Perhaps it is, but not because you're going to have a date with Laura. Laura is trying to lead you to a pay-per-view porn Web site.

If you want to check her out, go ahead (other than that you'll have to delete the infinite number of pop-up windows she'll open), but in the end, you'll be disappointed.

Internet-dating site operators try hard to intercept these solicitations, but these sex solicitors are swift and fleeting in getting out their first messages and then deleting their postings before they can be caught.

 If an e-mail seems unbelievable, it probably is. You may have to experiment some before you know what a realistic e-mail looks like on an Internet-dating site. Start with a bit of skepticism.

## Legit sexually oriented dating sites

Although it may not be your cup of tea, some people, men *and* women, do seek purely sexual liaisons on the Internet, and some dating services cater to them. Even if you don't plan to partake, you need to know they exist so that you don't accidentally stumble into one unaware.

For example, Matchmaker.com, an otherwise mainstream site, also has a community called Alt (easily confused with Atl, the abbreviation for Atlanta). This community is for singles and couples seeking various forms of sex-only relationships. So if you find yourself flipping through the profiles of *Alt*ernans instead of Atlantans and find the postings a bit racy, check your community settings before engaging your eyeballs.

The same is true for a pair of sites run by the same company: Friend Finder and Adult Friend Finder. The two couldn't be more different, with the adult version being very adult oriented, giving new meaning to the word *friend.*

# Steering Clear of Those "E-Mail Order" Brides

In your Internet-dating site travels, you may come across an e-mail version of mail-order brides set up to look like a dating site. You'll soon realize that your first date is at the wedding chapel, but you'll have to spring for the transportation . . . to a former Soviet Republic not so near you.

These sites typically charge fees for sending e-mail to the posted women. Whether they're the same women described and shown in the photos can't be known until you visit them, so the possibility of being disappointed after a very long trek is great.

These sites border on scams — with the border lying somewhere between Eastern Europe and Fantasyland. To boot, they're just not Internet-dating sites as we define them, with a true interaction between males and females. Furthermore, although we think that long-distance relationships are entirely possible and sometimes desirable (we started that way!), the distances involved, usually transoceanic, make getting to really know someone very difficult, if not impossible.

# Chapter 6

# A Tour of the Sites: Your Inside Guide

*T*his chapter is unlike the rest of the book. It's a mini-directory intended to help you evaluate specific dating sites and give you ideas about what to look for in sites that aren't listed.

We can't possibly cover all the available online-dating sites, so we don't even try. The Internet has hundreds, and new ones arrive every day. So, instead we pick a few national sites that seem to span the range of the mainstream and report on them in quite some detail. Then we list the URL (Web address) for many more sites with no explanation. We encourage you to look at our detailed evaluations in this chapter and apply that framework to other sites you're considering. After you start using any site, you can understand why we focus on the features we did. We think you will find them important to your online experience.

If you're trying to find Internet reviews of online-dating sites, we need to warn you that much of what you find isn't objective due to one reason: Almost all the reviewing sites are "referral sites," which means if you click on a hyperlink to a dating site (from the reviewing site), the reviewing site receives a small payment! If you sign up for that dating site, the site pays the review a BIG payment.

So it's difficult for these sites to be objective. You never know if a reviewing site is being paid. (Although if you're a techie, you can get a clue if you see the paying site deposited a cookie[s] in your machine for accounting purposes.)

Dating sites change their features and software frequently, sometimes even in response to books like this one. Therefore, some of the information you read may be out-of-date. Nevertheless, the intended audience of a site rarely changes, even if the features do, so much of what we put in our detailed section is useful.

If you find a site that you think should be in the next edition, please let us know at mail@onlinedatingauthors.com.

# Yahoo.com (Personals.yahoo.com)

Yahoo Personals (reachable via Personals.Yahoo.com or Yahoo.com, then select Personals) is part of the Yahoo! Web site that runs the well-known free e-mail site and search engine, Yahoo.com. As you would expect from a Yahoo product, its online-dating site has a clean and uncluttered look and is easy to use. It's not strong on frills, which many users ignore anyway, but instead has a big user base and a fast server. Although you don't need to have a (free) Yahoo e-mail account, signing up for one gives you access to additional features like IM (instant messenger) and a photo Web page, all reachable by the same user name and password.

## Pricing

- ✔ $19.95 for one month
- ✔ $42.95 for three months
- ✔ $89.95 for one year

Your subscription is auto-renewed at the pro-rated monthly value of your selected package. You need to cancel to stop this from happening.

## Free site tour

**Yahoo does offer a real tour.** You can see individuals' photos by age range and zip/postal code. You can also look at entire profiles and full size photos without signing up. You just can't initiate contact.

### Limited access usage

Yahoo's non-paying access, like many other sites, is unlimited in length but limited in function. You can sign up forever and for free. You can run searches, just like any other paid subscriber, and you can respond to e-mail messages, but you can't initiate e-mails or send IMs as a free user. You can however, send *icebreakers,* which are pre-fabricated messages that indicate your interest. You don't know if you're sending an icebreaker to a nonsubscriber, so they may not be able to respond to you. So if you're a nonpaying user and you get an icebreaker, chances are the sender is also nonpaying.

### Profiles

**Questions and answers:** Yahoo's profile consists of Q&A questions with a series of pull-down answers or check boxes. Some of the more critical questions are

- ✔ **Children — have/want?** Yes, Yahoo asks both questions (whether you have/want children), and they're *searchable* fields. See Chapter 5 for more about searching.

- ✔ **Religion:** Yes, Yahoo asks this question and it's searchable, but you can opt out.

- ✔ **Distinguishes marital status?** Yahoo does ask this question, and it does distinguish between single (never married) and divorced. If someone answers the question incorrectly (for example, by indicating "Single," when he or she is actually divorced), you can bet it wasn't a mistake.

- ✔ **Willing to relocate question?** No, Yahoo doesn't ask this question.

### Essays

Yahoo has one essay that isn't optional. You must type at least 120 characters. Yahoo was smart in requiring essay answers to contain more than a few words, and they seem to get their members sufficiently engaged in trying to write something useful. The site reviews the essays for appropriateness, and the site deletes e-mail addresses or HTML tags. Every time you make a change to your essay, Yahoo will review it again.

### Photos

Yahoo has an easy-to-use photo posting system, and photos are a key part of the overall profile. More than half of the members post photos after a few days. Thumbnail photos are quite readable. You can post up to five photos. A nice feature is that all photos display immediately when you open a profile, which saves time and wear and tear on your carpal tunnel.

### What you can find out about your prospects

✔ You can tell if your prospect is currently online, and try to reach him or her immediately by IM (instant message), but only if he or she has signed onto Yahoo Instant Messenger, a free program from Yahoo.

✔ You can tell when the prospect last logged on, which is a great feature that helps distinguish the active, committed dater from the *deadwood* (someone who isn't seriously interested in online dating, but hasn't removed his or her profile).

✔ You can tell when the prospect first signed up, which is useful to know how experienced he or she is.

### Chat/Instant Messenger (1M) features

**Can you turn IM off?** Yes, if you don't want to be bothered, you can disable it permanently.

**Can nonpaying members initiate IM?** No.

**Can nonpaying members respond to IM?** Yes.

**Do users know when you're online and able to IM?** Yes.

### E-mail system

Yahoo has its own e-mail system, making it an all-in-one site (see Chapter 5 for details). If you set the preference, it will send a message to your external e-mail box notifying you that you have mail awaiting you in the Yahoo Personals mailbox.

### Search tools

Yahoo can search its Q&A fields in any combination. You can search profiles that have photos only and by any age parameters, such as with no age bands. A nice feature of the search system is that you can do a full keyword search of an essay, title, or user ID. You can use this feature if you can't remember a subscriber's name, but remember an interesting phrase in his or her profile.

### Auto-matching services

Yahoo does have a computer matching service called Matches by Mail, and it mails the results to you. In addition, when you log on, your home page offers you a few suggested matches based on the criteria in your profile. A service called Mutual Matching is also available that suggests suitable matches.

## Other cool stuff

- ✔ **Audio:** Yahoo Personals has a voice recorder that records a message up to 30 seconds. It's slick, free, and easy to use.

- ✔ **Video:** Yahoo Personals also contains a video recorder. You must use a Web cam (you can't send a high-resolution video clip), so the video is less than stellar, but still fun and best of all, it's free.

- ✔ **About my match:** Yahoo has a Q&A section that asks users a lot of questions about what they want in a match. This feature is useful because it helps fill in the gaps about what a subscriber may have failed to mention.

- ✔ **Conversation starters:** When you send someone an e-mail, Yahoo includes a note with up to three conversation starters, which you can preselect from a list (such as "in a new relationship, do you like to take it slow, or do you start with a bang"). These may seem silly, but if you choose a provocative one, they do help get a conversation started.

- ✔ **If you liked him/her, perhaps you'd like this one too?** You know how Amazon suggests other book titles after it has figured out what your search pattern is? Yahoo does the same thing with prospects. Adjacent to every prospect in your search list will be the phrase "View similar profiles," which can lead you to prospects with similar physical specs.

- ✔ **Gotta have, maybe:** When you search, you can do more that specify the characteristics of the prospect you want. You can also indicate if they're deal breakers (essential criteria) or just wishes. That way, Yahoo ranks your search results with the "gotta have" matches first and the "sorta gotta have" matches next.

- ✔ **Active During.** Yahoo tells you if the person's profile is active and after 90 days deletes them. Many sites leave deadwood posted to artificially inflate numbers.

## Special interest groups

**Can gays/lesbians find matches?** Yes, simply put in the gender required.

**Can you search by ethnicity?** Yes. The following ethnic groups are searchable: Asian, Native American, Black/African, Pacific Islander, East Indian, White/Caucasian, Latino/Hispanic, Middle Eastern, various, and of course, "other."

**Does the site identify special sexual interests** (such as casual sex dating, swingers, couples, and so on)? No.

### *Safety issues*

**Blocking feature:** Yahoo has the ability for you to block anyone from making further contact.

**Abuse reporting:** Yahoo receives and responds to abuse reports.

**Surveillance by a live monitor:** Occasional, mostly in response to a reported problem.

**Can you be totally invisible?** Yes. Your search activities can be made invisible if you remember to turn off Yahoo IM in the preferences.

**Can you tell if someone has browsed you?** No.

### *Secret Sauce*

Remember this stuff so that you can use this site to its full advantage.

**How to stay on top of the search list.** In large cities, staying at the top of any search list is important. In Yahoo, the last people to log in are listed first in a search, so if you're online for a long time, you may want to log off every half hour to get back on top. Likewise, logging in at least once a day is a good idea.

**Remember to turn on your Yahoo IM.** Because Yahoo Personals uses Yahoo Instant Messenger to handle chat, you need to sign up for Yahoo Messenger (free) and set it to always be on. Otherwise, you may forget to activate it and you won't appear as "online" when you really are.

**Likely likeables:** Yahoo knows that people forget to tweak their "must-have" criteria even after they've returned to planet Earth and realize that "must have" is really "would like to have." So Yahoo offers suggested prospects you may have missed, but who are close to what you had specified. A nice touch.

# *Match.com*

Match.com (Match for short) is one of the biggest general interest dating sites. If you're a beginner to online dating, Match is a no-brainer place to start. It's a true middle of the road site that tries to be suitable for everyone, which has its advantages (and of course, disadvantages). The advantage is that it attracts tons of signups, and that, of course, is essential. The site's light breezy style, minimal essay demands, and smooth, quick sign-up procedure make it attractive. Furthermore, by keeping the profiles clean of offensive and suggestive language, it appeals to the mainstream dater's basic needs.

However, because of its easy participation, members sometimes skimp on information in their profiles. Almost everyone wants to read interesting details about their prospects, but nobody wants to write about him or herself. As a result, Match has decided that less is more, and enough people must agree because Match's sub-scriber base is very large.

Because most beginners usually have trouble writing about them-selves, Match makes the sign-up process easy. The difficulty comes later when you want to focus in on just the right person from the masses. Without tons of data to read, especially essays, you have to do a lot of digging on your own. Remember that the digging can be fun and Match's membership gives you a lot to choose from. That big database is especially helpful in smaller cities where find-ing sufficient numbers of prospects isn't always easy.

If you're an AOL subscriber, you can access `Match.com` via `LOVE@aol`, but it's still the same site.

### Pricing

- ✔ 1 month for $24.95
- ✔ 3 months for $49.95
- ✔ 6 months for $74.95
- ✔ 12 months for $99.00

Your subscription is auto-renewed at the pro-rated monthly value of your selected package. If you want to stop your subscription, you have to cancel the renewal before it auto-renews.

### Free site tour

**Match doesn't actually offer a tour.** The tour is more like a show and tell about Match's features, but you can't see photos of individ-uals, and you can't actually search or try out features. To do that you must sign up for the limited access usage, but it's free.

### Free limited access usage

Match offers free limited access usage, which is unlimited in length but limited in function. You can sign up forever and for free, but there are limitations. You can search all the profiles you want during the trial period. Anyone can contact you, and you can reply, but you can't contact anyone. You can only send a *wink* (a pre-programmed message) if you're interested in someone. After a few weeks into using the site, you'll be very tempted to reach for your Visa card and sign up. As we recommend in Chapter 4, pay the freight and start dating seriously.

As a paid subscriber, you can write to anyone. Only subscribers can initiate a chat (IM) session. But keep in mind: You don't have any way of knowing who is a paid subscriber and who is there on a free trial. Don't be too hurt if someone seems to be ignoring your contact; he or she may be a nonpaying member.

### Profiles

**Questions and answers:** The Match.com profile comprises mostly Q&A questions with a series of choices, mostly short phrases, which are optional. Some of the more critical questions are

- **Children — have/want?** Yes, Match asks both questions (whether you have/want children), and they're *searchable* fields. Match recognizes the importance of this questions and even asks about how *many* children and about adoption.

- **Religion:** Yes, Match asks this question, and it's searchable, but you can opt out.

- **Distinguishes marital status?** (Does Match distinguish between single, never married and single, divorced/widowed?) Yes, in fact, Match understands the sensitivity some people have about this question. Match further distinguishes between singles (never married) and divorced by adding "Committed relationships but never married."

- **Willing to relocate question?** No, Match doesn't explicitly ask this question, but it does ask how far (miles/km) you're willing to look for a prospect, so you have some idea whether he or she would entertain a long-distance relationship.

### Essays

Match isn't oriented toward in-depth essay questions, making it very easy to sign up. But of course, if you don't answer the essay questions, you won't find out as much about your prospects. Match does have one main essay question: "Describe yourself and who you'd like to meet," but even it's completely optional. Match also offers four other personality-related essays, which are also optional.

The site's staff reviews all essays before the essays go live. Every time you make a change, the site reviews the essay again. If you try to include your e-mail address in the essay (to avoid paying fees), the site blocks you, but many creative users still try to beat the system. Don't do it. It's not fair!

### Photos

Match has an easy-to-use photo posting system, and photos are a key part of the overall profile. A high percentage of users post photos after a few weeks. The photos are small but quite readable, and you can post up to 26! You can upload your photo, e-mail it to Match, or send it by snail mail and the site will scan it for you at no charge.

You can also easily save photos of interesting prospects on your computer if you click on the photo, and then click on Save As under the File heading. You can save them in your "Favorites" within Match.

### What you can find out about your prospects

✔ You can tell if your prospect is currently online; for instant gratification, you can IM (instant messenger) them. Be sure to give your prospect a little time to pick up your IM call. IM's startup takes a few extra seconds.

✔ You can tell when the prospect last logged on, which is a great feature that helps distinguish the active, committed dater from the deadwood.

✔ You can tell when the prospect first signed up, which is useful to know how experienced he or she is.

### Chat/Instant Messenger (IM) features

**Can you turn IM off?** Yes, if you don't want to be bothered, you can disable it on a per-use basis or permanently.

**Can nonpaying users initiate IM?** No.

**Can nonpaying user respond to IM?** No, and you won't know what users are unable to reply.

**Do users know when you are online and able to IM?** Yes.

If you reject an IM request from someone, they receive notice that you don't want to talk to them!

Furthermore, if you don't want to schmooze, you can go into stealth mode and make yourself invisible to other prospects who want to chat you up when you're busy surveying the terrain. However, you must reset to stealth mode every time you log on.

### E-mail system

Match has no e-mail system. You use your own private e-mail box to receive e-mails, and you remain anonymous as long as you don't put your e-mail address in your reply mail. You can send correspondence to profiles of your choice, and Match forwards it to their outside private mailbox. As a result, no person has access to another person's private mailboxes. Everyone's privacy is protected. Match also keeps an e-mail history on your Match homepage. It doesn't contain the text of your e-mails, but it does keep a handy list of your correspondents.

### Search tools

Match has several Q&A fields and almost all are searchable in most combinations. You can search profiles with or without photos or by any age parameters. You can search any city or zip code you want and get up to 500 profiles to peruse. A nice goody is the Keyword Search feature that allows you to run a search for any particular word in the prospect's text, so if beekeeping or spelunking is important in your perfect mate, you can seek one out with a few keystrokes. You can save searches, run them automatically, and have the results e-mailed to you.

### Auto-matching services

If you want to throw your fate into the machine's hands, you can let Match find you suitable matches based on the parameters you chose using its Mutual Match feature. Then Match notifies you of its findings via your private e-mail.

### Other cool stuff

- **Audio:** Match has a voice-recording system called Voice. For an additional fee, you can send voice messages to prospects by e-mail.

- **Video:** Match has a very slick video system. For an additional fee, you can upload it online as an e-mail attachment or Match can mail you a disk. The system gives you two minutes to say what you want, records decent quality, and allows you to send it to prospects as e-mail. Only paying members can view it.

- **Phone number "anonymizer":** If you want to telephone (or be telephoned by) a prospect, but want to be sure he or she won't have access to your phone number (remember: caller ID blocking isn't 100 percent secure), Match can link you through its phone system. The resulting call is truly anonymous, but it's not free. It has a per-minute charge.

- **Mobile match:** Using your mobile phone, you search and e-mail as if you were at your computer.

- **Personal Attraction Test:** Match has developed a personality test to measure the characteristics of attraction. It takes about 10 minutes to fill out, and you receive a customized report that details the type of person you're looking for and the type of person looking for you. You can then see the results of your prospects' tests as a way to focus in on the right personality.

### Special interest groups

**Can gays/lesbians find matches?** Yes, simply put in the gender you're seeking.

**Can you search by ethnicity?** Yes. The following ethnic groups are searchable: Asian, Native American, Black/African, Pacific Islander, East Indian, White/Caucasian, Latino/Hispanic, Middle Eastern, and of course, "other."

**Does the site identify special sexual interests** (such as casual sex dating, swingers, couples, and so on)? No.

### Safety issues

**Blocking feature:** Match has the ability for you to block anyone from making further contact.

**Abuse reporting:** Match receives and responds to abuse reports.

**Surveillance by a live monitor:** According to Match, the site doesn't monitor traffic, but does respond when notified of problems.

**Can you be totally invisible?** You can make your search activities invisible if you remember to turn off the IM system, but the date you were last online is always visible. So if you're dating someone and you want to keep looking, your prospects can see your visiting frequency on Match.

**Can you tell if someone has browsed you?** No. Match doesn't have a system for knowing specifically who is looking at you and vice versa.

### Secret Sauce

Remember this stuff so that you can use this site to its full advantage:

**How to stay on top of the search list:** In large cities, staying at the top of any search list is important. In the past, to stay on top, Match required you to change your profile regularly. That has changed. Now the prospects listed first are those who have most recently logged on. In a system as large as Match, log out and log on every hour or so, or you may slip way down the search list in a hurry. If you don't log on every day, you will likewise fall way toward the bottom.

**Deadwood (Who is unreachable?):** Match doesn't allow nonsubscribers the ability to reply (except for a brief period) so if you try in vain to reach someone and can't figure out why he or she isn't replying, that person probably hasn't paid. That person probably isn't worth the trouble if he or she won't pay to be listed.

**Show as much of yourself as possible:** No, we don't mean show as much *skin* as possible. We mean take advantage of the opportunity to say as much about yourself as possible. So many features on Match are optional (essays, Q&A, voice, video, and so forth). If you use them all, you tend to stand out above the crowd. Many subscribers are lazy and put in the minimum effort, and it shows exactly how serious they are.

# Lavalife.com

Lavalife.com (LL for short) is a unique site because it offers three strata of dating engagement on the same site. When logging in, you can select one of three dating communities:

- Dating (not looking for a long-term relationship, for meeting new people, without expectations)
- Relationship (looking for a long-term relationship)
- Intimate Encounters (looking for "something wild," meaning for many people, casual sex)

Each community has more or less the same format, but the Q&A varies a bit to bring out the different objectives.

## Pricing

Lavalife doesn't sell subscriptions by time. Instead you purchase credits. Each initial message costs five credits; a 20-minute IM session is five credits or ten credits for 60 minutes. Subsequent messages to the same person are free, and you can conduct any number of simultaneous IM sessions within the same 20/60 minutes for the price of one session. Anyone, with credits or not, can initiate a *collect* call. Like a collect telephone call, the party receiving the message has the option of paying for the message. The paying party can first look at the collect-party's profile before accepting the charges. Pricing is as follows

- 60 credits cost $14.99
- 115 credits cost $24.99
- 200 credits cost $39.99

Good news: LL doesn't have an auto-renewing system that sells you new credits when you run out. The credits don't expire.

### Free site tour

LL has a fun free tour that allows you to look a photos and complete profiles within a specific age range and geography. Of course, on a tour, you can't contact anyone or receive messages until you subscribe.

### Limited access trial

LL's trial period is unlimited in length but limited in function. You can sign up forever and for free. But there are limitations. You can search all the profiles you want, anyone can contact you, and you can reply for free. You can send anyone a *smile,* (a prefabricated message indicating that you're interested, but nothing more.

As a paid member, you can write to anyone. Only paid members can initiate a chat (IM) session, but you don't have any way of knowing who is a paid subscriber and who is a free trial member.

### Profiles

**Questions and answers:** LL allows you to complete a different profile for each of the three communities (Dating, Relationship, and Intimate Encounters). The Q&A questions are basic with a series of choices. Some of the more critical questions include

- ✔ **Children — have/want?** Yes, LL asks both questions (whether you have/want children) and they're searchable fields, if that is an important criterion for you.

- ✔ **Religion:** Yes, LL asks this question and it's searchable, but you can opt out.

- ✔ **Distinguishes marital status?** (Does the site distinguish between single, never married and single, divorced/widowed?) No. In fact, LL doesn't even ask the question for the Dating and Relationship communities, but interestingly, it does for Intimate Encounters.

- ✔ **Willing to relocate question?** No.

### Essays

LL has only one essay ("Tell us about yourself in your own words"), and it's optional although most people seem to give a short answer. If you do write one, you must type a minimum of 100 characters. LL isn't oriented toward in-depth essay questions or even Q&A, which makes it one of the easiest sites to sign up. As a result, you can't find out as much about your prospects unless you ask them.

### Photos

LL has an easy-to-use photo posting system, and photos are a key part of the overall profile. Many users post photos after a few weeks. The photos are small but quite readable, and you can post up to ten. You can upload the site your photo over the Internet, or send it by snail mail and the LL staff will scan it for you at no charge.

LL has a very unique system called Backstage Photos. In addition to photos posted for all to see, you control access to another set of photos in the backstage. If you're uncomfortable with having your photo publicly posted, particularly for the Intimate Encounters section, you can admit prospects to your backstage when they contact you. What LL allows you to post in the backstage is significantly relaxed over what LL allows as a public photo.

### What you can find out about your prospects

- ✔ You can tell if your prospect is currently online and contact them by IM.

- ✔ You can tell when the prospect last logged on if the prospect has allowed that in his/her preferences.

- ✔ You can't tell when the prospect first signed up, which is useful to know how experienced he or she is. You can see when the prospect last altered his or her posting, which indirectly gives you useful information.

- ✔ You can operate in stealth mode to a degree. If you set your preferences to be invisible, people can't find you in a search. However, if someone knows your user name, he or she can see how often you log on.

### Chat/Instant Messenger (IM) features:

**Can you turn IM off?** No, if you don't want to be bothered, you just ignore it.

**Can nonpaying users initiate IM?** No.

**Can nonpaying users respond to IM?** Yes.

### E-mail system

LL has an all-in-one site. If you set the preference, LL can send a message to your external e-mail box notifying you that you have mail awaiting you in your LL mailbox.

## Search tools

Most of LL's Q&A fields are searchable in any combination. Its only weakness stems from the small number of Q&A questions in the profile.

## Auto-matching services

LL has no matching service.

## Other cool stuff

✔ **Backstage Photos.** This feature provides a partial solution for people who simply can't bring themselves to post a public photo. The Backstage Photos feature avoids the need to set up a separate Web page and maintains complete anonymity. The true purpose of Backstage Photos is to allow only people you authorize to have access to more of your photos.

✔ **Three sites in one.** On LL, you can easily post profiles in three communities with very different objectives at the same time, and the profiles can likewise be different. Yet, you pay only one fee and have one convenient account to receive messages.

## Special interest groups

**Can gays/lesbians find matches?** Yes, simply put in the gender required.

**Can you search by ethnicity?** Yes. The following ethnic groups are searchable: Asian, Native American, Black/African, Pacific Islander, East Indian, White/Caucasian, Latino/Hispanic, Middle Eastern, and of course, "other."

**Does the site identify special sexual interests** (such as casual sex dating, swingers, couples, and so on)? Yes, in the Intimate Encounters section.

## Safety issues

**Blocking feature:** LL has the ability for you to block anyone from making further contact.

**Abuse reporting:** LL receives and responds to abuse reports.

**Surveillance by a live monitor:** LL claims that it doesn't monitor messages but does record them in case there is a need to investigate postings.

**Can you be totally invisible?** Yes. Just change your preferences and you can have different preferences for each of the three sites within LL.

**Can you tell if someone has browsed you?** No.

### Secret Sauce

Remember this stuff so that you can use this site to its full advantage:

**How to stay on top of the search list:** In large cities, staying at the top of any search list is important. LL lists those people who are the most recent log-ins at the top. If you're logged on for too long, you may want to logout and log on again. If you don't visit for several days, you will fall through the cracks.

**Hello Canada!** LL is headquartered in Canada and consequently has a very sizable Canadian membership. If you're looking to meet someone from Canada, LL may be the place, but still the majority of its members are in the United States, so you won't feel left out if you can't say 'eh.'

# JDate.com

Unlike the other sites in this chapter, jdate.com isn't a true mainstream site. JDate is directed toward Jewish singles, although you don't have to be Jewish to post. We take you through this site because it has user-friendly software with plenty of great touches. We also want to show you that niche market sites can be as powerful as their big-brother mainstream sites. If you're interested in niche online dating, use this site as a template.

One aspect of Jdate.com (JDate for short) you will find intriguing, if not initially a bit scary, is its vast capability to allow two-way eavesdropping or *snooping* as we prefer to call it. Although you can turn off all these features, when activated, your perusing habits are reported to the persons you have perused. For example, if you open 20 profiles for a full look, each of the people you looked at will know that you looked them over. At first, you may feel a little freaked out, but use this feature as an icebreaker, and it may even lower your rejection rate, because the people who've looked you over probably left with a positive impression. But, if you don't like any of these features, you can just turn them off. The switch is deeply buried in the Preferences area.

JDate strikes a nice balance between enough information about your prospect without being so demanding that many people give up before completing the sign-up process. Although JDate's pricing is definitely on the high end of dating sites, it essentially controls that niche market and buyers are willing to pay. In any event, online dating is still the best bargain in terms of cost versus benefit compared to traditional dating.

### Pricing

- ✔ 1 month for $ 28.80
- ✔ 3 months for $79.95
- ✔ 6 months for $149.95

Your subscription is auto-renewed at the pro-rated monthly value of your selected package. If you want to stop it, you have to cancel the renewal before the end of the period. Auto-renewal gives you some sort of guaranteed protection against price increases, but read the fine print carefully to figure out what that means.

### Free site tour

JDate has a nice free tour that allows you to do a basic search and dig deeper into the profiles. Of course, you can't contact anyone, but you can get a good idea if any sufficient prospects are available in your area before you sign up, which is important for niche sites because some regions may not have adequate subscribers.

### Limited access usage

JDate's trial period is unlimited in length but limited in function. You can sign up forever and for free. But JDate, more than other sites, encourages users to pay by severely restricting the functionality of free users.

You get free and unlimited access to the database for searching. You cannot read e-mail nor reply to e-mail unless you've paid. As a trial member, you can't initiate a real e-mail message, but you can send a *tease* (a message selected from a limited list of canned phrases) to anyone, paying member or not. Nonpaying members can respond to an instant message, but can't initiate one. If you're a nonpaying member and someone sends you a tease, you can only send a tease back. Therefore between nonpayers, you have the equivalent of tease versus tease and neither prospect knows why the other doesn't write a real message. (The site doesn't tell you who are subscribers, though many people say so in their essays.)

 Every site has more nonpaying users than paying (although JDate probably has the highest paying percentage of all sites). By being a paid member, you have way more access to prospects than your competition that didn't pay. So if you want to reach more prospects fast, buy the subscription.

### Profiles

**Questions and answers:** The JDate profile comprises Q&A questions with a series of choices, mostly short phrases. Some of the
important questions are

- **Children — have/want?** Yes/No. JDate asks if you have kids
  and whether they live with you, but not if you want more kids.
  It's not a searchable field, so if that information is important to
  you, read each profile carefully and ask follow-up questions.

- **Religion:** Yes, JDate asks this question and it's searchable, but
  you can opt out. On JDate.com, the Jewish dating site, the
  answer is a bit of a no-brainer, so the site asks what religious
  sect you're affiliated with.

- **Distinguishes marital status?** (Does the site distinguish
  between single, never married and single, divorced/wid-
  owed?) Yes.

- **Willing to relocate question?** Yes, but it isn't word searchable.

### Essays

JDate has five essay questions that aren't optional (meaning you
have to answer them). Don't fret. They're easy to answer and can be
interesting and informative to read. You must type 100 characters or
you'll be trapped in a continuous loop until you do. Some people
beat the system by typing in gibberish, but doing so leaves a pretty
poor impression of your intelligence or typing skills. Although we
were told that the site doesn't accept such nonsense, the site seems
to post it (as long as your gibberish is *clean* gibberish).

The site reviews all essays before the essays go live. Every time
you make a change, the site reviews your essay. If you try to
include your e-mail address in the essay (to avoid paying fees), the
site blocks you, but some users try to beat the system. Don't do it.
It's not honest and you look sneaky.

### Photos

JDate has an easy-to-use photo posting system, and photos are a
key part of the overall profile. A high percentage of users post
photos after a few weeks. The thumbnail photos are small but
readable, and the display photos are compressed but clear
enough. You can include up to four photos. You can upload a
photo from the Internet, e-mail it, or snail mail it to JDate, and the
site's staff will scan it for you at no charge. On JDate, you can't
post a private photo, viewable only by members. If you post a
photo, everyone can see it. The site doesn't allow explicit photos.
You can easily save others' photos to your hard drive.

### What you can find out about your prospects

✔ You can tell if your prospect is currently online, and they can then reach you on IM.

✔ You can tell when a person was online last. Someone who hasn't been online since Al Gore invented the Internet probably isn't a serious dater.

✔ You can operate in stealth mode and make yourself invisible, which is useful if you don't want to be bothered — or discovered by your boy/girlfriend. Stealth mode is selectable and remains selected until you change it.

### Instant Messenger (IM) features

JDate probably has the best IM software in the business. It is fast and has an easy-to-use IM feature. If you don't want to use it, you can turn it off permanently (go to your "Preferences" on the site). Keep in mind that a subscriber can initiate an IM session but a non-subscriber can't. A symbol on screen tells you who is online so you can IM them if you want. *Note:* If your screen has been idle for a long time, you may want to refresh it (press F5 on a PC), which checks to see if the prospect is *still* online.

### E-mail system

JDate uses an all-in-one system. JDate supplies all members with an on-site e-mail box. You remain anonymous as long as you don't put your personal information in your reply mail. The e-mail box has a subfolder system for organizing your mail. If you want to save e-mail to your drive, you have to use cut and paste the mail to your word processing program.

The site automatically sends e-mail alerts to your private e-mail account. *Note:* Some e-mail systems consider these alerts *spam* (junk e-mail) and may toss them. E-mail remains in your box as long as you remain a subscriber (unless you delete it). *Remember:* Save your mail before your subscription expires or it will disappear!

### Search tools

JDate has a reasonably powerful search tool, but it can't search all fields. Searching outside your geographic area is easy; just change your zip (postal) code, area code, or city in the search screen.

Searches default to the profiles that have photos, which means if you don't post a photo, people probably won't come across your profile.

A search may return you a huge number of hits if you don't narrow the scope, and because JDate doesn't report the number of hits, you may unknowingly be wading through an awful lot of pages before you hit bottom. *Note:* Prospects in stealth (invisible) mode won't show up in a search.

Finally, JDate doesn't have a way to conduct a key word search (for example, looking for a specific word in an essay). A key word search is useful if you're trying to find an essay you read but can't remember who wrote it.

Your search results can also indicate if you have contacted a particular prospect in the past. Everyone you have looked at is tagged as: looked at before, IMed before, exchanged e-mail, and so on. This feature is helpful if you're searching late at night and not thinking clearly.

### Auto-matching services

JDate has a computer matching system called Your Matches, which uses your prior search criteria as basis for formulating match prospects. The site e-mails the results to you.

### Snooping stuff

JDate sites have a feature that may seem kinda freaky at first, but works out to be very useful and entertaining. Unless you turn it off (default is on), the site reports to a prospect any time you look at his or her profile. The site also reports to that prospect anyone you list as a favorite. The result: You know who is checking you out. It works as a fun icebreaker. For women (especially), if you peruse a guy, you can almost count on him sending you an e-mail — unless he isn't a paid subscriber. If you don't want all that attention, you can turn it off this feature permanently, but you will miss some fun!

### Special interest groups

**Can gays/lesbians find matches?** No. Instead, the company has a specific gay/lesbian site called glimpse.com.

**Can you search by ethnicity?** Yes, but because this site is primarily Jewish, the choices of ethnic groups are appropriate to this niche.

**Does the site identify special sexual interests** (such as casual sex dating, swingers, couples, and so on)? No.

### Safety issues

**Blocking feature:** Yes, JDate has the ability for you to block anyone from making further contact.

**Abuse reporting:** JDate receives and responds to abuse reports.

**Surveillance by a live monitor:** Occasional, mostly in response to a reported problem.

**Can you be totally invisible?** You can make your search activities invisible if you turn your preferences to "deep cover" mode, but the date you were last online is always discoverable to anyone who knows your user name. So if you're dating someone and you want to keep looking, it won't be a secret to your boy/girlfriend.

**Can you tell if someone has browsed you?** Yes, if they haven't turned off that feature.

### Secret Sauce

Remember this stuff so that you can use this site to its full advantage.

**Why are people teasing each other?** If someone teases you, the chances are high that he or she is a nonsubscriber. If you tease that person back, he or she can't tease you again, unless he or she subscribes. So if two people exchange teases, the likelihood that both people aren't subscribers is high, and they'll never end up communicating. At that point, both of them have to fork over some dough (highly recommended idea) to get messages through to each other.

**How to stay on top of the search list:** In large cities, staying at the top of any search list is important. In JDate, you get to the top of the search heap by logging in. If you stay online for several hours, you will gradually drop down the list with new log-ins after you. If being on top is important, you have to log out and log in frequently.

**Deadwood** (Who is unreachable to a paying member?): JDate does not allow nonsubscribers to reply to subscribers. It also prohibits nonsubscribers from reading mail from subscribers. Thus, all non-subscribers are largely deadwood because they can only send teases and respond to instant messages.

# Considering a Whole Lotta Other Sites

The following is a listing of other sites that are equally interesting as those sites in this chapter, but space limitations prevent us from doing a full review. You can find many excellent national main-stream sites in this list, as well as we also list specialty sites that are directed to niche and local audiences. Sites can come and go quickly, and some change their flavor overnight, so approach each one with due care.

If you come across a site you think should be added to this list for the next edition of this book, or any dead links, please let us know at mail@datingauthors.com.

americansingles.com

asianfriendfinder.com

collegeluv.com

craigslist.com

christiansingles.com

datecraze.com

datemeister.com

datingdirect.com

drdating.com

dreammates.com

eharmony.com

emode.com

epersonals.com

equestriansingles.com

facelink.com

friendfinder.com

friendsearch.com

friendster.com

glimpse.com

gay.com

hifisoulmate.com

humorandlove.net

iwantu.com

jmatch.com

jmates.com

jumpdates.com

kiss.com

loveaccess.com

lovecity.com

matchmaker.com

megafriends.com

mingles.com

neodates.com

nerve.com

oneandonly.com

onetoonematch.com

overthirtysingles.com

plentyoffish.com

realsinglesdating.com

sciconnect.com

singlesnet.com

spiritualsingles.com

thesquare.com

ucandate.com

udate.com

usamatch.com

# Part III

# Jumping Aboard for the Online Time of Your Life

The 5th Wave          By Rich Tennant

"I posted my online profile and got over a dozen responses within the week. They were so impressed with what they read, that they all wanted me to write their online profiles for them."

## In this part . . .

When you finally sign up to a site and begin to peruse you first list of prospects, you're likely to have a couple of reactions: Where did all these people come from, and why didn't I know about this years ago? Welcome to the amazing world of online dating! Then come your first jolts: You mean I have to write an essay about *me?* And I have to post my photo for the entire Internet world to view? And finally, you will desperately want to write to someone and it will occur to you: What does one say to a person at the other end of the Internet?

In this part, we waltz you around all these impediments so that when you finally initiate your first e-mail contact, your profile will look polished, your photo will say "pick me," and no one will know that it's your first day online.

# Chapter 7

# Signing Up for a Trial Run

*In This Chapter*

▶ Figuring out the difference between a real trial run and a come-on

▶ Getting familiar with the issues of trial runs

▶ Knowing what to do with your trial period

*W*hen you look at the incredible number of online-dating sites, you may wonder how you're ever going to pick one — especially the *right* one. All the sites want you to join, and consequently they go out of their way to draw you in. Unfortunately, some of the come-ons are just that. But don't fret. In this chapter, we give you tips on how to test the sites and find the good ones.

## A Tour of a Site Isn't a Trial Run

Virtually every online-dating site has an almost carnival-like home page designed to dazzle the uninitiated. Most sites show luscious couples (who presumably met on the site) in a tight embrace, and you can just sense their urgency to get out of that photo and find a private place. Many of them also feature Java-enabled flashing signs offering you a tour and a free trial. Your goal is to cut through the crap and get down to the business of figuring out what makes that site tick.

But if you're like us, you don't want to have to sign up just to see what's going on behind the home page. The people who run the sites know that people want a quick look, so they often offer something called a *tour* for you to get acquainted with their sites. Sounds good, eh? Well, not so fast. You need to know that a tour is very different from a trial run, which does require some level of signup. And as fate has it, we don't agree on whether tours are worth the effort.

# A tour is a complete waste of time!

Most tours present an image so far from reality that they tell you nothing. In fact, because they're skewed to the best graphical experience, you'll probably draw conclusions about the site that aren't at all true.

For example, most tours show only prospects with pictures posted, leaving you with an impression that most, if not all, people post their photos. The reality is that different sites have vastly different photo posting rates, which greatly affects the number of photos actually posted, but you'd never know that from the tour.

Furthermore, key ingredients of a *good* site include quality profile questions (questions the site asks, which become the personal profile you post) and quality answers (answers showing real effort taken by the subscribers). On a tour, though, you rarely see the questions, let alone the answers.

Yes, tours are easy to take, but they're intended to draw you in with insufficient, if not false, information. Skip the tour, check out the features available at the various sites (see Chapter 6 for details), select a site with features that best suits your needs, and take it for a trial run.

# Hey, a tour is quick and easy, so go for it!

Michael is right to a point. A tour is a total sales job, but it's such a no-brainer that you may as well go for it.

Unlike with a real trial, you don't have to sign up for anything to take the tour. You get to look at who is on the site. You may even see a large number of potential dates. And on some sites, you can view the entire profile.

Because the tour puts the site's best foot forward, if you see something distressing, you probably won't like the site. If that's the case, you can quickly move on and try another.

Bottom line? A tour isn't perfect, but it's quick and free.

## Locating a tour's jump-off point

Finding the starting point for the site's tour is sometimes difficult. Just keep hunting around the home page until you spot it.

# Finding a Site That Has a True Trial Run

Okay, say you've done your research and know what features you want in a site (for the scoop, see Chapter 5). You're ready to go to the home page and begin the trial run sign-up process.

Before you take the trial-run, take heed: The trial run's purpose is to get you to subscribe and send money, which is entirely fair and reasonable. Be aware that everything about the trial run is designed to get you over that threshold. Therefore, you find that trial runs have a fair number of teasers, usually related to features that aren't included in the trial run. They shunt you off to the credit-card payment page before you've figured out whether you like the site (see the "Visual seduction: The fine art of getting you to subscribe" sidebar in this chapter).

A true trial run lets you test most of the site's functionality without paying, at least for a period of time. Notice some of the features you should have access to during a true trial run:

✔ **The ability to post a full profile and answer all questions.** This level of access is fairly common. Keep in mind that site operators want your money, but they also need postings to attract other potential subscribers. It's a bit of a cat-and-mouse problem. People don't subscribe to a dating site if the site doesn't have anyone for them to date, so trial run takers can post full profiles and often appear indistinguishable from the real McCoys (thems that pays).

Keep in mind that during your trial run, you may be viewing a significant number of postings from people who are also on their trial run.

✔ **The ability to post a photo.** Most trial runs allow and indeed encourage you to post a photo.

Be aware that most trial runs are time limited. If you want to get the most out of the trial, you need to post your photo immediately on signup. The site's photo police usually take about two to three days to approve your photo (they're guarding against inappropriate postings), so you may be finished with your free trial before you even get your photo up. That pickle of a situation could skew your online experience entirely.

✔ **The ability to receive e-mail messages.** Most sites provide this feature free for the trial period. An e-mail account is a very strong incentive. If you get mail while you're just visiting, won't you be encouraged to stay awhile longer?

✔ **The ability to send e-mail messages or reply to ones you've received.** Ah! Free trials usually draw the line at sending or replying to e-mail messages. Yes, you can receive mail, but some trial runs don't let you reply to mail. If you try, the sites quickly send you to the Visa/MasterCard Central Command for a quick financial transaction. Expect to pay for those services. The question is can you figure out enough about the site without this feature to make a judgment? If so, finish the trial and sign up if you like the site.

✔ **The ability to communicate with or see all postings.** Some sites segregate users by their level of membership — typically, Silver, Gold, Platinum, and so on. Some sites don't let, say, the Silver members do certain things the Platinum members can do, including interact with people on free trials. Our two cents' worth is that understanding these differences is not important to you at the trial-run stage.

✔ **The ability to use the Chat feature.** With some sites, chat is the only way you can get someone's attention who is currently online. If you can't use this feature during your trial run, you can't get a flavor for how interactive the site can be.

✔ **The ability to store and recall your *favorites* (prospects you want to come back to later).** This feature is nice, but you can easily work around it with a pen and paper.

## Visual seduction: The fine art of getting you to subscribe

Be aware that during your tour, the site may regularly entice you to depart the tour and peruse a particularly alluring profile. Just as the image of your chosen babe/hunk is about to materialize, the site directs you to Visa/MasterCard Central Command and offers you the opportunity to subscribe then and there.

Just so you know, the only way you're going to see that enticing profile is to plunk down some plastic. We suggest that you push the "Back" key and rejoin your tour. You have plenty of time to subscribe later.

# Using Your Trial-Run Period Wisely

Dating sites wouldn't call it a *trial* period if you weren't supposed to try out the site, and *try* means jumping in with both feet. Remember these tips on your trial run:

- ✔ Answer most of your mail (except for lewd or other inappropriate messages). Saying that you just got on the system and don't yet have your bearings, but will get back to the person later is perfectly acceptable. (Just make sure you follow up.)

- ✔ Attempt to assess whether the site has enough people in your age category and geographic area who may be prospects. Keep in mind that new people are always coming in and others are always leaving, but the community size should always growing somewhat. If the site is too small to begin with, it may not grow fast enough for your needs. You may have better luck with a site that's more popular in your area.

- ✔ Browse hundreds of profiles of the gender you're seeking. If your city or area doesn't have hundreds of postings, switch to a different city or postal code to see more. The goal is to get to know what people write.

- ✔ Initiate a few e-mail contacts, which seems to be especially tough for women, who tend to prefer being a recipient. You won't figure out as much about the site if you go the recipient-only route. You have to take charge.

- ✔ Make a serious attempt at writing answers to the essay questions, realizing that your first attempts may be awful. This book contains chapters to help you write your answers (see Chapter 10).

- ✔ Post your photo immediately. Even a bad photo gets you visibility, and you can always upgrade it later.

- ✔ Try to assess whether the site asks prospects the questions that matter to you. For example, if you're looking for a person of your religion with an advanced degree and no children, then the site needs to have those questions in its Q&A section. Otherwise, you'll be asking a lot of prospects some very personal questions that they won't be comfortable answering early on.

In time-limited trial runs, usually lasting a week or less, the best day to sign up is Wednesday or Thursday. If you upload your photo immediately, the site will screen and approve it by Friday, and you'll have a fully functional system for the weekend, when activity is greatest.

You can't ask some questions in e-mail even though they're routinely answered in Q&A forms. Strangely, for example, it's a lot easier for people to state their religious affiliation on a Q&A form than to tell you in an e-mail. When asked directly, they find the question too personal, and besides, there's no easy way to opt out. On the Q&A form, though, if they don't want to answer, they have the option of selecting NOYB (none of your business), and you have your answer!

# Deciding What to Do After Your Trial Run

When your free trial ends (in a week or so, in the case of an unlimited but handicapped time duration), be ready to sign up for full membership or opt out for another site.

If you opt out and move on, take heart that you didn't waste your time. You'll be savvier at your next stop. And don't overlook the possibility that you may want to come back to the first site. Many sites send you reminders (more like pleas), asking you to come back. Sometimes, they even reactivate your free trial for a few days.

If you're offered a chance to return even for a few days, take the site up on its offer. For good reason, too: After you leave, your profile may remain posted for a few more days, and you may have mail sitting in the site's mailbox. You always have a chance that you received a letter from Mr. or Ms. Right. It's free. Why ignore it?

# Chapter 8

# Establishing Your Screen Identity

*In This Chapter*

▶ Picking a screen name and tagline that makes you stand out

▶ Making sure that what you write is what gets onscreen

*T*he goal of Internet dating is to find someone who is a match or have that someone find you. In this chapter, we show you how to improve your chances of the latter by choosing an appealing *screen identity* — the part of you that prospects see online at the very beginning.

## Making a Great First Impression

Assume that a man living in a major metropolitan area is looking for a woman 35 to 50 years old, with no other limiting criteria, and that *you're* such a woman, hoping to be found. Wanna know what you're up against?

We ran such a search on several sites and got more or less the same results for the Boston area and 100 miles around — more than 500 matches (or *hits* as they're called). In fact, at one site, 500 is the maximum number of hits allowed per search, so any woman who was match 501 or more was completely invisible to our sample search.

The thought of wading through 500 hits (especially on a dial-up Internet connection) is daunting, so we quickly excluded anyone lacking a photo, which got us down to 316 matches. And the 184 or so matches that just disappeared? Well, sorry Charlie. Not having a photo is the first point of exclusion.

Now say that the man living in said major metropolitan area takes the same approach we did and whittles down his list accordingly.

He then claws through about 100 postings looking for a match worth writing to. By sheer luck (or by clever manipulation of the dating site's ranking software — see Chapter 6), you're in that group of 100.

He clicks down the list, giving each posting a *quarter of one second* review, enough time to look at

- ✔ The photo, in a reduced size and cropped

- ✔ The screen name

- ✔ The tagline (opener phrase) of 50 characters or less

- ✔ The prospect's age or age range

- ✔ The prospect's location (where she lives)

That's it. So how are you going to stand out among 100 other matches?

How you stand out depends on the *package* of three important elements: photo, screen name, and tagline. So, what does your package say?

Whether or not someone writes to you may depend on the impression that your package (photo, screen name, and tagline) transmits. We've looked at plenty of postings, and have noticed that some people didn't give these elements much thought when they signed up. Fortunately, fixing them is never too late. You just need to be sufficiently motivated to do so. (Chapter 12 is all about photos. This chapter's got you covered on the other two elements.)

If you've already signed up, do a search for your own profile. Have another person look at it — optimally a friend of the opposite sex — to see what he or she thinks of it compared with others. Even if you like it, try changing something. Doing so may provoke some original thinking and probably improve your screen image. Besides, you may attract prospects that passed you by the first time.

# Choosing a Screen Name That Enhances Your Attractiveness

Every site requires you to establish a *screen name,* which is the name displayed on your posting and the name all initial prospects know you by. Some sites are generous, giving you plenty of latitude when creating it. Others take your choice and add some other identifier to it to make it unique.

At `Matchmaker.com`, for example, you can choose any name you like (subject to approval from the site's decency police), and the site then attaches a three-digit number to it. So if you want to be Mary, you'll probably end up as Mary123. No, not very interesting, and you'll occasionally get the remark "I didn't like Mary122, so I'm trying you." But, hey, at least you get to use the name Mary.

Similarly, on any of the American Singles sites, you provide a short name and the site may add a number to it. At `Udate.com`, you pick a short name, and the site adds a number if the name has already been taken. And at `Match.com`, you get a whopping 128 characters to divide up however you want between a screen name and tagline (see the following section for details on taglines). Most other sites offer similar formulas for designating screen names.

You can always take the easy way out by using your real name followed by the number that the site assigns you, like we mention earlier in this section. But we suggest that you consider using this opportunity to make your screen name unique and attractive. Remember, your screen name is your prospects' first clue to your personality and style. You can headline your hobbies, passions, or intellect.

Following are some real-life examples of interesting, or at least eye-catching, screen names. They're useful in that they give a wee bit of insight that may resonate for the right reader:

| | |
|---|---|
| SoulofWit | FitnFun |
| SkisAspen | IlovePez |
| ForceofNature | CatsandTV |
| ArtBabe | Imagine |
| NoAvgGuy | ClarkKent |

Our bottom-line take on screen name includes

✔ On sites where you don't have much flexibility in name selection, you have two basic choices: choose a person name (like Mary, Tom, Bobby, or whatever) or do something creative. Our advice: Be creative. You don't have much space to work with, so make the most of it.

✔ On sites that allow long screen names, they end up functioning pretty much the same as taglines, so treat them as such (see the section "Picking an Effective Tagline" later in this chapter for the scoop).

✔ Don't choose a screen name that's potentially objectionable. The site's decency police will reject it, or if the site does accept it, the name could be a real turnoff. Beyond the obvious four-letter words, avoid screen names with sexual innuendo, which is a bad idea for men and downright dangerous for women. Names like Hard-one, EZ, and Hotbod aren't particularly endearing. Except for the raciest sites, you don't find those kinds of overt, in-your-face sexual messages. Everyone likes to be enticed, not hit over the head with a blatant sexual message.

✔ On some sites, searches retrieve matches alphabetically. Guess what letter is the No.1 choice on those systems? You may want to start your name with A, like A-Datable or A-Mary. Yes, starting your name with an A is a bit odd, but getting to the top of the list is your goal.

# Picking an Effective Tagline

In addition to displaying a screen name, many sites allow you to display a phrase, called a *tagline*. Some sites, such as Match.com, let you choose a long screen name and a long tagline. That option can be a bit overwhelming, though, so we recommend going with a relatively short name and focusing your creative juices on the tagline. If you try to be too creative with both, they tend to conflict and create a confused message.

Do a search on your site to see which is more prominent — taglines or screen names. Focus on refining whichever one is more visible.

## Figuring out what to write

Taglines are difficult to write. Good ones, though, are mighty powerful. People work in advertising agencies making their entire career on just one tagline. (Think "Where's the beef?")

As in advertising, the key to a good tagline in online dating is

✔ Conciseness

✔ Simplicity

✔ Sincerity (or, alternatively, humor)

In the world of marketing (which, in the end, is what online dating is all about), the goal is to reach the right customer, not every customer. This goal is called *strategic positioning,* the process of defining who you are in a way that your customers understand whether they're a good match for you. Likewise, in the world of online dating, your goal is to present yourself in a way that tends to attract the right kind of person, not every available prospect.

The obvious first step is to think about the kind of match you want. Focus on the less superficial stuff, not how tall or suave or sexy you want your prospect to be. Then you need to combine that thought with something about who you are. And from there, create your tagline.

If that advice doesn't work and you're still drawing a complete blank, you have three choices:

- ✔ **Take the first few words from your essay and call it a tagline.** Be careful that you're tagline doesn't put your prospect asleep.

  Some sites, like any of the American Singles sites, automatically use the first few words of your essay to generate your tagline. This feature can cause some serious embarrassment if you aren't careful (see the section "Checking how your tagline gets displayed" for the scoop). Don't be dull. For example, say that you started your essay like 50 percent of all postings: "I'm youthful, spirited, happy, healthy. . ." That's what your tagline will be. This tagline isn't horrible, and it won't injure anyone, but that tagline won't excite anyone either.

- ✔ **Consider borrowing from someone else's clever opener.** Don't fret here. Plagiarism is okay in online dating.

  Note that copying a tagline from someone else is only a good idea if the tagline is *really* good and it fits you.

- ✔ **Switch to humor mode and have fun.** After considerable research, good humor is always appreciated.

## Using a tagline that pulls double duty

The first purpose of a tagline is to quickly say something about yourself that invites a person to look further. The second purpose is to create some point of further discussion — an icebreaker that provides a prospect with an easy topic to start a conversation.

For example, we read a cool tagline from a woman that made us read on:

Skydiving is the coolest experience on (or off) this planet. . . .

But what if you're not a skydiver and not even interested in being one? Then switch into humor gear. A funny line can be a great icebreaker, and you don't have to be particularly funny to write funny. Try these starter ideas:

- **Use an interesting quote from your favorite writer, humorist, or wag.** Google is teeming with quotes from Mark Twain, Dorothy Parker, and Woody Allen, to name a few. The quote needn't be hilarious, just engaging. For example:

  "Way down deep, I'm very shallow." (Dorothy Parker)

- **Tweak the opening line from your favorite poem or literary piece, giving it a funny twist.** If someone is familiar with your reference, you can begin conversing about something you both already have in common. For example:

  "It was the best of dates, it was the worst of dates." (Our apologies to Dickens.)

- **Use a line from a funny commercial — even one from your childhood.** Most people enjoy pop culture references.

- **Quote your favorite bumper sticker or a friendly reminder from your utility bill.** Don't be afraid to be inventive.

- **Put the words *funny taglines* (or similar phrasing) into your favorite Internet search engine for suggestions.** We did, and we got the following:

  - "I'm boycotting shampoo!!! Demand True poo!"

  - "Everything I need to know I got from watching *Gilligan's Island.*"

  - "I run with scissors."

  - "Where are my sunglasses? Oh here they are."

  - "In time, we all become that which we most hate. That explains how I became a plate of liver and onions."

  - "I used to think I was indecisive, but now I'm not too sure."

# Checking how your tagline gets displayed

Remember the game "Telephone" from when you were a kid? You whispered something to the person next to you, and at the end of the chain, you compared what you started with to what the last person heard. Well, guess what? You may notice a bit of Telephone in how your tagline gets posted. You need to check to make sure that the site didn't turn your tagline into a scarlet letter.

The sites that allow long taglines don't always display the entire line in search results. Sometimes only a limited number of letters gets posted on a search. (The entire tagline is visible when your prospect opens your photo and full profile.) For example, American Singles uses this system to create a tagline from your essay.

Table 8-1 gives some examples of good taglines gone bad (no, it's not the name of a new TV reality show) when various dating sites didn't display the entire tagline in search results.

| Table 8-1 | Fumbled Taglines When Sites Didn't Display Them in Full |
|---|---|
| *What Was Intended* | *What Appeared* |
| I'm easy to get along with. | I'm easy |
| Most people say that I'm big hearted. | Most people say that I'm big |
| I'm 52, but I'm a doggoned younger person than my age. | I'm 52, but I'm a dog |
| People say they love my self-confident attitude. | People say they love my self |
| Remember to stop and smell the roses. | Remember to stop and smell |
| With me, boredom is always a thing of the past. | With me, boredom is always a thing |
| Please help me get off this site by being my match. | Please help me get off |

*(continued)*

**Table 8-1 *(continued)***

| What Was Intended | What Appeared |
| --- | --- |
| I'm real easy on the eyes. | I'm real easy |
| Come and see the finger lakes with me. | Come and see the finger |

You really can't tell how the computer can chop your phrase. You just need to check — after you establish your profile. And like the story of the Emperor's new clothes, people may not tell you. They just won't write you, and that's the problem.

# Chapter 9

# Yeah! Multiple-Choice Questions

. . . . . . . . . . . . . . . . . . . . . . . . . . . . . . . . . . . . . . . . . . . .

*In This Chapter*

▶ Looking at the questions that trip people up the most

▶ Choosing the answers that are right for you

. . . . . . . . . . . . . . . . . . . . . . . . . . . . . . . . . . . . . . . . . . . .

*W*hen filling out your profile, the first critical part is answering a series of questions, which we call the *Q&A*. The questions are all objective, meaning you choose from various scripted answers. (The other serious part of filling out your profile is answering a series of open-ended, subjective questions, which we call the *essay* part of your profile. See Chapter 10 for the gruesome details on that.)

For the most part, the Q&A part falls into three categories:

✔ Who you are

✔ What you're looking for

✔ Other silly questions

Your answers to *all* the questions can determine who finds you when doing a search, so pay more attention to them than you think they're worth.

In this chapter, we cover the main questions you'll encounter in a Q&A and give you important advice about how to answer them so you can attract compatible prospects.

## Getting Past Your Grand Illusion

You may think that answering questions about yourself is easy, but after you start, you may find it a bit challenging.

The first surprise most people have is that they can't remember the last time they needed to know the answers to the kinds of questions in the Q&A. For example, you may even need to check your height and weight (at least you have a starting point when you put down your stats).

If you haven't dated in a long time — like if you're recently divorced after a long marriage — you probably have tons of catching up to do. One area you need to get up to speed on is that of *reality*. You aren't the kid you were when you last dated. And, frankly, that's good. What you may have lost in baby-smooth skin and agility you can now compensate for in sophistication and class. If you date age-appropriately, we hope you won't mind that you can't compete with the 18-year-olds.

After you move past the illusion of your former youth (have you?), you can get down to business and answer the questions objectively.

# Chugging Through the Q&A

The questions themselves come in three basic flavors. These questions are your first opportunities to reveal some basic aspects of yourself to your prospective matches. Needless to say, being as truthful as possible is key.

- **"Just the facts, ma'am" questions.** These questions include topics, such as eye color, hair color, height, weight, and so on.

- **More personal stuff.** These questions cover income, religion, ethnicity, and such (although many people consider height and weight pretty personal).

- **The touchy-feely stuff.** (Guys, get used to it.) Some sites have boatloads of these types of questions, asking how you feel about various topics. A few examples of touchy-feely questions include the following:

    - How do you feel about housework? One available choice is *can't do it/can't do without it.* (Michael here. That's definitely my choice.)

    - Are you caring?

    - Are you patient?

    - How much willpower do you have?

Our aim is to give you some insight into where the most trouble lies so that when you evaluate the answers, you have some sense of what is likely to be false or at least obscure.

No matter how you answer the Q&A, go back later to see whether you need to change any of your answers. If you read enough profiles, you probably have a sense for which answers are okay and which are problematic. The wrong answer can cost you plenty of prospects. Go back and review them from time to time.

## Marital status

Jeez, how hard can that question be? Well, many people screw it up, and not necessary intentionally.

---

# Finding your perfect match E-style: A tale of two sites

Although some sites are migrating toward reducing the effort required to get a profile posted, a counter trend does exist. Such counter-sites come in two flavors: The first, emode.com, offers you a battery of tests whose results are displayed as scales along side the usual profile data and photos. For example, *Temperment* is scaled from fiesty to easygoing, *communication style* from motivating to supportive, and so forth. The objective is to give you additional tools to help define your emotional match and get beyond the mere physical. Otherwise, emode.com operates much like other sites, where you look at photos and data to pick your matches.

Another site goes one step further by interposing its judgement in place of yours. At eHarmony.com, you don't get to do any window shoping amongst the photos. Intead, you answer a massive set of questions akin to the MMPI (Minnesota Multiphasic Personality Inventory) and you let eHarmony offer you such suitable candidates. In effect: "If we ask you enough questions, we can do the matching for you." Kind of a "let *our* fingers do the walking" mentality.

If you think that other online-dating sites are too visual, you don't have to worry about that with this site. The site doesn't have any photos to look at, at least until eHarmony gives you access to the people it thinks are right for you.

If you want to try it and you have about an hour to complete the forms and 60 bucks (U.S.), give it a shot. But you have to take the questions seriously or you'll have wasted your day. Like the MMPI, if you lie, the site will know it and reject you. And we can tell you form experience, the questionnare is *long*. (Judy here, I answered the questions and received several potential matches as determined by the eHarmony powers that be. I felt that there was something paternalistic about being sheparded toward potential matches based on my psychological profile. Besides, I was looking for a mate who best complements me, not one who is necessarily the most similar to me).

A "Single" option on marital status means one of two things: The person isn't now married, or the person has never been married. Some sites are smart enough to use the term "Never Been Married," but not all sites do.

Now you may be thinking, "If I put single instead of divorced, what's the big deal?" Well, it could cost you some matches. Some people are very fixated on that data. We found that

✔ Many women won't date a man in his 40s or older who has never been married. It may also be true in the reverse, but women seem to place more importance on this factor than men.

✔ Many people won't date someone who is separated. Reason: Your prospect may return to the ex, or he or she isn't over the trauma. This prejudice may be more prevalant in women for separated men.

Before making your selection, understand the various marital-status terms:

✔ **Divorced.** This category is pretty much of a no-brainer, but beware that being divorced is a legal matter, and your true status does matter to some people. Almost divorced is like a little pregnant. Can't be.

✔ **Married.** If you're married, you shouldn't be on the site, right? Not necessarily. Some sites are specifically intended for married swingers or open marriages. *Married, but looking* sites aren't everyone's cup of tea, but if you and your spouse are into swinging, at least you have an honest outlet. On the flip side, if you're contacted by a married person on a conventional dating site, your first question ought to be "What's the story?" or more likely, NEXT!

✔ **Separated.** Although some states do acknowledge a legal separation, very few people obtain this decree. So separated means anything from sleeping in a different room to a different house.

If you see someone listed as "Separated," ask the person how separated he or she is, as in how many feet the person lives from the ex. You'll find some frauds in this category. Separated is a fairly safe place for them.

✔ **Single.** If you've never been married, select this choice. If the site offers a "Divorced/Widowed" category and you fall into either category, then "Single" isn't your right choice. If you want to conceal your divorced or widowed status and explain the situation later (it isn't an outright lie, after all), okay, go ahead, but consider our warnings.

✔ **Widowed.** If you're widowed, choose this category. Note that not many people lie about this one. People who reveal this information are also usually pretty willing to talk about their situation.

✔ **Delusional.** Regrettably, no sites offer this category, but darn well they should! Delusional in this sense is a person who thinks he or she is capable of a relationship but obviously isn't. We want this category for all people who are

- Very recently separated and who think they're ready for a relationship

- In serious need of a sexual relationship (and believe that sex = relationship)

- Still an emotional mess even though their divorces are long over

# *Age*

Welcome to the mother of all lies. Many people have discovered that cheating on age is easy. Better yet, they know their prospects will have a difficult time proving otherwise.

If people lie, they usually lie about five years or so (downward, if you had any doubts). Some people do have at least a reasonable basis for some of the deception. The majority of men seem to be looking for younger — and sometimes *much* younger — women (sometimes to the point of absurdity). In addition, some of the search engines group the age search in blocks or age bands of five or ten years. If a person is 35 and wants to search for someone who's 30 to 40, the person will be missed on many sites that categorize in age blocks of 25 to 34 and 35 to 44 unless he or she lies and puts his or her age on the lower (25 to 34) age band.

Should you lie? If you're a woman, evidence indicates that lying isn't a completely bad idea. But you need to correct your error in your essay, pointing out why you did it. Again, make the correction in your *essay,* not two years later when you're applying for a marriage license. Here's a good way to do it:

> One last thing. I'm not 44. I'm really 45. I'm young at heart and body, and this site groups people into 10-year age bands and I just crossed one. Please excuse my deception, but you wouldn't have gotten this far if I didn't. Everything else in my essay is true, and in any case, it is true that I was 44 a few short months ago.

## Lies — tall and grand

Remember a skit on *Saturday Night Live, Weekend Update,* some years ago? The anchorperson reported that Congress had raised the age of retirement from 63 to 68 . To compensate, however, he said , they also raised the age of birth to 5.

And the same goes with the age game.

We hear that people lie a lot on their profiles. It's probably so, but when we asked people to tell us what percentage of their profile was true, most people said most or all. (Of course that could've been the biggest lie of all, but we don't think so, by the way we asked the question.)

# Height and weight

The second most significant shock of online dating for me was finding out how important height was to women when they had the opportunity to "spec" a man. (The most significant shock was how many great women were online.) In fact, I found that the shorter the woman, the taller the man had to be. I am (only) 5-feet-10-inches tall and suddenly felt in need of elevator shoes. Guys do pick up on this predicament pretty quickly, and we think men inflate their height as much as women deflate their weight.

The first time I stepped on a scale in Europe, even though I knew it was in kilograms, I was so happy. I even thought (briefly) of swapping the scale for those shampoo bottles. No woman is ever light enough, and like age, weight is difficult to discern in a blurry photo. With speed limits, people assume a 5 to 10 mph (10 to 20 km/hr) grace factor, and we think that a lot of people use this same logic to adjust (yes, downward again) their true weight. Some sites are sufficiently aware of this "downsizing" that they only ask you to provide general information. Some provide weight bands like age bands.

# Body type

Probably a better measure of one's weight and fitness all in one is the body-type question used on many sites. Matchmaker uses a list like this:

- ✔ Chiseled, I work out every day

- ✔ Toned, I keep fit

- ✔ Skinny, I could use some carbohydrates

- ✔ Voluptuous/Portly

- ✔ Large but shapely

- ✔ Rotund

- ✔ I look like a reflection in a fun house mirror

On that list, height-weight proportionate seems to include the widest latitude of people and is therefore the least reliable. If you use it, expect to be queried on it.

# *Income*

This Q&A question is fraught with controversy. So much so that we don't agree on the best way to handle it.

Almost every site offers you the chance to list your income (almost always in income bands). You can always choose an opt-out answer. Some are cute (Only the IRS knows for sure), some are a bit in your face (None of your ^%#&^* business), and some are proverbial (Tell you later), which really means "tell you *never.*"

On most sites, the choices start at U.S. $15,000 and go up to $150K or so. Some multinational sites indicate the amounts in local currency, so don't forget that the $ symbol also can stand for Mexican pesos, Hong Kong dollars, and, of course, Canadian dollars, so your mileage may vary according to the type of dollar.

Your choices are to

- ✔ Give the true number

- ✔ Misstate your income (upwardly or downwardly — we've seen both) depending on your objective

- ✔ Refuse to state your income (by selecting the obscure choice)

### *Never state your income in any form*

I didn't state my income and didn't like any of my prospects to state theirs, either. It suggests, at least to me, that men with a higher income are trying to state that they're more worthy of dating — a better catch, so to speak.

Wait and discuss this subject later. Besides, you have many other ways to determine likely income when you put all the pieces together: occupation, house, car, manner of speaking, and so on. Yes, you may be wrong, but if you need better data, then you're shopping by price, not by quality.

Finally, with time and experience, I've developed a sense about when people aren't being completely forthright. Likewise, you can develop the same sixth sense about income information. One way to deal with the numbers is to divide them by two or presume that they're pesos until proven otherwise.

### *Income info can help you at times, so why not use it?*

I must say that I don't entirely disagree with Judy on this. But that said, I did list my income. (Judy told me later that she nearly skipped over me as a result. I was saved by a funny line in my essay.)

I fully realized that a segment of the dating population places high regard on a person's income, and that segment overlooks other (glaring?) flaws in prospects for the possibility of a stable financial future. They aren't necessarily gold digging or inflicted with the sugar-daddy syndrome. Their thinking is more like *safety in numbers.*

Some profiles are gushing with clues: "You need to be *financially stable,*" "We should go on our first date to an *upscale* restaurant," or "We'll travel the world" (when it's obvious that one party couldn't possibly afford it). In the more sexually oriented sites, you find some offers of sex for upscale-living exchanges. You'll see a new spelling of an old word that makes everything crystal clear: "I am looking for a *generou$* man."

So considering all that, why post your income? As a man, I was truly interested in someone who wasn't just looking for a mate in order to be financially rescued. If a woman listed her income, it was an important piece of information. I sought to attract women who would see my income, and feel that we could be compatible based on our lifestyles and professional backgrounds.

You just need to go into the income question with eyes wide open and a sharp skill for ferreting out the true gold diggers who'll never love you.

## *Education*

Although we don't have more than anecdotal evidence, we think that the typical online dater is better educated than the typical single person elsewhere. It makes sense, too. To be online, you need to know how to use a computer, type, and *write*. In addition, you need to have some money to spend and, most of all, *perseverance*. Many people attain these qualities through higher education, particularly the perseverance and writing skills.

Many people consider educational achievement important. All sites ask the education question and, frankly, offer pretty much the same choices for answers, ranging from "High school graduate" to "Postgraduate degree."

# Religion

This question can be tricky. Do you post your official religious affiliation? Obviously post it if you want someone of the same faith. But what if your prospects' religion doesn't matter that much to you, and you don't want to dissuade someone just because you're a follower of, say, Zeus or Thor?

Some sites give you help by using a follow-up question:

How important is your religious affiliation?

Other sites let you off the hook by allowing you to choose "spiritual, but not religious."

# Occupation

In North America, people are very fixated on what others do for a living — as much if not more than how much money people make. Unlike age, sex, height, or weight, you have tons of latitude with this category, and you can even get points for creativity.

Each site handles this question differently. Some sites have objective occupation lists that are pretty long but never really very specific.

Match.com is pretty vague with a relatively short occupation list but it covers all the choices, and because it only lists a few, anyone using the site can include occupation in a word search.

American singles.com uses a very detailed and lengthy list, but it isn't searchable, meaning you can't look for a 6-foot-5-inch (200 cm) blonde Norwegian who is a military MP. You just have to wade through the mountains of 6-foot-5-inch blonde Norwegians.

Matchmaker.com has a searchable Q&A with a limited number of choices, but the site includes an essay question similar to this:

> What type of work do (did) you do? How long have you been (were you) in that line of work? Do (did) you enjoy it?

# Smoking, drinking, and drug habits

All sites ask about smoking and drinking habits. A few ask about drugs (although some include it with drinking). Although the smoking data may be accurate, at least at the far ends of "Never" and "Heavily," don't count on the reliability of drinking consumption. Few people with drinking or drug problems are honest about their situation.

If these issues are concerns, and they should be, you may want to indicate the following in your essay:

> If you're into drugs of any kind, or if you drink more than socially, please spare us both the time and trouble and skip me.

We know this statement is pretty extreme, but this area is where you find plenty of delusional people. The warning won't be totally effective, but posting it upfront can help.

# Children

You probably have tons of legitimate questions relating to children but unfortunately few sites ask them. The basic question is always there:

> Do you have children?

Yes and No are the only choices. Sometimes this critical question is there:

> Do they live with you?

Yes, No, and Sometimes are typical choices. Here's what's almost always missing:

> Do you want more children?
>
> How old are your children?
>
> Would you be willing to accept a partner who has children?

Many people list their children's ages in the essay, which is a great idea. Doing so tips off those people who aren't comfortable with children of a particular age to not make contact. Unfortunately, some people shield that information for a long time because they've encountered rejection over their circumstances. Doing so is a really bad idea. It always fails, and it's way more painful.

## Pets

A few sites ask about pets. Like questions about children, they all should. Some people are seriously allergic to certain pets, making Snookums a complete deal breaker.

Here are the missing questions:

> Are you allergic to any pets?
>
> How many pets do you have? (A person with 12 dogs shows up the same as a person with one dog, but there's a world of difference between the two people.)
>
> Are you a pet lover? (This question is vague, but having it answered in some form is still helpful.)

If you have pets and they're important to you, put that information in your essay. Surely you want compatibility on that score, too. On the other hand, using a tagline like "Love me, love my dog" is probably overstating the relationship (we hope), and so is posting yourself with Fluffy being the prominent creature in the photo. See Chapter 12 about what should go into your photo.

## Medical issues

Dating sites totally abandon this area. All mainstream sites ignore disabilities of any kind, allergies, nonlife-threatening conditions, and serious medical conditions. Considering that the over-50 age group of Internet daters is one of the fastest growing segments, the omission is pretty absurd.

If you have a medical condition, and allergies are the most common, you may as well put it in your essay. If you don't, you'll have to bring it up eventually anyway, and some people consider it a deal breaker. If you're uncomfortable about shutting the door to anyone with a mammal in the house, try something a bit light, like this:

> By the way, if you have a cat, I need to warn you that I'm allergic to some, but not all, cats. The breed doesn't seem to matter. I just have to try him or her out on a test run. Perhaps if we meet and see that we have potential, your cat and I can have some quality time together.

## Sexual orientation and other sexual topics

Most mainstream sites are pretty consistent about making your sexual orientation known upfront. When you sign up, you state what you are (male or female) and what you're looking for (male, female, or both). These categories are almost always searchable, so you'll have little trouble staying on the track you want.

If you're looking for more specialized sexual relations, you need to go to a site that's more sexually oriented. Adultfriendfinder. com is pretty thorough in what it covers, has a massive membership, yet it's not specific to any sexual orientation. Men: Listen up. Such sites have a very high percentage of postings of women who aren't what they say they are. Beyond that, you can choose from a multitude of sites for any known (and some unknown to us) forms of sexual experimentation. Note that most of these specialized sites aren't mainstream (meaning they don't have mass audiences), so the software may be more primitive.

# Chapter 10

# Yikes! The Essay Questions!

* * *

## In This Chapter

▶ Procrastinating may be the best first step

▶ Checking out your prospects and competitors before writing your essay

▶ Writing a killer essay

* * *

**M**ost online sites require (or at least encourage) you to fill blank screens with answers to open-ended yet personal questions. Everyone hates to write 'em but loves to read 'em.

Just like an online photograph, an essay sets you apart from the crowd, and you can't get by without one. In fact, the essay is where the online rubber meets the road.

Fortunately, you don't have to attack the essay questions by grinding gears with pure brute force. In this chapter, we take you through the process in small, easy maneuvers so that you can get the essay done and look good. Trust us, answering the essay questions doesn't hurt (much).

Don't be tempted to opt out of the essays forever. A few sites let you weasel out of doing them but don't do it. Even if some of the essays are optional, short answers are better than no answer. Your effort (or lack thereof) really shows in this part. You'll attract much better (more compatible and appropriate) matches if you spend the time on your essays. Remember that a blank essay is like a blank stare. Not very attractive.

## Overcoming Writer's Block

You're sitting in front of a big, blank screen confronted with one of life's great questions: "Who am I?" Whatever you write will be visible to the entire Internet world, and if that isn't a daunting task, we don't know what is.

To get past the essay mountain, you have two choices: brute force over the top or around the pass. For this task, take the pass. This section leads the way.

## Procrastinating sometimes isn't so foolish

An easy and relatively painless way to write your essay is *not* to write it. At least not quite *yet.* However, many sites require a minimum number of written words, any words, before the site accepts your profile.

In order to meet the minimum requirement — a way we've seen a few times and don't recommend — is to totally blow off the essay by typing keyboard trash (random meaningless letters just to make the quota). What the reader thinks: "He/she doesn't care enough to write anything at all, although *I* had to slave over my essay. NEXT."

A better way is to type something simple but honest. Inform your readers that you're not avoiding this challenge forever — you need a little extra time. A little humor can save you, too. Try some of these placeholder examples:

> *Screen name:* **Man, under construction**
>
> *Essay question:* Describe yourself
>
> *Essay answer:* The man isn't under construction. He's fully assembled, and all required batteries are included. It's the essay that needs work. I'll return to it shortly — well, within the warranty period.

> *Screen name:* **Sneak preview**
>
> *Essay question:* Give a detailed description of yourself
>
> *Essay answer:* Coming soon to a dating site near you, a really engaging and captivating essay about myself. Alas, I haven't written it yet, but I promise I will, and it will be PG (pretty good).

> *Screen name:* **Modern major general**
>
> *Essay question:* About me
>
> *Essay answer:* This attempt at an essay is merely my first maneuver at storming Dating Beach. I'm awaiting mental reinforcements to hold my ground. For now, I ask you to accept this foothold, but as General MacArthur said when he left, "I shall return." Over.

You don't have to be funny, just sincere.

You can put off your *real* essay response for a bit, while you get your dating sea legs. But be aware that unless you've posted a photo, you're essentially invisible. No one will take you seriously, even if you initiate the e-mail exchange. Put yourself in your reader's place. With so many profiles to look at, why even slow down for a profile that's just bare bones?

## Sidestepping the procrastination trap

Writing a placeholder essay answer has risks. If you find that you're receiving lots of mail and getting a good response rate to e-mail initiatives, why finish the essay?

First of all, if you're getting responses based only on your photo, remember that all these contacts are based solely on your appearance and little else. If you're trying to meet someone who's a real *match,* you need to put some of yourself online. Your essay isn't just an advertisement. Your essay is also a way of informing others that you may not be a good match.

If you're especially attractive (or you have a very attractive photo), you may get an avalanche of mail. But you, beautiful person, have a special problem. Although the situation is extremely seductive, the number of inappropriate prospects you have to reject may, in fact, dishearten you. So know that the danger of not completing your essay applies to you tenfold. If you want people to see that you're more than your beautiful photo, then your only hope is a complete essay.

## Reading Others' Profiles as Research

Okay, you posted your photo and a placeholder essay. Perhaps you're even running down the clock on your trial period. (For more on trial periods, see Chapter 7.) To get past your essay mountain, the next step in the minimum-pain plan is to study how *others* got over their mountain. In other words, look at your prospects and the competition.

When scoping out other profiles, we strongly suggest that you start with prospects (usually people of the desired gender) rather than your competition. Look at the great prospects waiting to meet you, before dealing with the reality that you're competing for them.

When looking at your prospects' essays, control your urge to contact them right away. Search out ideas for your essay. If you write to anyone now with an incomplete profile, you'll spend a number of e-mail exchanges explaining why your profile is unfinished. Note that at many sites, you can designate and save favorite profiles for later review. Use that feature now and come back to your favorite prospects after you've written your essay.

## Looking for clues in prospects' profiles

Well, actually, you need to read prospects' profiles for *two* reasons:

- To figure out what prospects are looking for in a potential mate
- To get a sense of the site's level of explicit language

Regarding the first item, you only need to look at a few dozen profiles before you can sense what we're talking about. Of course, you immediately find the obvious.

In my experience, I quickly noticed that many women put great stock in a man who is

- Funny
- Tall
- Stable, especially financially

I found that men are looking for a woman who

- Isn't overweight
- Is attractive
- Has a full set of teeth

I'm just kidding on that last one, but I noticed that many men have a hard time getting past the physical.

If you use a keen eye, you can find that many essays suggest other aspects of compatibility that men and women consider important. Everyone notices things differently, but the main point is that by reading enough essays, you get a taste of what prospects want in a partner, as well as what entices you. And when you read something that interests you, write it down and keep a list. (For example, you may notice a common interest in a particular sport, hobby, or lifestyle.)

While reading prospects' essays, review the essays that catch your eye to see whether they contain common themes. Then incorporate those themes into your profile. For example — Judy here — I was attracted to men who appeared to be intelligent by virtue of their good writing. I decided to change the style of my essay to match theirs. I didn't need to add the word *intelligent* to my list of desired attributes.

You're not trying to write an essay that isn't true. You're reading other essays to find out what people care about. You still want to tell your own story.

Switching gears, the second reason for reading prospects' profiles is to sense the site's level of explicit language. Online-dating sites can differ vastly in the people they attract, and you can even find dramatic differences within the same site if it has different "communities." For example, on Lavalife.com, you can select which level of sexual explicitness appeals to you, from PG to, well, not-PG (most users opt for PG). If you choose not-PG, you certainly need to be comfortable with the language of that community. Furthermore, writing your essay in the same language as your prospects is equally important.

For example, on Lavalife.com's Intimate Encounters section, the usually tame sexual decorum on other communities is abandoned for something more in your face (for example, something where discussing your fondness for latex, lace, or leather may be appropriate). Still, occasionally, you see a person who wrote an essay for Disney World. That kind of essay really looks out of place when parked in the cyber version of the Playboy mansion.

## Extracting the best from your competition

After you peruse a large number of prospects' essays, you're probably chomping at the bit to hit the virtual road and meet someone. But hold on just a twitch longer. Remember, you don't have a presentable essay yet. Sure, the placeholder beats a blank essay by a mile, but it won't suffice if you're trying to get the attention of one of those hot prospects you just reviewed.

Now grit your teeth and check out your competition. You may find that most of your competitors' essays are downright lousy, but you may also find a few pearls of genius.

Your goal when reviewing competitors' essays is a bit different from when reviewing your prospects' essays. With competitors, you're looking for choice lines, phrases, and lead-ins that catch your eye. Don't copy verbatim what others write, but glean the idea and combine it with your own personality to come up with a new idea. Don't be afraid; be original.

If you find a great line you just can't resist, try to borrow from competitors well outside your local dating community.

# Putting It Off No More: Drafting Your Essay

You've looked at the essays of some juicy prospects (yet controlled your urge to fire off an e-mail) and collected some nuggets of wisdom about what your prospects want to know about you. You've held your nose while zipping through your competition's essays and extracted a rare bit of brilliant prose from a few. Now get down to business and write your own essay.

## Some major do's

If you follow certain guidelines when writing your essay, your chances of success — of meeting *the one* — are greatly improved. Our advice is to put the following guidelines on your Always Do list.

### Avoid even a hint of deception

You should never lie under four circumstances: under oath, to a customs or immigration official, to your parents, and in your online essay. If you lie in either of the first two situations, you can spend time in prison. If you lie in your essay and you're caught (and you will be), you probably won't get a chance to explain why it was necessary to lie. (And if your parents catch you in a lie, well, you're probably grounded.)

We Internet daters are a highly suspicious lot. Our baloney-meters are set to *MAX,* and our prospects' phasors are set to *poof* (online dating speak for "dump"). Prospects have good reason to challenge inconsistencies because no honesty police are watching over what's written.

# Beware BOB879

Sometimes suspicion reaches the level of absurd, and here's a story that proves it:

We know a man who didn't want to reveal his real name, Kevin, as his screen name. So for online-dating purposes, he simply created a screen name that would suffice — Bob (the system made him BOB879). Such an innocent thing, yes, but it was enough to get Kevin poofed (dumped).

How? Well, he was exchanging e-mail with a seemingly desirable woman. Initially, he didn't put any name at the end of each message, but at one point, he finally signed an e-mail with his real name, Kevin. That act caused the woman to give him a thorough e-tongue lashing about how men are frauds, and she never wrote to him again.

People are extremely sensitive to minor inconsistencies in your story. Avoid them from the get-go by not putting the seeds of one in your essay and always clarify any inconsistencies that come up later, before you get called on them.

The main way to catch a real fraud is to find something that doesn't jive between the essay and other e-mail communications.

## Be honest

If you can't be honest about something, don't mention it at all. For example, if you know your athletic ability is important to some people and you claim to be a tri-athlete, don't substitute running, biking, and swimming for remote controlling, cheese-doodle eating, and beer-can smashing.

## Describe the nature of the relationship you're looking for

Are you looking for a long-term relationship? A casual friendship that may become more? Or a date for this Saturday? What you're looking for will have a big impact on who'll write to you.

## Express your interests

Sharing your current interests not only reveals something about your character, but also ensures that you'll meet others with similar interests. For example, one man told about his graduation from microwaving to gourmet cooking and mentioned that he was looking for someone to continue the culinary quest.

## Focus on your priority issues

Focusing on your priorities attracts the right kind of person. If starting a family is important to you, make sure you let others know. Your priorities may be an attraction for some and a non-starter for others, but don't worry about the latter. You don't want to start an online relationship with someone who doesn't share your view on this issue.

### Include interesting descriptions

Express feelings rather than statements or facts. If you're a mountain climber, tell about how you feel pitted against the unrelenting forces of gravity (while constantly on the edge of death) instead of saying, "I like to mountain climb."

### Interject humor

Dating (and finding a mate) is pretty serious business, but a little lightheartedness can help break the ice. That said, don't mess with the really serious questions (like "What am I like?" "What am I looking for in a mate?" and "What is the meaning of life in 500 words or less?"). You still have ample opportunities to have fun without being considered shallow.

## You so funny

We found Matchmaker.com to be fertile ground for using humor without jeopardizing your "datability." Matchmaker is somewhat unique in that it asks plenty of essay questions. Because some questions are silly and border on meaningless, you have a golden opportunity to use humor to fill the spaces. Trust us, it works miracles!

Consider these example questions and two ways of answering them:

**Matchmaker question**: Do you belong to any clubs, teams, or special-interest groups?

**Typical answer**: I'm a member of the local health club.

**Answer with a touch of humor**: I belong to AAA, but I never attend the meetings. I know I should. Call me irresponsible, but that is why I have AAA.

Michael here: This answer got me a lot of mail, all positive except from one woman who said she wouldn't date me because she wouldn't date someone with a drinking problem.

**Matchmaker question**: If you were to meet someone for the first time, what would be the perfect setting?

**Typical answer**: A candle-lit restaurant by the ocean.

**Answer with a touch of humor**: In a small room with a single incandescent light bulb hanging from the ceiling. Yes, it may seem like an interrogation room, but isn't a first date a bit like that? Want ambiance? Okay, two light bulbs.

HE SAID

# Goddesses need not reply

I rewrote my essay many times, which was a natural progression. I could tell by the kind of e-mail response I was getting whether I was attracting someone who was right for me.

Like all guys, the first thing that came into my mind was: Write to the best-looking women. Pretty quickly I found that line of thinking to be not only flawed but also a singularly bad idea.

I decided that I was not only going to avoid goddesses but also officially swear off them.

Here was my answer to the "describe your perfect date" question:

> "She (that is a minimum requirement) needs to be in good physical condition, a good runner, no rust, and attractive, but under no circumstances may she be a goddess. (Sorry, goddesses, please check with Hunk276. He's your guy.)"

That answer (only a portion shown) got me a lot of mail from very desirable women as well as some mail from a few very infuriated women (from the Union of Concerned Goddesses).

## Keep your essay fresh

Your essay is a work in progress. Unless you're the William Shakespeare of online dating, your first few attempts at writing an essay are going to read like something Bart Simpson wrote, which is okay. You have to start with *something,* or you'll never get online.

In addition, experiment by changing your profile from time to time. If you're getting inappropriate responses or people just don't get it, you need to try something new. (For example, if you're getting a lot of lewd, sexual e-mail, perhaps something in your essay is being taken the wrong way.)

## Keep it relatively short

The right amount to write isn't rightly definable.

If that vague little nugget doesn't help you know how long your essay should be, maybe you could try Supreme Court Justice Potter Stewart's method of identifying pornography: "I know it when I see it."

Not so helpful?

Try this rule that works better:

- ✔ Check out how much *most* other people have written. Those essays are too short.

- ✔ Read the longer essays and take note of how far you got before your mind started to wander. Those essays are too long.

- ✔ Write more than too little and less than too much.

Most people don't write enough in their essays, and some don't write anything at all. You don't want to be one of them. A few people have literary e-diarrhea (they hit the maximum allowed character limit on each of their essay questions), and their whole essay reads like a self-help session. You don't want to be one of them either.

If you have a lot to say, spread it across several of your essay questions instead of crowding it into one answer. Better still, save the detail for your e-mail exchanges.

### Mention special activities and achievements

If you've won the Nobel Peace Prize, (casually) mention it, but hold back that you're a former Supreme Court Justice for later conversation.

Actually, people are interested in much more trivial achievements, like your golf handicap.

### Say what you're willing to try

Share something you haven't done yet. The activity doesn't have to be extravagant like hang-gliding or hiking the Appalachian Trail. For instance, one man wrote about his desire to cut back on his career and spend more time with a mate to travel the world.

### Share your future goals

Include how your partner fits into your future goals. If you're hoping to take your life in a new direction and want your partner to join, your essay is a good place to let him or her know. For example, if you plan to quit your job and join the Peace Corps or open a martini bar in the Caribbean, you want to attract someone who is intrigued.

### Show the real you

What's important in your life? Your inclination, at first, may be to reveal as little as possible about yourself. Trouble is, if you don't say much about who you are, why would anyone want to contact you?

# How to bring out a big achievement and not scare off prospects

Educational achievement intimidates some people, but you can take some of the seriousness out of it. (Women with advanced degrees often intimidate men.) For example, if you're a lawyer, you may just say, "I watched so many *Law and Order* reruns they waived the bar exam for me."

Remember, you're basically anonymous until you reveal your identity. This anonymity gives you quite a lot of freedom to show your traits before you reveal your identity.

## Tell an anecdote

Go ahead and share a story or some interesting past event in your life that reveals something about your character and experiences. Stories are great because they add realism to your essay. They don't have to be very long — just a few sentences.

For example, one woman wrote about discovering how to skydive and mentioned that the experience opened her up to trying new experiences (and probably cleared her sinuses).

Another woman wrote this:

> After a lurid and steamy career in international finance, at 45 I settled down to write and teach creative writing part-time. I'm now 52. (Yes, I know I put 49 on my profile, because no man, no matter how old, searches past 50.) I ran my own business for the past 10 years and now am really sticking my neck out by leaving the 9 to 5 and writing/teaching full-time. I have one son who is 32 years old. He's an engineer and happily married. My family is small but important to me, though no longer the center of my life. Favorite pastimes include walking (on the beach, but we don't have beaches in Nebraska), in the mountains (I know, we don't have them either), or in corn fields (YES, we do have those!); travel; theatre (and even theater); museums; concerts; board games; reading; and hanging out with kids (for some reason, this feeds my writing). Also love to talk. Not surface stuff but psychology, cosmology (not cosmetology), current events, and art — all which interest me deeply. I'm a good listener too, at least that's what my friends say. Picture me wearing blue jeans and a slightly contemplative look, head stuck in a book or gazing at the cloud formations in the sky. I'm still a dreamer with a strong connection with reality.

# How to brag without sounding arrogant

How do you say you're great without saying you're great? Many people use the old standby "My friends say that I am (insert glorious character traits here)," but we dare you to bring forth said "friend."

If you're going to create a fictitious friend and tell prospects "Here's what my friend says about me," why not create a fictitious friend who's famous? For example:

"He's a lot taller than he looks." Napoleon Bonaparte

"Relatively speaking, he's a smart guy." Albert Einstein

"She looks fantastique in a swim suit." Jacques Cousteau

"He has a commanding presence." Norman Schwartzkopf

Another way to introduce just about any topic is to borrow a well-known gag from television — Letterman's Top 10 list. For example:

"Here are the top reasons why I'm a good date:

I'm well grounded, and I obey all the laws of gravity.

I never run with scissors, especially at the airport.

I'm adventurous enough to eat my own cooking.

I just cleaned my house — wish you could have seen it (I may even do it again)."

Nowhere did this woman list her attributes, but she subtly wove them into a meaningful life story. A touch of humor made her real without seeming silly or superficial. We all have life stories as simple as this one. All you need is the willingness to craft an essay with care and the recognition that this essay may be the most important thing you ever write.

### Write about you

While reading your competitions' essays, you may be tempted to cut and paste a few phrases right into yours. But remember that your essay needs to reflect you.

Keep focused on the fact that the right person for you is rarely the right person for someone else. If the cosmos weren't lined up that way, we'd all want the same person, and that would be really messy.

### Write as if you're having a conversation

Keep your ideal match in your mind while conversing in your essay. Instead of saying "He/she will like sailing," try "If we're a match, you and I will likely spend many happy hours island hopping in our sailboat."

A great source of amusement is the predicament of dating itself. Dating (traditional as well as Internet dating) has its absurd side. Everyone knows it and won't mind laughing with you.

A great many people make laundry lists of what they want in a mate. I found the "describe your perfect match " question on `One2Onematch.com` to be an irresistible opportunity to feed back what I had read in hundreds of essays. Here's what I wrote:

> My ideal match should be rich, sexy, and have a beach house on the coast. Otherwise, I'm not very particular. Oh, did I mention blue eyes, blonde hair, and a perfect body? And while I'm at it, I should tell you that it's essential that you be low maintenance. Actually, no maintenance would be best, but a semi-annual maintenance check and level check would be acceptable. But then again, I'm not picky. It is NOT necessary that you feel as comfortable in jeans as an evening gown. It's only important that you have more than two sets of clothing. As to your height, after reading a few essays, it appears very important that short women have very tall men. I can't figure out why, but perhaps they're on to something. Perhaps it has something to do with light-bulb changing. Therefore, no women under 6-feet-6-inches (210 cm) need apply. My trailer home is full of light bulbs. Finally, if you're the girl-next-door type, please tell me what exactly you're next door to. If you're zoned "Industrial," you may be my type. Some guys say that if you're rich, beautiful, and your father owns a small country, that gives you extra points. In my opinion, it isn't important how you got those extra points, just so long as you have them. My minimum threshold is 745 (points). P.S. I posted two identical photos of myself. One for you and the other to give away. Just trying to be helpful.

Frankly, I was looking for someone with a dry sense of humor, and that answer definitely drew out that kind of prospect.

## Some major don'ts

Just as doing certain things increases your chances of meeting *the one,* doing certain other things pretty much guarantees failure at online dating. Our advice is to put the following guidelines on your *Always Don't* list.

### Don't apologize

The classic apology that never belongs in any essay contains the infamous words "I don't know why I am doing this..." or "I don't like talking about myself, so..." or "I can't believe I am here, but..." Every one of these phrases begs the question "Why bother to go online if you can't get over the newbie factor?"

We all had to write the essay. Don't waste our time and yours with such phrases. Okay, if it helps you get started, write the phrase, finish the essay, and then delete the phrase.

### Don't be negative or list demands

Everything in writing — especially on the Internet — is amplified in its force and effect. Negativity is especially dangerous. Avoiding negatives may be impossible, but you can with a little creativity.

Even if finding a mate who is taller than 6 feet, (190 cm) weighs less than 170 pounds (78 kg), has blue eyes, a beard, and is toned and buff is essential, listing these demands only makes you appear cranky and spoiled. E-mail negativity is stronger than in-person verbal negativity. Can't tell you why. It just is.

If you must have a specific ideal in a date, a *spec-date,* turn the negatives into positives (and then reconsider whether those characteristics really matter that much anyway). Use these examples:

- ✔ You can easily rewrite "I don't date men under 6 feet (190 cm) tall" with a positive spin: "I love the feeling of a man towering over me. I am 5-feet-9-inches (170 cm) in heels." Or maybe this: "I'm already 5-feet-9-inches and I love to wear high heels. Guys who still tower over me are a real turn-on."

- ✔ Rewrite "If you aren't slender, we aren't a match" to eliminate its negativism: "Me: athletic, trim, in shape. You: pretty much the same."

- ✔ Spin "I can't tolerate smokers, so although it's okay with me if you smoke, we won't ever meet" into "I have to warn you that I'm seriously allergic to smoke. I know I may miss out on a lot of great guys, but if you're a smoker, please accept my apologies or see whether (really) quitting is an option."

- ✔ Change "I work out every day and them some, so I need a guy with a six pack that can bounce quarters" to "I'm in really good shape, and working out is important to me, so I hope it's important to you."

Don't write your essay to be a litany of what you need and want. Your essay is supposed to be a subtle advertisement of who you are. Make your essay sufficiently clear — in a positive way — that inappropriate prospects will realize they're not a match for you *before* making contact.

### Don't be too sexually explicit

We think sexually explicit language is such an important topic that we cover it in detail in Chapter 11 (which, by the way, is devoted entirely to matters of sex).

### DON'T CAPITALIZE

Knowing why some people use capitalized letters all the time is difficult to understand, but when someone types in ALL CAPS, LIKE THIS, IT SEEMS LIKE THEY'RE SHOUTING. Yes, we know that using the Caps Lock key makes typing so much easier, but it reads like a beacon of disregard for the reader. It says, "I don't care how hard or annoying reading all caps is; typing in all caps is so much easier on my fingers, and after all, which is more important — my fingers or your eyes?"

By the way, typing in all lowercase letters with no capitalization, although not quite as annoying, isn't much better.

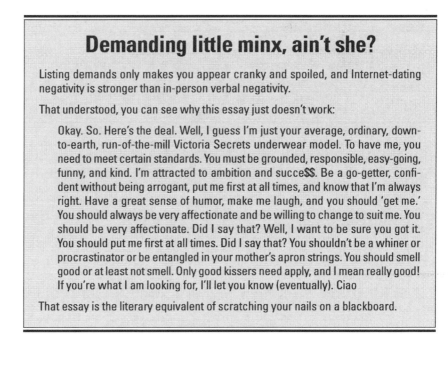

# Demanding little minx, ain't she?

Listing demands only makes you appear cranky and spoiled, and Internet-dating negativity is stronger than in-person verbal negativity.

That understood, you can see why this essay just doesn't work:

Okay. So. Here's the deal. Well, I guess I'm just your average, ordinary, down-to-earth, run-of-the-mill Victoria Secrets underwear model. To have me, you need to meet certain standards. You must be grounded, responsible, easy-going, funny, and kind. I'm attracted to ambition and succe$$. Be a go-getter, confident without being arrogant, put me first at all times, and know that I'm always right. Have a great sense of humor, make me laugh, and you should 'get me.' You should always be very affectionate and be willing to change to suit me. You should be very affectionate. Did I say that? Well, I want to be sure you got it. You should put me first at all times. Did I say that? You shouldn't be a whiner or procrastinator or be entangled in your mother's apron strings. You should smell good or at least not smell. Only good kissers need apply, and I mean really good! If you're what I am looking for, I'll let you know (eventually). Ciao

That essay is the literary equivalent of scratching your nails on a blackboard.

### Don't give a laundry list

Laundry lists are great for the Laundromat but not as an entice-ment for dating. Look at this example:

> I'm attractive, classy, smart, confident, urbane, romantic, sen-sual, affectionate, charming, easy going, sociable, creative, sensitive, high strung (but worth it), blue eyed, well read, well traveled, and a divorced mother of two beautiful children to whom I am deeply devoted, and I like the theatre, long walks on the beach, window shopping, intimate conversations, and clever repartee.

All she left out was the sesame-seed bun.

Compare the previous response to this approach:

> I spent ten years as a market maker on the floor of the New York Stock Exchange working 12-hour days, until I relocated to D.C. to work for the Treasury Department. Now I've moved to New England to get away from it all. I teach third graders how to add and subtract (just like at the Treasury). Now I get my summers off, hopefully to enjoy them with someone I meet here.

No laundry list there, but she still expressed that she's passionate (at least about her work), probably very intelligent, professional, creative, and risk taking. So much better than a list, and her essay *begs* you to ask her questions. Her essay is an automatic icebreaker.

### Don't mention the trauma of your prior relationship and/or marriage

If you rant about a prior relationship, you're saying that you're not ready to let go of the past (or that you're a vindictive jerk/jerkess). Although your past-life experiences are important, they're a no-win situation in your essay. Even if your ex was a psychopath who was convicted of treason and you were totally justified in leaving him or her, by mentioning the situation, you only raise more questions, none of them enticing. In your essay, advertise your most attrac-tive self; don't hang out your dirty laundry.

### Don't pontificate

Save pearls of literary genius for later. Essay readers are graduates of short attention–span theater and aren't interested in long quotations, passages from novels, or poems. Unless you select a great quote or phrase that directly relates to who you are, save it for a later, more intimate exchange with someone you know will be interested.

### Don't say everything in your essay

Save some for later discussion. Try to resist the urge to put your entire life's story in the essay. You may have many great tales to tell. Just slip a few tantalizing morsels into your essay, and an interested reader will know to ask for more.

### Don't use clichés

Clichés are very tiring. "I love walks on the beach at sunset." (Isn't that the definition of cliché?) Using them only reinforces that you may be as boring as what you write. Phrases, like fruit, are better when fresher.

### Don't use words you don't know or others may misinterpret

If you've been studying for the SAT recently, you know having a vocabulary of obtuse words can get you into a prestigious college. If you normally use such words in your regular speech and they don't come off clunky or forced, using a few of them in your essay is okay. It may help you find an intellectual equal. Unfortunately, though, misusing such words in your essay may cost you a great date.

Nobody likes a smart aleck. Write like you speak.

## Some bonus nuggets of advice

In addition to the definite do's and distinct don'ts of essay writing, follow these few other tidbits.

### Add a final touch of spice: an audio file

Pictures are worth a thousand words, so posting a photo is a must (see Chapter 12 for details). But don't overlook the power of an audio file, which makes your profile distinctive.

An *audio file* is a digital tape recording of something you want to say to your prospects. You record the file from your PC (or, with some dating sites, by calling a special toll-free number), and readers can play it back through their computer speakers.

Few people bother to add an audio file to their essay so those who do become a curiosity of sorts, which makes the effort worthwhile. In most dating sites that have audio, the site earmarks your profile with some kind of noticeable icon indicating the presence of the audio feature.

Does anyone bother to play audio files? You bet. So what do you say? Michael here: I opted for humor by quoting a Verizon Wireless commercial ("Can you hear me now? Good."). But you may prefer something more mundane.

What you say in your audio file doesn't really matter. What matters is that your prospects get to hear your voice. Like a good photo, a soothing voice can be very attractive. If you have a good voice, use this opportunity to stand out.

### Avoid abbreviations and acronyms

Once upon a time abbreviations had their place. Writers of personal want ads, paying $1 per word, crafted some amazing acronyms, like SWFISOSDMFF (single white female in search of single divorced male for fun). Later, techno-geeks found great joy in using acronyms to amaze and impress mere mortals, like TWAIN (technology without an interesting name) interfaces.

But with your essay, consider most abbreviations and all acronyms to be verboten. (Oh, yes, avoid foreign words, too.) Trying to communicate with someone you don't know (and can't see, hear, or touch) is already hard enough. Quirky language, like TTYL (talk to you later) or BTW (by the way), may seem obvious to you, but who knows how your recipient is interpreting it. The best rule is to save shortcuts for later communications, when you and your prospect can get a better feel for mutually understood terms.

Alas, not everyone you write to will have read this book (although we can't understand why), so others won't be taking our advice of avoiding the use of acronyms and abbreviations. For help in deciphering all that online alphabet soup you may encounter, turn to Chapter 3. It contains a brief introduction to commonly used Internet acronyms, abbreviations, and *emoticons* (pictographs made from keyboard characters).

### Check grammar and spelling (twice)

Bad grammar and spelling gives a poor first impression. Fortunately, software is available for spelling correction and, although much less reliable, grammar checking. Unfortunately, almost none of the dating sites provide such spell-check software in their system, (and *never* in their instant message [IM] software). So you have to muster all your discipline to run a spell check on every message you send — at least until you know the person and your spelling weakness are forgiven.

# Chapter 11

# Dealing with Matters of Sex

*S*ome therapists say that for a healthy relationship to work, you and your other half need to balance the six Fs:

✔ **Family.** Both parties share similar views on loyalty and devotion, as well as on the importance of each other and their children.

✔ **Finance.** Both parties have similar attitudes about spending and the significance of money (or lack thereof).

✔ **Friendship.** Both parties share a fundamentally great friendship with other benefits thrown in.

✔ **Fun.** Both parties have comparable ideas about what's enjoyable or at least can enjoy each other's preferences.

✔ **Fighting.** Both parties agree on what's a fair fight. (Even an unfair fight is okay if both parties agree on the terms.)

✔ **Sex.** (Yup, in the therapists' formula, this one also starts with F but not in print.) Both parties fundamentally agree on what's okay and what's not, without either party feeling inhibited or stretched by the other. (This task is trickier than it seems.)

That last F — sex — is one of the greatest forces of nature, on par with water and wind. Sex is such an important part of dating and relationships that it's the entire focus of this chapter.

In researching this topic, we talked with hundreds of online daters and read all the literature and research we could find. In a nutshell, we discovered some interesting tidbits. Everyone wants to hear about sex on the Internet, but few want to talk about it. We also found that no one single truth exists about sex in online dating; instead, many truths exist. In this chapter, we tell you some of those truths.

Giving advice on sexual topics in a book is the surest way to get into trouble. After reading this chapter, some women may complain that we base our assumptions on stereotypes, present or past. Some men may have the same complaint. We ask for your indulgence in advance, because we're telling our story for the mainstream public based on the people we talked to about the subject. If your predilections aren't mainstream, perhaps none of this discussion applies to you. In such a case, we say to proceed at your own risk.

# Determining Your Objective: Casual Sex or Relationship

Even the tamest online-dating site provides some opportunity for you to express your interest or disinterest in sex, so rest assured that you can get your message out. What we want you to know, though, is that what you write about sex is going to determine, to a greater degree than you can imagine, how your prospects respond. In short, be very careful with this topic, no matter how you feel about it.

Furthermore, sex is an important part of most healthy relationships, so the question isn't so much whether sex is going to happen but when (even if that means engagement or marriage way down the road). What you need to decide upfront is what you're looking for — a relationship or casual sex. In other words, is sex your primary objective? Or is your primary objective intertwined with the development of a more complete relationship? Knowing the answer helps you determine which dating site to use and what to expect in terms of online sexual communication.

The younger you are, the more likely you are to accept premarital sex as a well-established part of mainstream thought. (Yes, we know significant groups disagree with this concept, and some religiously oriented dating sites take quite the opposite view.) And the Midwest is far more conservative than either of the coasts when it comes to sexual issues.

In our research, we discovered several interesting tidbits regarding sexual communication among the various types of dating sites, including:

✔ **Most mainstream dating sites are geared for people who are looking for a long-term relationship.** These sites don't promote or discourage sexual contact between their members, but they do make some effort to keep the *public* portion of their site free of language that may offend anyone.

These sites don't want to shock first-time users who may be timid or wary of joining. They typically keep all serious four-letter words out of your essay and prohibit nude photos. The Howard Stern radio program is far more offensive and sexually suggestive than any mainstream dating site.

To make sure they're not prudish, so if you want to find an even moderately tasteful way to say what you want, the sites won't block it. E-mails aren't normally monitored because they're not public. (Some sites sporadically monitor chat room dialog.) The only time an issue arises is when someone reports an abuse to the system monitor. Most mainstream sites enable you to block mail from anyone for any reason. We suspect that if you get blocked by too many people too frequently, your activities may be monitored.

Some mainstream sites are skewed toward a younger audience, 20s and 30s, such as Nerve.com and Lavalife.com, but that only changes their orientation from finding a *mate* to finding a *date.*

✔ **Entirely different from mainstream dating sites are casual-sex dating sites, geared for people who aren't looking for a long-term relationship or even a dating relationship.** Although these sites make up a very small percentage of online-dating sites, they don't necessarily have fewer subscribers (both male and female). The site operators tell us that the subscribers aren't commitment-centric daters, so these sites may not be the best place to find a marriage partner.

These sites permit heavy sexual overtones. If you're not looking for a casual-sex partner but happen to come across one of these sites by accident, the experience can be a bit shocking.

✔ **Combination sites have a lot of mainstream users as well as special "communities" of casual-sex seekers.** What makes these sites unique is that you can sign up as one type (mainstream) and cross boundaries into the casual-sex portion without paying any additional fees.

Because Lavalife.com is a combination site, it recognizes that your essay for a long-term relationship is probably very different from an essay for a casual encounter, so the site allows you to have multiple essays.

✔ **Other sites masquerade as dating sites but aren't about dating at all.** The most common masquerade site merely delivers viewers to porn-for-sale sites. Another common type offers foreign (mostly women) brides for sale. These sites don't help the online-dating industry gain respect, but because no standards on terminology exist, the masquerade continues. These sites are pretty easy to spot.

# Speeding up intimacy

"Do online daters really get intimate more quickly?" The closest thing to a right answer is that, yes, they may. Here's why:

Internet dating involves many small steps along a path that ends in a face-to-face meeting. First comes e-mails, and then a phone call — sometimes more than one. Then maybe more e-mails come, finally followed with a meeting.

In many cases, the first meeting occurs long after the first contact (which, by the way, is almost always the case in long-distance relationships — see Chapter 20 for more on long-distance relationships). As a result, both people feel that they know each other much better than they would have on a blind date, even though technically the meeting is still something of a blind date.

On a first date that's a traditional blind date, very few people end up in bed. Making that leap with no foundation is just too much of a stretch for most people. But on a first face-to-face date that transpires from an online-dating site, the chance for early intimacy (though still not likely) is greater due to the many e-mail and phone exchanges that occur before the first meeting.

**Warning:** Many people report that if they engage in long e-mail exchanges and phone contacts, they tend to build fantasy expectations of the first face-to-face meeting. Those expectations do have their own momentum, which can lead to earlier intimacy. However, those same fantasy expectations are probably also the cause of many first-meeting disasters. The greater your expectations, the more likely you're going to feel disappointed if they're only partially met.

You may have experienced this situation in a smaller way if you ever e-mailed someone for days (or weeks) and then finally heard the person's voice on the phone and it didn't match the voice you had imagined. Usually, people get past that kind of letdown quickly, but if the photos, voice, demeanor, and body language don't match what you've conjured up in your mind, you're likely to walk away from the first meeting crushed. Best advice in such a case? Make the first meeting short. Then get back on the phone in a day or so and talk and keep sending e-mails. See whether you can close the gap *in your mind* between the phone prospect and the real prospect.

# Addressing Sex (or Not) in Your Profile

If you subscribe to a mainstream site, the site won't ask you overtly sexual questions for your profile, but that doesn't mean you won't have ample opportunity to lace sexual innuendo into your answers. We aren't just talking about essay questions, like "What do you think is sexy?" or "Define sexy," but multiple-choice questions with available answers that run the gamut from sexually neutral to unmistakably sexually provocative.

## All sexual info will be scrutinized

You need to realize that some people can take an honest answer involving a sexually provocative question out of context because such an answer is word searchable on most systems. For an example of the ramifications, consider this Q&A found on one service:

> Question: "What is my favorite indoor activity?"
>
> Available answers: Shopping, table tennis, sitting by the fire, reading, watching TV, movies, bowling, sex.

Selecting *sex* as your answer, when in the context of a thoughtful essay, may not seem particularly provocative. Problem is, a subscriber can easily run a search for all people who are looking for sex. If that's your favorite indoor activity (and we found many people who said so), would you feel okay if it were taken as your *primary* indoor activity?

 We asked a few women who listed sex as their favorite indoor activity to temporarily remove that tidbit from their profile. The number of lewd e-mails they received dropped. In short, what you write may not be what people see.

 Be careful about tucking sexual answers into otherwise nonsexual questions. Some of these answers are pretty funny in the context they're placed, but remember that some people doing word searches don't necessarily view your answers in the same context.

Lest you feel discouraged, we found some code words that provide generally acceptable ways to express a healthy sexual interest without being lewd or lascivious:

- Passion
- Passionate kisser
- Hugging
- Affection
- Intimacy
- Kissing
- Warmth and closeness
- Physical relationship
- Physical compatibility

On the other hand, the following terms and discussions often turn off people who are seeking a long-term relationship:

- Sex
- Sexual ability
- Names of body parts (anatomically correct names, including Latin and more earthy terms)
- Names of specific sexual acts
- Mention of previous sexual conquests

## Every sexual response has at least two interpretations

Internet dating is no more sexually provocative than real dating. After all, a person's clothes, makeup, and tone of voice can be very sexually engaging in person but completely lost on the Internet. Likewise, although you find a photo provocative, without eye contact, you lose much of the sizzle. In addition, the feedback you get from eye contact gives you an immediate idea of whether your message succeeded or whether you really screwed up. Try that in e-mail!

Internet daters must work with mere words to create the sexual tension that's part of regular dating. And they have to craft those words entirely in the dark. Furthermore, although most of us have developed a level of skill at nonverbal sexual communication (body language), most of us still need to discover a comparable skill on e-mail.

Considering those challenges, putting sexual info in your profile can be risky because some people may misconstrue the meaning. Here's what we found:

✔ Anything that *can* have a sexual meaning is usually taken as such. Consider, for example, the question — how you would end a first date. Answering "anything goes," is fairly obvious what you mean, but what if you answer "light petting" (an actual choice) or "I'll introduce you to my parents"? Do those choices mean sex is part of the night's activities? To some people, the answer is certainly yes. Be sure you're okay with that interpretation.

✔ Men are especially eager to assume the most sexually provocative meaning to whatever you write. Hey, they're wired that way. If you want to make sure that we get the message, don't be confusing in your e-mail.

✔ Women, you'll get far more lewd and possibly offensive e-mails from men (and some women) if your Q&A answers include sexually provocative choices.

✔ If you want to be even a little bit provocative, switch to a casual-sex site. Your moderately provocative posting will seem tame compared to the competition.

# Figuring Out the Right Time to Talk About Sex

Even if you follow our advice in this chapter, know that we're not suggesting that sex, sexual innuendo, and flirting aren't part of Internet dating. They are, and without them, online dating would be dull. But like most aspects of life, talking about sex comes down to *timing*.

We can't say when the timing is right for you and your prospects, but we do have a few choices for you to consider bringing sex up:

✔ In your profile — Q&A and/or essay

✔ In the initial e-mail contact or early contacts

✔ In the first phone contact or later e-mail contacts

✔ After the first meeting

✔ After several dates

> ✔ In e-mails after meeting in person
>
> ✔ After the wedding
>
> ✔ Never

We both agree that you should avoid sexual provocation in your profile's Q&A answers unless you're fully prepared for the consequences. (And to be fair, we found both men and women who understood what they were doing and were completely comfortable with their choices.) But we differ on when is the best time to bring up sexual topics, such as the importance of sex in a relationship, previous sexual experiences (good and bad), expectations, and so on.

## A woman's perspective on timing

Face it. Guys seem to always be interested in sex. Sometimes women are, too, but usually not as quickly or indiscriminately as guys.

For women: You need to know that given a chance, guys usually find the most sexually suggestive meaning to anything you write. Neither they nor you can win this struggle between what you write and what they read, so I recommend keeping sexual choices out of your Q&A and essay.

And, for men, the same advice goes out to you: The best thing you can do is keep your sexual innuendo in your holster until you get to know the woman better. Avoid sexual choices for your Q&A and keep sexual info out of your essay.

Furthermore, don't raise sexual issues or discuss matters of sex until after the first phone call or, better yet, the first in-person encounter because so many e-mail contacts fail to make it to the first meeting. Why bother getting into sexual topics if the relationship isn't going to advance that far anyway?

Not that sexual compatibility is unimportant to me. It's very important, but personally, I'm not willing to discuss such a personal topic with anonymous strangers. Besides, I can think of so many other important things to discuss early on, such as family, concept of commitment, and culture.

Bottom-line advice? Don't be so eager to talk about sex, and chances are you'll get there sooner than you think, but at a time that's right for both of you.

# A man's perspective on timing

Most of the women I interviewed had strong opinions about the importance of finding a sexually compatible partner. Many women were particularly unhappy about past sexual relationships, and they were adamant not to repeat that experience.

For men: Know that sexual compatibility is important to many women. You can still share your feelings about sex — but do it in a subtle manner.

I agree with Judy that the Q&A is a bad place for innuendo, but the essay may be okay if you're extremely discrete and abstract. For example, saying that you consider intimacy to be an essential element of a long-term relationship is hardly saying anything that would surprise a woman. By saying it in an appropriate way, in the right context, you can send a signal that it matters to you, too. Explaining that intimacy is more important than a quick romp in the sheets doesn't hurt. Your choice of wording is key.

And for the record, this advice doesn't just apply to men. I found that both parties want reassurance that maintaining vibrant sex is an important part of any relationship.

On a personal note, when I was dating online, a discussion of sexual compatibility (finding someone who shared my feelings that sex is integral to a long-term healthy relationship) was sufficiently important that it was worth taking some measure of risk to find out whether my prospect's views were compatible. So I approached the topic early — after several e-mail exchanges but well before a first meeting. I discovered that more women than I could've imagined shared similar concerns.

So my bottom-line advice? Approach sexual subjects early — after several e-mail exchanges but well before a first meeting — as long as you tackle them tastefully and with respect and concern.

# The best time to talk about safe sex

*Safe sex* (or, more properly, *safer sex*) is a topic that ought to come up at some point right? Everybody has trouble bringing up this subject, but online daters may have the advantage. For prospects that turn out to have real potential, you will move from email, phone and of course, meet in person. Our advice: even though you have other forms of contact, don't abandon e-mail. E-mail gives you the unique ability to talk about difficult subjects with less emotion, threat or chance of embarrassment

If you're going to discuss safer sex through e-mail, approach the subject soon after you meet, but way before you have an immediate expectation that the next meeting will be intimate. This timing makes the discussion more abstract and not necessarily suggestive.

# Chapter 12

# Selecting the All-Important Photo

*L*ike it or not, appearances do matter in *any* form of dating. When you meet people at a bar or other in-person venue, you first notice a person's appearance. In person-to-person contact, looks give us clues, right or wrong, about what a person may be like. Unfortunately but realistically we often make mistakes about people by drawing on our prejudices when we see their appearance.

Internet dating doesn't really change our behavior at all. It just delays us from getting very accurate information because we draw our visual clues from a single and often fuzzy photo, which is hardly as valid as a three-dimensional person in living high-resolution color. Regardless, even a single photo is vitally important in Internet dating, and this chapter explains the reason.

## Unleashing the Power of the Online Photo

In online dating, you make a tradeoff. You lose the sense of touch, smell, and sound, but you gain other insights, many of which may also be critically important to you (like number of children, marital status, religion, and such). And we think the tradeoff is good in the long run.

However, if you don't have any visual clues upfront, you may end up with the nagging feeling that your online communications were a complete waste of time if your prospect's look didn't turn out to be a good fit. Besides, photos help demystify the already some-what mysterious nature of online dating.

Although online services try their best to cajole you to post your photo, they don't force you to do so for one very important reason: They want your money, and if you don't sign up on a site that insists on a photo, they lose your money. They know you probably won't have a very effective online experience, but from their point of view, having an unhappy customer is better than no customer at all. (Plus, they figure that after you see how many people have photos posted, you may change your mind.) Bottom line? Don't skimp just because the site says photos are optional. They're not optional in terms of success.

Do you want to know the real power of the online photo? Read on:

- ✔ If you post a photo, you'll get roughly 10 times the number of contacts as profiles without a photo. Several dating services have actually measured this criterion through direct testing, and they've always come up with pretty much the same result. Losing 90 percent of possible responses may be okay if you live in Tokyo, Bejing, or other cities where the populations are enormous, but in all other places — even New York City — you can't afford to lose those prospects.

- ✔ Posting a photo dramatically reduces your nonresponse and rejection rate. Many people simply don't respond to an e-mail contact from a nonphoto person. You find that many people (especially women) say exactly that in their essays.

- ✔ You don't need to be a babe or a hunk for a photo to work for you. A decent photo demystifies you and makes you a person with a face, not just a block of text.

If you're still unconvinced about the importance of a photo, browse others online to see what they're doing. You'll find this direct relationship: Beginners have a lower percentage of photo postings, and more-experienced users (about a month online) show a dramatic increase in photo postings. You'll quickly realize that successful online dating requires a photo.

# *Facing the Consequences of Not Posting a Photo*

Some people get it right away: Online dating is just impractical without a photo. Others don't understand and wander around in no-photo darkness for a while.

We want to spare you the 40 hours of wandering, so read these fundamental reactions people have to profiles with no photo postings:

- ✔ **Men without photos:** Women find profiles with no photos suspicious, perhaps ominous. Is he trying to hide his identity? Is he married? Is he a criminal? Does he look like Mr. Potato Head? Women are unquestionably more cautious than men in general and even more so online.

- ✔ **Women without photos:** Men are suspicious, too: Is she particularly unattractive? You know how visual many men are. No matter how witty, clever, or intelligent you are, men just have to have a look at you. You may consider a visually fixated man to be unworthy, but assuming that all men who want to have a visual clue about you are fixated on looks is unfair.

- ✔ **Anyone without a photo:** The overall reaction is this: Why aren't you taking the same risk of exposure as the rest of us? Many people have told us that fairness and balance regarding photos are really important to their comfort level.

***Note:*** Dealing with exchanging photos if they're not posted in the first place is difficult. The reason is that the underlying message is more complicated than it looks at first glance.

Say, for example, that you write this:

> Hi, Man123. I saw your photo and profile and think we have a lot in common. Please write me if you see the same potential in my profile. By the way, I didn't post my photo because [insert any number of reasons here], but I would happy to e-mail you a photo, if you like.

But the reality is that he sees this:

> Hi, Man123. I saw your photo and profile and think we have a lot in common. Please write me if you see the same potential in my profile. By the way, I didn't post my photo, but I will grudgingly

send you one, if you're so shallow as to need to see my face before you decide whether I'm worthy.

Furthermore, if a person agrees to see your photo and then suddenly loses interest, you'll question why he or she rejected you on the basis of your appearance alone. Such prospects may try to find a polite way to extricate themselves from further communications, or they may just *poof* (disappear altogether). Many prospects don't bother to reply because they don't want to be put in that awkward position in the first place. We know of no way around this dilemma. After one such experience, most people simply avoid profiles without photos, even if the prospect offers a photo later.

# Getting Over the Excuses for Not Posting a Photo

People rationalize all sorts of reasons not to post their photo online. Six reasons immediately come to mind:

✔ **Excuse No. 1: I'm embarrassed about doing Internet dating.**

Yep, everyone seeing your photo knows you're dating on the Internet. But how do they know that? Because they're also on the Internet for the very same reason. Somewhere between 5 to 20 million people are dating online.

✔ **Excuse No. 2: I'm insecure about how I look.**

Remember, when you meet people in other settings, you're a walking photo. Look at the cross section of people with photos posted. Some are good looking, and some aren't. Most are just like everyday folks.

✔ **Excuse No. 3: I want people to see my character, not just my looks.**

You don't believe in finding true love on the basis of how one looks but instead how they act. Okay, you can return to planet Earth now. You're attempting to change human behavior singlehandedly. Like it or not, appearances matter in any form of dating.

✔ **Excuse No. 4: I'm famous (or infamous).**

Granted, this excuse doesn't apply to most of us, but even famous people use online-dating services. If you're one of those rare people, you can still post a photo. Simply use a more obscure one — maybe one with a different hair style or clothing. You can also use a photo with distant view where you're wearing a hat. Yes, prospects may have a difficult time seeing you, but at least they know you're a serious online dater.

✔ **Excuse No. 5: I don't have a scanner or digital camera to post my picture.**

This excuse doesn't cut it either. Almost all online services receive photos by snail mail and scan them for you. Think of another excuse.

✔ **Excuse No. 6: My dog ate my photo and insists he will eat all future photos.**

Now we're talking! The fact is, if you have no intentions of posting your photo, and are willing to limit your chances of success online, you may as well give a lame excuse like this one. The others are just as lame, but you'll get points for being an original.

# Working Around the Photo Impasse

So a photo is strictly out of the question for you, huh? Well, fret not. We can still offer some advice. We engaged our crack team of lawyers (that would be Michael) to find you a couple of loopholes, which provide partial solutions to the no-photo problem.

## Posting your photo on a secret Web page

One method for working around the photo impasse involves using a Web site that hosts your photo but only reveals it to those people whom you authorize. You provide the photo's Internet address and username when you send an e-mail to a prospect. An example e-mail may look like this:

Hi, [insert prospect name here].

I liked your essay, and you look great. I was particularly attracted to your occupation as a rat farmer. I have often dreamed of leaving the rat race and settling down on the rat farm. If you find my profile interesting, let's exchange some e-mails.

Billy Bob

P.S. I'm sorry I didn't post my photo, but I just don't feel comfortable posting my photo because [insert excuse here]. I know how important a photo is, so I posted mine at `http://photos.yahoo.com/dummiesbook`.

If you go to that site, click on my album and you can see some pictures of me.

Always include this link in your first message to all prospects you write to. They're probably unwilling to ask for your photos (because they may feel shallow if they reject you after seeing your photo). Sending your photo link with your message eliminates that resistance and they will almost certainly take the time to look at your link.

 Many of these services are available on the Web, and some are free. yahoo.com has a very nice one. You will also find one at facelink.com. Of course, you can also set up your own Web page. They aren't linked to your private e-mail address, so that remains secure.

 When selecting a place to post your photos, read the fine print. When posting on some free sites, you're automatically granting them the right to sell your photo! In addition, be sure the site has a mechanism for deleting your photo and closing your account before you sign up.

Remember, offering to send someone your photos isn't the same as sending them your photo link, unsolicited, with your first e-mail. Asking you for your photo is often difficult, and may appear shallow (see the section "Facing the Consequences of Not Posting a Photo" for the reasons), so you need to offer the Web address containing your photo with *every* new e-mail you send.

 Use the "post your photo on a secret Web page" workaround only if you're willing to be proactive and write e-mails to anyone you're interested in. We know from our research that women especially prefer receiving mail instead of initiating contact. If you're one of these women, you can't use this workaround. This approach also requires that your reader be willing and able to find your photo.

## Posting your photo outside your hometown

If your concern isn't that your picture is posted but that people you know in your community may see it, a simple workaround is available. Instead of setting up your profile in your hometown, select a different community or zip code when registering.

SHE SAID

## Facing down the fears of going photo-public

When I first faced the question to post or not to post, I was unsure of what to do. Because so many people are dating online, I figured that as a physician surely a few of my patients would see my photo there (and they did).

I procrastinated for several days. In the end, I realized that I was Internet dating because it was the most practical method for me to meet people. I wanted to succeed. Why should I sabotage my effort by leaving out the most important ingredient — my photo?

How this workaround works depends on which dating service you choose. On some sites, the region or community your profile appears in is a choice you make at signup. You can change your apparent location by just altering the zip/postal code in the confidential information section of the setup *after* paying by credit card. You can make the change to your zip/postal code at any time and as many times as you want. If you put in a zip/postal code that isn't the one on your credit card, your payment may be rejected.

When using this workaround, know that you won't receive e-mails from people in your local community because they'll consider you an outsider in their midst, and most people don't want to bother with long-distance relationships. So people who intend to be proactive and initiate all contact (just like with posting a photo on a special photo Web site) should use this approach. You also have to explain why you're located in the wrong community, which may be tricky in the suspicious world of Internet dating, but you can explain it if you're sincere.

Here's an example of how to do so:

Hi, [insert prospect name here].

I noticed in your profile that you're a page-turner for the string section of the Cleveland Symphony. I have been to that symphony many times, but I have never seen you there. Do you hide behind the violas? Anyway, it seems that we may have a lot in common, and if you agree, please write back.

Barbara

PS: I know it looks like I am from Toledo, but I really do live in Cleveland. I posted myself in Toledo because too many people in Cleveland know me. I'll tell you all about it when you write.

# Dealing with the Attractiveness Issue

Whether you're not so attractive or totally to die for, you've probably got some reservations about posting your photo online, such as

"What if nobody responds because they think I'm a dog?"

"What if they don't want to date a grandma?"

"What if they only want me for my body?"

This section helps you sort through both ends of the attractiveness-issue spectrum.

## What if you're not gorgeous?

Most of us look okay. Not stunning but not ugly. We try to improve our looks to some degree through chemicals, hairstyles, and clothing, but in the end, we live with what we have. The question for us ordinary-looking folks is this: If I'm not superattractive, would I be better off without posting a photo?

The answer is absolutely not! In this respect, the Internet is no different from other forms of dating. Everyone wants a different look, and everyone's perception of what's attractive is different. Yes, if you're not drop-dead gorgeous, you won't have thousands of drooling and mostly inappropriate matches trying to get your attention. You're much more likely to have fewer and better matches trying to make sincere contact with you.

A lot of prospects are out there, and most wouldn't make a good match. However, you're only looking for one match — the right one. That person also needs to be a realistic match for you.

## What if you're too good looking?

Oddly enough, this dilemma can be a bigger problem than being unattractive, at least in terms of getting tons of mail from people who consider looks an adequate basis to select a date/mate. Of course, for those of you who are truly magnificent, this issue isn't new to you. You've lived with your looks all your life; people see you for your appearance instead of who you are.

If you've figured out a way to overcome this dilemma in real life (or you depend on it for getting what you want), you find that it works pretty much the same way on the Internet. All you need to do is post a dreamy photo of yourself and then figure out a way of filtering through the mountains of e-mail.

 If you're a very attractive woman, you'll be especially affected (afflicted) by the flood-of-mail phenomenon. You'll also find that the vast majority of men won't even have read more than a few lines of your essay. Wanna test the theory? Bury an important point about yourself deep in your profile — a point that no one could ignore — and see whether your "suitors" mention it. For example, somewhere in the middle of an essay answer, add this statement: "I would really appreciate it if you read my profile carefully before writing to me because it's important to me to know what we have in common. Please mention these similarities when you write." You may be startled by the lack of response to your request.

We hear you: So why is receiving a flood of e-mail such a big pain? It depends on your ability to ferret out the matches that are possibilities from the ones that are obviously of no interest. After you get past the ego boost, you may find managing the flood of mail difficult, let alone figuring out whom you should reply to.

As it turns out, some very attractive people (mostly women) have concluded that they're better off without a photo. We strongly advise against this thinking. A more effective approach is merely to post a less revealing or more obscure photo. (We tell you about photo manipulation in the section "Creating a Better Photo 101" later in this chapter.)

# Avoiding Photo Blunders

Knowing what type of photo works best for you is important because that photo is the single element of your profile that everyone views with interest. In fact, you may not realize it, but your photo is subject to *intense* scrutiny, and people may draw a host of (possibly inaccurate) conclusions about you based on what they see — or think they see.

Moreover, be aware of these common photo blunders:

- ✔ **Photos with a not completely cropped arm or shoulder of another person.** This *faux pas* begs the questions "Whose body part is this? A former spouse or significant other? And just how recent is the photo?"

- ✔ **A series of photos with the same clothing and background, in multiple poses.** We find that men have a proclivity for this one, and it just looks cheesy and forced. If you're going to post more than one photo, use a little variety, please. Surely you've been photographed more than once in recent history.

- ✔ **Photos with the subject on a chair, feet closest to the viewer (especially the soles of shoes).** This blunder gives the impression of arrogance and disdain for the viewer, even if unintended. In some cultures, showing the bottom of your feet to someone is a real put-down.

- ✔ **Photos with a bevy of gorgeous young things on your arms (men, take note).** If you're trying to convey that you're a sex magnet and supremely popular, showing pictures of your past exploits isn't the way to attract people for dating purposes. Posting these types of photos is really a form of self-sabotage and discourages those people looking for a serious, monogamous relationship. Instead, show how alluring you are with your witty prose and clever communiqués.

Some advice to guys: Including a bevy of blonde (or brunette) beauties photo is the kiss of death. Are these women former sex partners, girlfriends, or women currently pursuing you? Either way, potential prospects don't want to see them or know about them. If you're pursuing a prospect online, she wants to feel a bit exclusive, even if she knows you're on the Internet trolling for women every night. I know the picture is an illusion, but at least don't put those babes in your prospect's face every time she brings up your profile.

Some advice to women: If you post a photo of you with Arnold Schwarzenegger, I may have a sudden attack of inferioritus maximus and go to the next posted profile. If Arnie is a close friend, let me know over coffee.

- ✔ **Photos with your face partially obscured by sunglasses, branches of trees, or the Washington Monument.** You're transmitting the following message: "I'm hiding." Viewers don't appreciate playing *Where's Waldo*.

# Uncovering the Truth about Pets, Babies, and Glamor Shots

When choosing a photo to post with their profile, some people tend to go to extremes with — either very glamorized shots or very folksy ones — without regard to the person they're trying to attract. This section points out a few photo clues that should raise your suspicion about some prospects.

## Glamorized photos

Remember the saying "lies, darn lies, and statistics"? Well, they should have included photos in the most extreme category of deception. After much research, we can report one absolute truism: One two-dimensional photo can't possibly portray a person's look accurately. Additional photos, taken under different lighting conditions and different environments can create a more accurate composite, but one photo is simply too little information.

Now add the fact that professional photography is designed to exploit the deceptive nature of 2-D photography, and you better be chanting to yourself *caveat emptor* (buyer beware) when perusing photos.

Not that we think posting your best photo is bad. Indeed, you're foolish if you don't, but to avoid sticker shock on your first meet, always post a second snapshot to create some balance.

 A general rule that we used with amazing accuracy is this: A person always looks better than their worst photo and worse than their best photo. So if you keep that in mind when you meet someone, you will rarely be disappointed.

 If your prospect has posted only one photo and you're planning to meet, ask him or her to send you another. Tell your prospect about our photo advice in this section and that it can make the meeting go smoother. If your prospect objects, he or she may have posted a fraudulent photo, and you'll be quite shocked at the first meeting.

Use these tips to spot a glamorized photo:

✔ **Mysterious backgrounds.** Pros use various diffusion backgrounds to remove shadows. Because no snapshot was ever taken with such a murky gray-blue sky, you'll have no problem spotting this clue.

✔ **Perfect eyes.** Eyes are really hard to photograph. Outdoor light is often so bright that you may squint. Indoor flash photos produce red eye, unless they're professionally lighted.

✔ **Perfect lighting.** Natural outdoor light usually produces soft shadows, even on cloudy days. Amateur flash photos have harsh, usually unpleasant shadows. Glamorized photos never have any shadows because the lighting is dispersed by diffusion umbrellas.

*WARNING!*

If you're thinking of using a glamorized photo, remember that a fair number of experienced online daters will avoid you, having been burned before.

*TIP*

If you really love your glamorized photo and want to use it in your profile, always include a plain old homegrown snapshot to go with it, which provides good balance.

## Fuzzy photos

If you see a photo that looks like it was taken by Voyager 19 as it swung by Saturn, then take heed: Something is *very* wrong (like the prospect is probably trying to hide something).

Today clarity of digital photography is every bit as sharp as film photography. Even photos that have been scanned at local photo shops are capable of extremely high resolution. People have no legitimate excuses for submitting dark, shadowy *X-Files* like photos.

## Photos with Fido or Cuddles

Many people include their pet in their photo. Although some people view this kind of photo as evidence of their compassionate, animal-loving nature, it can send a different message: "Love me, love my animal." If you're an animal lover, too, then this type of photo from a prospect isn't a red flag. Otherwise, take heed.

Note that the door swings both ways. If you're okay with that same possible interpretation, bring on Bowser, Snookums, or Sweet Pea in your own photo. If not, keep Four Paws in deep cover.

Furthermore, our bottom-line advice is this: Your prospect can meet your pet in due time. For now, focus on you and introduce the pet later.

If you do decide to post a photo of you with your pet, don't make it a shot of you with Fluffy snuggled up to your face. The message is "You're competing with my pet for my affection. You may lose, but I'll always have Fluffy to love." (One woman who posted a duet photo with her cat wrote in her essay: "I have a cat. If you can't love her, I'm really sorry 'cause it just won't work. Men come and go, but a cat is always there, somewhere.")

## Photos with babies

Babies, like kittens, are great additions to any advertising campaign, but in the dating campaign, they send mixed messages. The most prominent message is "Please take care of me and my baby." Beware when you see photos of prospects with their babies (as well as when you post photos of yourself with your baby).

It's a given that you'll have to love both the prospect and the baby (or the prospect will have to love both you and your baby) in order for you to end up as Mr. and Ms. Right, so why look so needy in the photo? Letting others know you have young children is essential, but the message is best kept in the written essay part. It just comes out too strong in a photo.

If the baby isn't yours, just a beloved niece or nephew, mention it in the text or caption if that's possible. But keep in mind that some people will see a young child and not even pause to read the fine print. We realize that you are trying to show that you are good parent material, but you may be passed over by a prospect who just isn't interested in beginning a new life raising another's child.

## Photos giving the wrong age impression

One of the main frauds online daters complain about for both sexes is age deflation — misstating one's age by shaving off a few years. Some people misstate their age by a few years in their essays, and some misstate their age by leaps and bounds in their photos — by posting *really* old ones. In the online-dating world, a two- to three-year old photo is the limit for the photo to not be considered a misrepresentation.

So how do you spot that a prospect posted a really old photo?

- If a child is in the photo, does his or her age correspond with the stated age of the prospect's children mentioned in the essay or in e-mail exchanges?

- Did the person place more than one photo with his or her profile? If so, do you notice a significant age disparity between the photos?

- Does the photo show a slimmer, lighter person than the profile text would indicate?

- Is the prospect still wearing his Nehru jacket or doubleknit polyester leisure suit?

- Does the prospect have a freshly coiffed Farah Fawcett 'do?

If you really want to use an old photo, indicate its age in the essay text and also post a fresh second photo, likewise explaining its age in the text.

If you misrepresent your age in your photo (or your text, for that matter), get ready for a troublesome encounter at your first in-person meeting. People don't like being tricked. If you pull this shenanigan on someone, no matter how desirable you really are, they're not likely to overcome the initial fraud.

## Photos featuring wealth or status

As one online dater put it, "You can't know what someone is thinking, or if they're thinking at all."

A message to the guys: Whenever I see a photo of a guy featuring his 735I BMW or Lincoln Navigator with oversized balloon tires, I conclude that he had something on his mind other than showing me some reliable transportation. Guys have a weakness for displays of wealth. So take my advice: You're probably sending the wrong message. Keep the car in the garage and show a big smile instead. Women are suckers for a cute guy who is wall-to-wall smiles.

A message to the women: If you want to ensure that your prospects press the Next Profile button when they see your photo, bedeck yourself with enough jewels (or other status element) for Prince Charles' coronation. Including such obvious attempts at displaying wealth or status in your photo sends up a red flag. Many guys may give you a pass. Why take that chance?

Some objects may be an important part of who you are. Those kinds of objects are appropriate for inclusion in your photos. For example, straddling your Harley or sitting at your baby grand piano tells people something significant about your interests and lifestyle.

# Deciding Whether to Post Multiple Photos

Most sites let you post several photos, and about 10 percent of the people who post photos do post several. Should you?

Depends. There are two reasonable points of view.

## Yes! Post several photos (more than two)

If you post more than two very different photos (not just different camera angles but entirely different settings), you give your prospects a composite view, which is much more realistic than any single photo or two.

If you really want to use a photo that's a bit old (more than two years), post several photos and indicate in your essay when each was taken. Doing so quickly absolves you of any liability for posting an old photo. If you look more or less the same, it also points out that you're aging gracefully . . . and slowly.

## No! Post only one or two photos

Photos are notoriously misleading. No amount of additional photos really makes up for the fact that the camera is designed to create a fantasy. By posting too many additional photos, you don't solve this problem, but you do create a new one: too much emphasis on vanity.

We've reviewed hundreds of profiles with more than two photos. Usually, if people post more than two, they post five or six. The message is very clear: "I am good looking. See me in so many good-looking poses. Resistance to me is futile." In fact, if you read the essays of most of these multiphoto posters, you find that they often reinforce this fixation on appearance in words as well as pictures.

Whatever you decide to do about posting multiple photos, under no circumstances should you post two of the same photo. Crazy? You bet. Does it happen? All the time! And we can't figure out why people do it. Perhaps posting the same photo twice is an idea carried over from those high school photo sheets: One photo is for you to keep, and the other is for you to give to friends. (Yes, we know that it doesn't make sense on the Internet, but we're desperately trying to find the cause of this phenomenon. If you can figure it out, please tell us.) Whatever the reason, don't do it.

# Creating a Better Photo 101

When we were dating online, we saw a lot of photos that never should've been posted. Not counting all the *don'ts* we mention throughout this chapter, many people just don't take the time to select photos that portray them best. We notice this trend more with people who post multiple photos where they appear quite good looking in one photo along with another photo that's simply awful.

## Selecting a good preexisting photo

Remember these heads-ups when selecting a photo to post:

✔ **Attitude counts.** Nothing is more irresistible than a big smile (unless you're missing a few teeth). When people look at your posted photo, they imagine that they're about to say hello to you. If you smile, every time they view your photo, you're encouraging them to contact you.

✔ **Friends can be more objective than you.** Have a friend (preferably of the opposite or desired gender) pick out your photos. And remember who your viewers are when choosing a friend to do the task. If your friend doesn't like any of them or says none of them look like you, trust his or her judgment. Besides being far more objective than you, your friend probably has the proper hormones to know what a good photo choice looks like.

✔ **Natural photos make you a natural person.** Snapshots are usually more interesting than posed shots, although they're much harder to find. Action shots of you engaged in an interesting activity are very alluring, even if bizarre. For example, we saw one shot of a woman with a snake around her neck. Repulsive to some, yes, but irresistible to investigate. She made sure she explained in her essay that she wasn't a snake charmer.

Action photos rarely provide an adequate view of yourself in a single photo. If you post one, adding a simple portrait shot to fill in the missing pieces isn't a bad idea.

If you want to show that you're height/weight proportional, consider posting a full-length shot. Weight fraud, by the way, is the No.1 objection of men. (Height is the No.1 objection of women. Age fraud is No. 2.)

✔ **Technical quality counts.** Look for photos with good skin tones, no spooky shadows, and no scratches and dents, which make your image look, well, scratched and dented.

## Taking a good photo of yourself

Without turning this book into *Photography For Dummies* by Russell Hart (Wiley Publishing, Inc.), check out this neat trick for figuring out how to take a good photo of yourself:

1. **Collect a large pile of your old photos.**

2. **Invite a friend of the opposite sex (unless you're seeking a same-sex relationship) to go over the photos with you.**

   Looking through your photos is a buddy activity, like swimming, skiing, and drinking, and should never be done alone.

3. **Divide the photos into four piles:**

   • Great shots of this century

   • Nice shots, but they don't look like you

   • So-so shots

   • Who is this man/woman, and why did they let him/her out of that mutant ward shots

4. **Don't ignore piles 3 and 4.** They're instructive in figuring out what doesn't work.

5. **Look at each aspect of the really good photos and the really bad ones with respect to the following:**

   • **Composition.** What else is in the photo? What color of clothing enhances your features? For example, if you have blue eyes, you probably already know that your eyes appear much bluer if you wear a blue shirt. What kind of smile seems genuine?

- **Lighting.** Do you look best in flash or natural? Which direction is the best light from? Head on? A bit to the side? Consider all options, including side light, diffused light, and shadow effects.

  Flash photography works poorly on people with very fair skin because the light penetrates and reflects back in an altered state. In fact, most people look awful under flash lighting. Rcd-cyc is obnoxious too. You can fix red eye photos, though, so don't discard them immediately.

- **Photo angle.** Which profile is your best? Do you look sinister if you look away from the camera?

  For example, I can't be photographed from below face level (meaning with the camera shooting up). It changes the entire shape of my face (or at least I don't like that shape).

6. **Using the information from your photo analysis, have your friend take some snapshots, get them developed quickly (or instantly, if digital), and have another pow wow to pore over the photos.**

7. **If you don't like any of the photos, do these steps again with your newfound knowledge of what works; if you do like any of them, kudos on a job well done.**

Consider these final thoughts:

✔ Don't settle just because getting a great photo is hard. A bad photo is like a doormat that says *Go Away.*

✔ If you like one photo from your past, but it was taken too many years ago (two or more), use it as one of your photos, with the other(s) being fresh. Just remember to point out the age of each photo in your essay.

## Getting your photo digitized

If you own a film camera or are working with existing photos (prints), you need to get your photos digitized to have the dating site post them. Although a few sites still allow you to mail in your photo, don't do so. If you do mail it in, you won't get your (treasured) photo back, but more importantly, you can't decide how your photo gets *cropped* — that all-important decision of what gets into the photo and what gets cut.

Getting your photo digitized is actually trickier than you may think. Not because cropping a photo is difficult, but because many of the commercial places that *can* do the job have no idea what they're doing. Words like JPEG compression, scaling, and sharpness control mean nothing to the discount-store clerk with a one-hour photo. Granted, many consumer products, like Aventix film cameras, provide digital prints along with the paper ones, but the digital prints are of such poor quality that you often can't use them.

Your best bet is to go to a reputable camera shop. Have the shop make a high-quality digital scan of your photo and put it on disk for you. (Alternatively, if you have a friend with the skills and a scanner, ask your friend to do this task for you.) Then you can transfer the photo from the disk to your PC and do your own cropping, scaling, or whatever else you want to do.

You can do much more with your digital photos before uploading them to your online dating site. Be careful not to get carried away because the prime directive is to produce a photo that, although pleasing, is in fact an *accurate* portrayal of you so no one is surprised later.

If you want to know more about digital photo manipulation, we happen to have just the book for you: *Digital Photography For Dummies* by Julie Adair King (Wiley Publishing, Inc.).

# Part IV
# Initiating Contact: You've Got Mail

The 5th Wave          By Rich Tennant

@RICHTENNANT

I'M JUST HAVING TROUBLE DATING A GUY WHOSE NAME DEFAULTS TO "LOONY FRUITCAKE" ON MY SPELL CHECKER.

## In this part . . .

**D**ating and sales have a lot in common. You have to attract customers, get them interested in hearing your story, and then close the deal. Where dating differs is that both the buyer and seller need to like each other equally or the deal isn't worth closing.

This part is about attracting customers (prospects), engaging them in e-mail exchanges, dealing with the occasional rejection, and closing the Internet deal (that is, meeting them in person). Because online dating is so fundamentally different from face-to-face dating, you may want to treat it as an electronic version of old style dating, but it's not. We show you how to use the Internet to maximize who you can attract and how to get to know them well enough to decide if a first meeting is worth it.

# Chapter 13

# Getting Matched Up

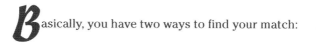

## In This Chapter

▶ Examining two ways to meet your match: reactive and proactive

▶ Getting a handle on who you are and how to search for what you want

▶ Ferreting out the real prospects from the deadwood

*B*asically, you have two ways to find your match:

- ✔ You go to the trough. You're proactive in seeking out matches and making the first contact.

  or

- ✔ You let the trough come to you. You subscribe to an online-dating service, post your profile and photo, and let matches seek you out. You're reactive rather than proactive.

If you've ever been fishing, you recognize these two methods. If you're looking to come away from a day's fishing with a catch, you're going to immediately see the virtue of the first option of being proactive. If you're in no hurry, you find that the second option takes a bit less effort, but you may have a dry stretch or even lose interest.

Unlike fishing, though, online dating isn't (or shouldn't be) just a hobby. It's a means to an end, and although the means may be enjoyable at times, online dating is simply a conduit for meeting someone and quitting the dating scene. Also unlike fishing, you may endure a fair amount of rejection, which you may find painful. (Fishermen don't seem to take rejection from fish personally.) Regularly occurring rejection may discourage you from continuing your quest.

In this chapter, we show you how to make the most of both methods.

# Sittin' by the Dock on the Bay: Reactive Matching

Okay, you've made up your mind to go slow. You won't seek out matches (too intimidating), although you don't mind perusing the available matches, hoping various prospects will contact you. In other words, you're going to use the "Choose me, me, me!" method of matching — reactive matching. As you may guess, we don't think much of this method, but if you must use it, then you need to know how to optimize your chances of being a chosen one.

But first, take a timeout for some tidbits:

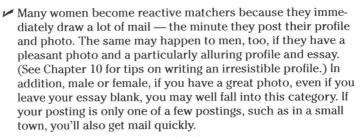

✔ Many women become reactive matchers because they immediately draw a lot of mail — the minute they post their profile and photo. The same may happen to men, too, if they have a pleasant photo and a particularly alluring profile and essay. (See Chapter 10 for tips on writing an irresistible profile.) In addition, male or female, if you have a great photo, even if you leave your essay blank, you may well fall into this category. If your posting is only one of a few postings, such as in a small town, you'll also get mail quickly.

If you find yourself receiving a small tidal wave of mail immediately after posting your photo, don't assume that the flood will continue. Most dating sites identify you as a new posting with a flag icon. Experienced online daters, who are lying in wait like gators with one eye cocked, will seek you out. After your newness fades, so will your popularity. You'll have to switch to a new strategy to keep the seekers seeking.

✔ Having a new posting on an Internet-dating site is a real advantage (for you and the site), and site operators are fairly liberal about making it appear that you're new when you're not. Showing an ever-increasing number of new postings is in the sites's best interest, so they often award new status to those people who've freshened up their profile — say, changed their essay or posted an extra photo (Match.com, for example). If your site does so, take advantage of that opportunity by refreshing your profile (and doing it repeatedly). Likewise, if you're looking at new postings, you may want to look closely to see whether those postings are really new or just recharged.

✔ If you see a posting that's indicated as new, you can usually tell whether it's indeed new or just refurbished. Many dating sites indicate a posting's start date or at least show how long a profile has been posted. Although dating sites grant new status to profiles that have changes, they don't change the start date. If the two don't match, the profile has only been updated. Of course, nothing is wrong with contacting someone who has been online for weeks or months (we actually recommend it as an advantage), but if you're a seeker of newbies, these postings are false positives.

# Optimizing your chances of getting mail

In short, making your posting inviting is the key to getting mail. Inviting means that your *front-page listing* (what people see from a search report) is irresistible. A great photo is worth a thousand e-mails, but you can't and, frankly, shouldn't want to be contacted by thousands.

Consider these quirky ideas:

- ✔ **Post a monochrome (black and white) photo.** If you find that everyone has posted vibrant, Technicolor photos, then you'll stand out immediately if yours isn't in color. As it turns out, monochrome is actually more flattering than color because it hides skin imperfections and allows you to highlight contrasts, such as between skin and hair.

- ✔ **Post a caricature, cartoon, or other sketch of yourself.** Your display photo won't be a photo at all but a drawing of yourself. Granted, this idea is a bit eccentric, but it may work well for some artistic people.

  This strategy is somewhat risky because some prospects may just pass you by as being strange, but at least they'll notice your posting. If you couple the drawing with a helpful tagline, like "This is how I feel, but my real photo is inside my profile," you should overcome resistance. Post a real photo as your second photo.

  Don't use a drawing as a way to avoid posting your real photo because it backfires. If you use a caricature, make sure it's highly inviting and not demeaning. A big sweet smile works great.

  Note that a few sites reject caricatures or other drawings, but if you submit your real photo simultaneously, you improve your odds of getting past the photo police.

- ✔ **Include an interesting object in your photo.** When people are paging through tons of photos, something included with your head shot that yells out "What the heck is that?" may get you noticed. Consider a Jackson Pollack mural, or Mt. Rushmore. This idea is tricky because the *thumbnail photos* (the little photos that appear first in a search) are really small on some sites. But not on all. If your site has bigger photos, take advantage of them. (As to what constitutes an object of interest, refer to Chapter 12. Take heed that in our view, pets and children don't qualify because of the mixed message they give.)

✔ **Add some pizzazz to the look of your tagline.** In addition to writing a great tagline or screen name (see Chapter 8), use your keyboard to get attention. Use a well-placed exclamation point, question mark, or some offbeat characters. You can even use a few capital letters but do so sparingly. If you don't, it appears that you're shouting.

If you get prospects to stop on your photo and tagline, the next step is to get them to write you. Your essay and Q&A answers need to do the trick, and you increase the attractiveness of each in very different ways. We devote Chapter 9 to answering the Q&A questions, and Chapter 10 covers writing your essay. Check out those chapters for the full scoop.

## *Realizing the truth about search engines*

Your Q&A answers are exceedingly critical to your match-magnetism because many of the answers are specifically word searchable, and most people look for their match by using the dating site's search tools. These search tools, or search engines, are often biased in certain ways, and if you want to be found by one, you need to know its biases.

### *The photo bias*

Go to the search part of your online dating site. (On most sites, you need to be a real subscriber, not a trial runner, to get access to it.) Usually, you find a simple search option and an advanced search option. Somewhere in the search page you'll see an icon like this:

Profiles with photos only

Many sites checkmark that box as a default in which case, prospects without photos essentially don't exist.

If you don't have a photo, the searcher will only find you if he or she unchecks this box. This simple search is biased against postings without photos.

Furthermore, the searcher has so many options to select that he or she may not select the box to see nonphoto postings.

### The age bias

Suppose that you're a 35-year-old woman who wants people to find her in searches of women 30 to 40 years old. Surely being right in the middle of an age decade puts you in a good position, right? Not so if someone searches on any sites that categorizes using age bands instead of allowing the user to select the exact age range he or she desires. For example, an age band of 25 to 34 years completely excludes a 35-year-old, whereas, someone may search 25 to 35 years.

Furthermore, if you're just older than a 10-year mark (31, 41, 51, and so forth), most people who tend to search by decades will miss you.

### The geography bias

Many sites use zip codes (postal codes) and telephone area codes as a way to formulate a person's location. Zip codes are relatively innocuous, but area codes aren't. For example, if you're searching for someone in Minneapolis/St. Paul, you would be surprised to find that it includes four area codes. To do a complete search of the city, you need to remember all four area codes or you'll lose a chunk of your search area.

If you live in a metro area undergoing an area code breakup, don't list yourself in the new area code even if it's your true area code because it could be months, if not years, before users as well as your dating site start using it. Note that you must edit your signup information to alter your area code after you pay your subscription fee. If you simply sign up with the wrong area code, your credit card may be rejected because the code won't match what's on file with your bank.

As if one source of geography bias isn't enough, a second source exists: how many miles (km) you live from a city or zip code. If you live, for example, in a large metro area like New York, Chicago, or Los Angeles, you could easily live 60 miles (90 km) away from the central city and still consider yourself part of that dating district. On some sites, the default distance is 50 miles (80 km). To solve this problem, you can do the same trick on your zip code that you can do on your area code: Change it to a zip code more toward the central city.

### The head of the class bias

Many sites allow your search to rank the matches in many different ways, and in a big city, being at the bottom of the match list means you don't exist. For example, in New York, searching for men with blue eyes who are 40 to 50 years old could yield 1,000 or more matches, although some searches only display the first 500. Trust us, no one gets past a few hundred listings.

So who gets to be first? On the AmericanSingles.com sites, the search engine asks whether you want to search those users who logged on most recently or those who registered most recently. In other words, do you want the most frequent visitors or the freshest catches? The default setting goes for the most frequent visitors. So unless you go to the trouble of logging on frequently, you quickly drop to the bottom on the list. In a big city, like Chicago, you'll fall out of the top 50 within hours. In, say, Fargo, North Dakota, well, you probably don't have to worry about it at all.

# Fishin' for a Catch: Proactive Matching

Suppose that you have five key criteria that must be present in a mate. You'll vastly improve your odds of finding a match if you proactively seek out the few who match your five criteria instead of just sitting around, waiting for someone who's a five-point match to find you. Here's why:

✔ Your key criteria probably aren't all objective attributes (a 6-foot-tall [190 cm], blue-eyed, 170-pound [78 kg], athletic PhD, for example). Instead, your criteria are likely to be very subtle and subjective. If you want a serene, kind, passionate, romantic 6-foot-tall, blue-eyed, 170-pound, athletic PhD, you're going to have to read those essays with a very particular filter — that filter being *you.* In short, if you do the pickin', you've got a much better chance of doing the pickin' right. Why delegate and let people (or a machine) pick for you?

✔ If you're a male, you'll quickly find that women just aren't as proactive as men, so the numbers are just plain against you. Basically, men must seek out prospects, or they won't do very well. It's just the way of the online world. Sorry, guys.

✔ If you're willing to consider a long-distance relationship (as we did), you have no choice. Few people seek matches with out-of-towners. If you want to try a long-distance relationship, you have to make the first move.

✔ Many people aren't proactive in writing e-mails because they fear rejection. Yes, you'll suffer a fair amount of rejection from your proactive efforts, but remember, you're only looking for one partner in the end. The ones that reject you are almost certainly blind alleys. In reality, thank them (but you don't need to).

✔ Some people sign up for a site but don't pay their dues (subscription fees). Most sites allow them to remain posted, but prohibit them from writing to you. We call these postings the Living Dead (or deadwood). Problem is, you don't know which ones they are. If you're waiting for someone to write you, but the person doesn't have the power to do so, you may be waiting in vain. Be proactive, and the problem doesn't exist.

## *Looking at your proactive search options*

Several interesting options are available for you to proactively find your match:

✔ Use the site's search engine to find matches.

✔ Use the site's auto-match tool to let the computer do the work.

✔ Watch who's online.

✔ Hang out in chat rooms and watch the traffic.

---

# Waiting for Godot

People who sign up for a dating site but don't pay their subscription fees are often allowed to remain posted but not permitted to write to prospects. We affectionately call these people the Living Dead.

One online dater related this story to us about how he discovered the Living Dead too late:

> I once spotted a profile that really caught my eye. I was an unpaid poster on a site that didn't allow unpaid posters to write e-mails, but I could respond to them. I changed my zip code to be located in her hometown, and I even adjusted my essay to more closely fit what she was looking for. I waited a few weeks, but she never contacted me. Darned if she didn't disappear after a few weeks, never to return. I assumed she met someone and it wasn't me. Later, I figured out that she was probably one of those postings that couldn't write to me, either. By trying to save the cost of one month's subcription, I may have missed the love of my life.

### Using the site's search engine

The section "Realizing the truth about search engines," earlier in this chapter, explains the biases of the search tools for the benefit of reactive subscribers. Take a look at that section because you need to consider those factors when doing a proactive search.

Here are some additional tips:

- ✔ **Be prepared to peruse hundreds of profiles.** Look past the photos and taglines and get down to reading the essay questions.

- ✔ **Come back often.** New people get posted every day.

- ✔ **Dig deeper than your competition.** If most people are looking for matches that show up on the top of the list, start from the bottom. If most people are looking at profiles with the stunning photos, ignore them and move to other ones that please you.

  You need to realize that almost no one looks as good or bad as their photos. Photos are just a guide. Furthermore, many people get overlooked because their first photo is unattractive. But often, their subsequent photos are much better. Dig deeper and look at all photos, not just the first one posted.

- ✔ **Don't delay.** Subscriptions expire. People give up. Most sites tell you when a person's subscription is about to expire. So if you see that a person has only one day left on his or her subscription, send a quick e-mail that includes your private e-mail address in case the person wants to contact you after expiration. Take note that some sites let people stay on as deadwood (another way to reference the Living Dead) after they expire, but they become the Living Dead who can't reply to you.

- ✔ **Don't rely too much on objective Q&A answers.** People often fudge height, weight, and age. If you want a 6-foot-2-inch, 39-year-old guy with blonde hair, he's probably not quite that tall, that young, and has a bit of a bald spot (invisible in the photo). The searchable Q&A answers aren't as useful as they may appear.

If you write to someone whose membership is about to expire, in addition to including your private e-mail address in your message, remember to print the person's entire profile, including photo and screen name. If you end up getting a message from the person on your private e-mail, you may want to re-read the profile to refresh your memory.

If you reply to someone's private e-mail address, clearly identify who you are and where you came from. "Hi, I'm Jack123 from yahoo.com" is all you need. Most people forget to include this information and expect the recipient to divine this information from cyberspace. On top of that, they may be annoyed that the recipient doesn't make the connection because they want to believe that they're the recipient's only e-mail correspondent. Crazy but true.

### *Looking at the most common searchable criteria*

If you're a tech-head at heart (or a psychology major), you're going to love playing with the search tool on most sites. And the more you play with it, the more interesting combinations you'll come up with. On a few sites, you could search for a woman who weighs 115 pounds, is 5-feet-10-inches tall, has gray eyes and Technicolor spiked hair, lives with her parents, is divorced by annulment, is in the military, has a master's degree, drinks like a fish but doesn't smoke at all, practices Wicca, lives 50 miles from you, was on the site last week, and joined two months ago. (That is, if you cared.)

All the search combinations and possibilities sound great, but we strongly warn you that setting non-negotiable criteria can be a huge mistake, reducing your chances of online-dating success. Look over this list of the most common searchable fields on many sites:

- ✔ **Age.** This criterion is sometimes searchable only in bands (ranges). If you'd accept a 40-year-old, is a 42-year-old too old? Also, know that some people aren't completely honest about their age.

- ✔ **Astrological sign.** The choices are the usual 12 plus some opt-outs, like Stop or Neon. If you're a regular reader of tabloid journalism, you may appreciate this mighty important piece of information. Most sites calculate it from your birthdate, which you supply at sign up.

- ✔ **Body type.** Some sites don't actually request weight in lbs/kg but only a type. The usual choices are slim/slender, average/medium, muscular/buff/toned, height/weight proportionate/average, voluptuous/portly, or similar. The one to watch out for is proportionate/average, which can be the catchall for not perfect but not grotesque, or it can be right on. You never know. More importantly, people probably aren't lying about this one. They just don't see themselves the way others do.

✔ **Drug use.** This one's much like smoking. The choices are usually none/never, occasionally, and regularly.

✔ **Education.** The choices are often high school, some college, bachelor's, master's, and PhD/professional degree. "Some College" is a suspect option. For some people, it means anything from "nearly graduated" to "went to tons of fraternity parties." And for the record, PhD/professional degree includes various postgraduate degrees, from MD to PhD to JD.

✔ **Eye color.** The choices are usually the primary eye colors of brown, green, blue, grey, and so on. If you have mixed colors, or wear color contact lenses, we guess you get to choose whichever one you like best. That means this criterion is highly subjective. If you must have someone with blue eyes, and your search makes it an absolute requirement, you probably have a 50/50 chance that your hits have true blue eyes.

✔ **Expectations on how to end a first date.** This search is a rather dangerous one, too. The typical choices are a handshake, a hug, a kiss, meet your parents, and such, but a few zingers are available for those who haven't read our chapter on sex (Chapter 11), including light petting, your place or mine, pure sexual ecstacy, and anything can happen. If you're banking on this question to provide you with useful information, you'll find yourself very disappointed.

✔ **Favorites (food, sports, music, and so on).** Hard to imagine these factors being deal breakers, but if you're looking for a sushi-eating, rap-singing triathlete, now you have your chance.

✔ **Hair color.** What can one say about this? Is it before or after an application by ChemLawn? And do they even have their own hair?

✔ **Height.** The search ranges for this criterion are usually selectable in inches or centimeters. People aren't very honest in this category. When searching, allow for several inches above and below your standard.

✔ **Location.** Usually, but not always, sites base location on data from the signup information. It's usually accurate, but some people need to change their zip code to get into dating circles larger than their hometown (see the section "The geography bias," earlier in this chapter for more). If you search on this field, providing for a wide area around your search location (50–75 miles or 80–110 km) is a good idea.

✔ **Profession.** This one is very risky to search on, so few sites allow it. People just have too many ways to describe their job, which makes searching it difficult.

✔ **Religion.** Usually, many choices are available, including "Not Part of My Life". Many people choose not to say, even though they have strong religious or cultural convictions. If you exclude, for example, anyone who's not Catholic, you'll miss many Catholics who chose not to say.

✔ **Spirituality.** Some sites pose these questions in different ways, but they all come down to how devout you are. The only reliable answers are at the ends of the scale: maniacally religious and heretically irreverent.

✔ **Sex (gender not quantity).** This one is a pretty reliable search criterion, although a few masqueraders are always out there. They're pretty easy to wash out in e-mail exchanges, though.

✔ **Smoking.** This search criterion usually comes in three choices: none, socially, or regularly. You can bet that the none answer is reliable. Don't count on the reliablility of the other two.

✔ **Weight.** See what we said about height earlier in this list because it's equally applicable.

✔ **Willingness to relocate.** This question happens to be a very important criterion if you're prowling territories outside your hometown. Sadly many sites don't use it. American Singles sites are among the few. This answer can be invaluable if you're hoping to lure someone away from their home turf. Don't assume that the answer "Not Willing to Relocate" is a certainty, but it may indicate that the person has other reasons why he or she can't move (children, family, job, house arrest).

### Getting extreme results (finding no one or finding everyone)

Most sites offer two levels for a search: basic and advanced. The basic search is usually best at finding

✔ People who've signed up recently (or since your last search)

✔ People within a certain geographic distance from you

✔ Specific age ranges of interest

## Q&A to the limit

Udate.com takes a big departure from some other sites. Udate's Q&A is very extensive, and the site's search tool allows users to customize Q&A searches very specifically. In theory, matching by formula should be easier on Udate than most other sites, but it doesn't work out that way very often. Instead, users often don't answer the all the available questions, possibly due to exhaustion.

The advanced search varies from site to site but usually lets you search nearly every question in the Q&A. Some sites even let you search with levels of significance attached to each criterion. For example, if you want someone with red hair and green eyes, but green is only somewhat important, you can say so.

However, with advanced searches, you run the risk of excluding everyone, sometimes by accident. Here are some common reasons:

✔ If you try to search outside your community (especially using Matchmaker) but forget to remove your local zip code (postal code) from the search, you may end up performing an impossible search — if the search is set up to span only, say, 50 miles. For example, say you live in Boston but are searching in San Diego, and you forget to remove your Boston zip code. If the search only spans 50 miles, we doubt anyone in San Diego lives 50 miles from Boston.

✔ If your search criteria is people with photos who've only been on the system fewer than two days, you normally get zilch. Most photos take a few days to get approved and posted.

So what do you do if your search turns up nothing? First, simply exit the search area to ensure that you clear your search. Then just return and start afresh.

Note that the opposite predicament — doing a search and getting endless results — is less common but possible. Obviously, you need to narrow down your field. To do so, focus on age and geography and forget about eye color, height, weight, and such. Plan to read plenty of essays if you're lucky enough to live in a city with tons of postings.

When you search through the profiles, use the Favorites (also known as Hot List, on some sites) tool if one is available. The tool enables you to come back for a second look when you're not so giddy about seeing all the great choices you've found.

Writing everyone you find interesting on your first pass through profiles isn't particularly a bad idea. If you write to everyone that raises an eyebrow, you'll end up involved in many e-mail exchanges that you don't really want to be in. Spare yourself — and them — a lot of rejection. Park them in your Favorites file and come back again later to see whether you still feel as interested.

### Letting the computer do your matching

Almost every site has an auto-matching feature. Match.com's is called Venus; on Lavalife.com, it's Match (clever, eh?). They all work more or less the same: You specify criteria, perhaps even how important each criterion is to you, and let the computer's fingers do the work.

On some systems, you can save your criteria and have the search run repeatedly (like every day/week/month). The site mails you a list of matches with thumbnail photos, which can be nice to come home to after a hard day at the office.

We have to say that auto-matchers are a lot like weather forecasting three days out: a roll of the dice. Still, they're fun to use and may even introduce you to someone you overlooked.

### Following who's online

If you're into instant gratification, watching who's online as a means to decide whom to contact is a fun, albeit somewhat illogical, way to search.

Almost every site has a feature that tells who's presently logged in, and some sites even tell you what the person's doing (which can be fairly interesting). On Jdate.com, you see who's online via a flashing "e-mail me" on their profile. Other sites use similar tactics.

The clear advantage of watching who's online is that you know which people are actively seeking a match, and they may even respond to you right then and there. Talk about instant gratification.

On most all-in-one sites (see Chapter 5), you can send an e-mail immediately, and the prospects almost certainly see it. You can even tell whether they opened your e-mail and when.

On other sites that don't have this feature, you can get someone's attention by using the Instant Messenger feature. Sending an instant message (IM) isn't the same as sending a contemplative e-mail message, and some of people don't reply to IMs, but the feature is there, so think about trying it.

If you start instant messaging a person, getting back to e-mail, where more substantive information can be exchanged, is sometimes difficult. IM is a bit manic and tends to send a potential relationship into one-liner exchanges, which are often hard to sustain, and a lot of pressure exists to go immediately to the phones.

### Lying in the weeds in a chat room

We don't have a lot of good things to say about public chat rooms inside or outside of a dating site, but they're another way to look for matches. Just remember to be pumped on caffeine before you start as the maze of mixed up message traffic is going to test your cranial stamina.

Instead of engaging in a conversation with chat-room participants, just watch (lurk) and see who writes what and check out the prospects' profiles while they're chatting. The bonus is that if you see someone who's interesting, you also get to read more about him or her by following the chat thread you're (legitimately) eavesdropping on.

## Finding important data that's buried in the postings

Each site has tidbits of really useful data that can tell you a lot about a prospect's online activities. For example, on some sites, each posting lists what percentage of e-mails a person returns. A person with a very low response rate (under 15 percent) isn't being picky. He or she is being nonresponsive. Another critical piece of data to look at is when the person last visited. Some site indicate virtually down to the minute (online now, was here 45 minutes ago, 3 days ago. . . several months ago). This info is particularly helpful on sites where you can't tell whether a prospect has read your mail messages. With the time-since-last-visit feature, you can at least find out whether the prospect logs in often.

## Snoopware! It's a little scary and cool at the same time!

A few sites have a "snooping" feature that can report whether another user has perused your profile. Knowing that someone has looked you over may be a little freaky, but it creates a no-brainer icebreaker. AmericanSingles.com has the most sophisticated version of this. If you don't like this feature, you can turn it off, but the switch is well hidden.

# Chapter 14

# Exchanging E-mails

*F*orget what Mom said. Talking to strangers when online dating is okay because online dating is completely different. You're anonymous, and can safely approach any stranger who looks intriguing. In addition, on online-dating sites, the fear of approaching strangers is essentially eliminated because everyone on the site is there to meet others.

This chapter is all about talking to strangers — Internet-dating style. And the way to talk to strangers is through the magic of e-mail.

## The Importance of Anonymity

To enjoy the freedom of contacting whomever you like on online dating sites, you must be willing to stay anonymous longer than you may prefer. E-mail is by far the most secure way to remain anonymous (as long as you follow our advice in Chapter 18 on how to keep your private e-mail system free of personal identifiers). Phone contact is much less anonymous, and meeting in person (obviously) is a complete giveaway.

 The best (and safest) way to online-dating success is to capitalize on the inherent advantage of the Internet — that anonymity factor — to distinguish the likely hits from misses before going to phone contact and certainly before scheduling a meeting.

Resisting the urge to move quickly from e-mail contact to phone contact or a meeting is one of the toughest skills to attain in Internet dating. In some ways, online dating is so counterintuitive from the in-person dating experience, and it draws on a weak link for many people — *written* (e-mail) communication. Yet controlling that force and staying online a bit longer yields a much more pleasurable online-dating experience.

Internet dating remains safer than in-person dating only as long as you take steps to keep yourself fully anonymous. People get into trouble when they mix up the rules between online dating and in-person dating. Don't mix up the rules between the two dating forms!

A most important online-dating rule (and advantage) is staying anonymous. Don't give your full name, your phone number, your address, or any other identifiers. Stick with your first name until you both reach a comfort level to share more personal information.

# *Checking Your List: Ready to E-mail?*

You're at the threshold of making your first e-mail contact. But before you begin, make sure you've got the following all set up:

✔ You've posted your picture (see Chapter 12).

✔ You've completely filled out your Q&A (see Chapter 9).

✔ Your essay screams *great guy/woman* (see Chapter 10).

✔ You completed a search to narrow the field a bit (see Chapter 13).

✔ You've read through the essays of dozens of prospects from your search results.

✔ You saved all the prospects into the Favorites folder of your online site.

✔ You've selected a few prospects that you've just gotta write.

Now questions immediately come to mind:

✔ How many prospects should I write to at the same time?

✔ What do I write to them?

✔ What do I do if they *all* respond?

Relax. You're in the right place for the answers.

# Figuring Out How Many E-mails to Send at Once

In real-person dating, many of us have gone out with two (or more) people at the same time without the prospects knowing about each other. Not messing up what you've said to whom takes nerves of steel and an elephant's memory.

Internet dating, at least through the initial contacts, isn't quite as challenging. In fact, you're expected to be in contact with many people at the same time. Yes, you still have to keep everything straight, but unless you're singularly lucky, consider your first contacts practice runs because, statistically speaking, they aren't likely to result in finding your predestined lifetime companion (although you never know).

So just how many messages should you send out at one time? Well, unless you're sending instant messages to people who are online when you write to them, getting a reply often takes several days. Some people don't check their messages every day, and others like to spend a little extra time drafting a response. In addition, some prospects never reply.

Considering those facts, do start by having a half-dozen to a dozen initial e-mails floating out in cyberspace. (And don't worry about those who never reply. If they all responded, you'd lose track completely.) If by some chance everyone does reply, check out the section "Reacting to their Responses," later in this chapter. We also suggest printing out those e-mails you send out so you can keep track. This is especially relevant to the intrepid beginner.

Because e-mail relationships are so fragile, contacting too many people (more than a dozen is a reasonable limit) at the same time isn't wise. Yes, contacting people serially slows down the process, but as you get more experienced, you'll have a better sense of who has potential.

# What in Tarnation to Write

I still remember the first girl I called up for a date at age 15. It was a horrible experience, probably for both of us. (I ran into her decades later at a high school reunion, and she still remembered the phone call. I was banking on her having a more repressed memory than I, but no such luck.)

Well, initiating e-mail contact is a breeze compared to your teenage experiences. Of course, partly because you're not a teenager anymore, right? But another part is that e-mail provides an invisible shield that prevents anyone from hearing the insecurity in your voice and the shaking of your hands when you say, "Would you date me?"

Still, like in sports (and sex), technique (and timing) is everything. This section explains the techniques that work for the first e-mail.

## *Everyone loves themselves (so indulge 'em)*

Want to get someone's attention? Compliment him or her on something. Only Attila the Hun would strike you down in response to a compliment (and, frankly, we have it on good authority that even he'd say *thank you* if you complimented him on the number of towns he pillaged).

We know the "compliment them" strategy works. Your only risk is that you'll overdo it (as the salesman on Rodeo Drive did with Richard Gere in Pretty Woman — rent it, and see what we mean).

Most people compliment some aspect of a prospect's photo. (You have great eyes.) This compliment isn't the best choice, but it works as long as you're not fixated on the physical.

A better choice is to compliment something in the prospect's Q&A or essay. For example:

> I see that you do the *NY Times* crossword puzzle weekly. I never get it without cheating. How do you do it?
>
> Or
>
> You mentioned that you're a software engineer. I've worked with a lot of them, and they really have interesting work.

Even if your prospect hates his or her job (or is unemployed), the prospect can't help but comment, and then you have a chance to keep the ball rolling!

Never forget: Talk about them, not you. Ego is a terrible thing to waste.

# *Ask, ask, ask (for anything)*

When a person comes to you on a street corner and asks for directions, do you just walk away? Hopefully not. You give some help. Remember, the goal of that first e-mail is to open a channel, any channel, so you can start to get your personality out into the open. How about this:

> Hi, I see that you have a great photo posted. When I tried to scan mine, I always get a blank screen. Can I impose on you to tell me your tricks?

Okay, so we combined a question with a compliment. No one said you have to limit yourself to one device to make contact.

Here's another:

> Your Q&A says that you like to cook. Does that mean you're good at it? I like to cook, too, but I haven't found anyone on this planet who wants to eat what I cook.

## *The expansion of the universe theory*

Another way to kick off an e-mail exchange is to extract something from the essay and ask the prospect to expand on what he or she meant. For example:

> Hi, _____ (always use the prospect's screen name). I saw in your profile that you mentioned having a first date at an upscale restaurant. Could you tell me how far up that scale you were thinking? And seeing that we both live in California, would that be the Richter scale?
>
> Michael

 Always put your real first name at the end of every e-mail. You have no idea how disarming and enchanting it is to know the name of an otherwise mysterious person. Including your real name is simple and it changes the entire complexion of the exchanges thereafter. And don't add a salutation. Not Sincerely, not Yours truly, and certainly not Love. Just your first name.

## *Point of information, please*

You can also make a connection by asking someone to clarify something you didn't understand in his or her essay. This example came to mind when we saw a posting from a guy who had simply typed keyboard trash in place of his essay:

> Hi, _____. You said in your essay that you're a terrible speller. Don't apologize. I am too. But would you mind if I ask you to explain what you meant by this sentence: *kluroeh aldhiqgt lihoiuas yeroian 09bkljalfnl.* I believe I heard this phrase in that movie about the Navajo Code Talkers, but the verb wasn't at the end.
>
> Judy

## *Extracting hidden morsels from the prospect's essay*

The essays of prospects, whether good or bad, are their attempt at saying who they are. And the essays should bring up many questions in addition to providing answers. By referring to a prospect's essay, you make it clear that you've read the essay and that you're interested in what the person wrote.

Consider this example profile:

> Hello. The cultured world of Manhattan is where I grew up and inspires the lifestyle I cultivate in Los Angeles today. Yet I remain a simple girl at heart. I'm outgoing and love to live life to the fullest. I always make time for my closest friends and family. I love to bring people together. And I have lots of opportunity to do that in my position as vice president of a bicoastal arts foundation. I am passionate about the arts and value democratic ideals, and in my work I pull the two together. I have an incredible circle of friends with whom I like to get together to have lunch by the ocean, catch an art-house movie, go to a concert, attend an event, or picnic at the Hollywood Bowl. I love to entertain, and friends tell me the parties I throw are among the best and most memorable. I like to stay fit and do some form of exercise every day; my favorites are hiking, yoga, and weight training. I also like to ski, dance, and horseback ride.

This prospect has given you so many things to write about, but here's a no-brainer opening e-mail:

> Hi, ___. I see you're deeply involved with the arts. Can you tell me more about how you got involved? [Now offer something about yourself.]
>
> Jack
>
> P.S.: I live in Yellow Knife and have limited access to the arts, well, if you don't count the A&E Channel.

Even lame phrases in an essay can create inspirational e-mails. For example, in my hometown, we have beautiful lakes in the midst of the city, and people love to walk, bike, or skate around them. Consequently, every local essay includes "I love to take walks around da lakes." Such a line is so trite that I can hardly stand it, but it still makes for good e-mail fodder:

> I see you like to walk around the lakes. Have you ever tried walking the secret passageway from Lake Wobegon to the Mississippi River to the Fort?

The answers could be any of the following: Yes! Nope. Really? Where is it? For your purposes, all answers except silence are winners.

## Rolling the ball ever so slightly

Don't overwhelm your prospects with too much at once. If you ask too many questions, give too many compliments, or comment on too many aspects of their essay, they'll get suspicious about whether your e-mail is a programmed query.

If you're on the receiving end of such an e-mail, you can usually ferret out the fakes. For example, I once got a message from an attractive young (read age inappropriate) woman from an unnamed eastern European country. In her first e-mail, she wrote at length about many aspects of her personality and how we may be a match. I responded with a short reply: "How did you know all that?" She replied with an answer as long as her first, not responding to my question at all but going on about her virtues (which were many). She was apparently reading from the "How to Get an American Man" column in Pravda and was simply sending me the second reply in the list.

## *Offering some gender-specific icebreaker advice*

Some opening e-mails work for women and not men — and vice versa. Read the following discussion that applies to you:

- **Read the profile carefully.** This rule is obvious, but guys are so visual that a good photo can neutralize their short-term memory functions. Sometimes women write really critical stuff in their essay to see whether you're reading. The clues are so blatant that you can't miss them. But if you do, you'll be *poofed* (ejected from the cyber world in her mind).

- **Keep it brief.** Usually, this advice isn't a problem, but occasionally it is. The first e-mail should be one paragraph of about four sentences. If your prospects' eyes glaze over from reading your mininovella, chances are you lost 'em.

- **Interject appropriate humor.** If you're not funny, don't start your stand-up career now. If you have a talent for writing funny stuff, most people love it. Be sure to make fun of yourself, not them.

- **Don't comment on their photo (too much) and don't make appearance the only reason for making contact.** Even very attractive folks don't want to be dated only for their looks. In fact, such people may be even more put off by the comment "Hi, I saw your photo and had to write." Mentioning photos is okay, but you can choose a different way to break the ice. Finally, don't write someone simply because she has a great-looking photo.

  Saying that you're comfortable with someone's looks is far different than saying that you're in awe of the prospect's striking beauty. Once, after viewing a stunning photo (and after ten minutes of fantasizing about it), I regained my composure and tapped out this e-mail:

  Hi, _____. I must admit I was attracted to your photo. You have a look that feels very comfortable to me. It got me to read your essay, and I couldn't help asking if you have been horseback riding since your youth.

- **Don't mention other men/women (of any kind).** Most problematic is any mention of your ex-, good or bad. No one wants to know about them (at least not yet). Keep your mother out of the e-mail, too. Women do like men who respect their mother, but you can bring her up later.

- **Don't mention sex or virility in any form.** Don't even make references to bulls on your farm.

✔ **Don't provide any excuses.** This error is common. You need to get on a positive plane right away, and any excuse, no matter how valid, is counterproductive. Avoid e-mails like this example:

"Hi, _____. I saw your profile last week, but I couldn't write because I wrote your screen name on one of Rover's dog bones and darned if he didn't eat it. Fortunately, it didn't sit well with him and I got it back, although some of the letters were hard to read."

If you're a woman writing to a man, heed this advice:

✔ **Don't emphasize your vulnerabilities.** This advice applies to men as well, of course, but women seem more prone to it. For example, never write

"Hi, ____. I almost didn't write to you because I didn't have the courage, but after two martinis, it didn't seem that daunting. So here I am. I hope you write back, or I'll have to have that third martini."

✔ **Don't reveal any information that could jeopardize your anonymity.** Amazingly enough, I received phone numbers from women in their first e-mail to me. I asked them why they did it, and they said that they didn't like e-mail and wanted to move to the phone as soon as possible. Don't do it. Revealing your identity early in the online-dating stage isn't safe, and you lose a key advantage of online dating: anonymity.

✔ **Interject appropriate humor.** With women, this advice requires a bit more care. Although many women want a man with a good sense of humor, sometimes men are intimidated by a scathing sense of humor. If your essay is blisteringly funny, it may get laughs, but it may not get mail.

✔ **Never use phrases like "friend first."** Any phrase indicating that you're putting preconditions on a relationship is a turnoff. "Friends first" is the universal signal for "I'm not going to get intimate with you until I'm good and ready, Buster." You can send that message in several other tasteful ways. Preconditions are a bad way to start.

✔ **Comment on his photo.** Unlike women, men like to hear that they're good looking and are less offended that you'd date them just for that. They figure that they'll charm you later. Hey, if looks work, go for it.

✔ **Avoid early and overt sexual innuendo.** We write a lot about this topic in Chapter 11. Suffice it to say, you can get in big trouble in a hurry if your opening e-mail is sexual.

# *Reacting to Their Responses*

Don't freak. The chances that everyone who wrote will reply — and, frankly, that any one of them is the right person — are pretty small.

Depending on the region of the country you're making contact, your odds of having someone reply to your initial message vary. (The Midwest has the highest odds, and the East Coast has the lowest.) Of course, your odds, like your mileage, may also vary according to what you write.

Many reasons exist why many people don't respond, including:

- The recipient doesn't connect with the way you look in your photo. (If this situation happens too often, get a new photo.)

- The recipient doesn't like what you wrote in your essay.

- The recipient is presently engaged in another relationship but hasn't taken down his or her posting.

- The recipient is presently engaged in several other e-mail relationships and can't manage even one more.

- The recipient is on an all-expense paid trip to the Bermuda Triangle, and no one has heard from him or her for months.

- The recipient is part of the Living Dead. Such people haven't paid their subscription fees but are still posted. They can't write to you, but you don't know that. (Chapter 13 talks more about the Living Dead/Deadwood.)

Distinguishing the Living Dead postings (people who can't answer like those on a perpetual trial period) from the effectively deadwood postings (people who would appear to be able to respond but for some reason just aren't) is fairly easy. Just look at when the person last signed on. Almost all sites give you this information, so use it.

Now, as for the prospects who *do* respond to you — and you may indeed have many — take our advice: Just keep the e-mail thread going with anyone that interests you and terminate contact with those you don't see a future in. You need to be upfront about it. *Poofing* (disappearing without a trace) isn't okay when the e-mail exchanges have been going on for a while. (The nearby sidebar "Where are their manners?" lets you know when disappearing without a trace *is* okay.)

## Where are their manners?

Newbies to Internet dating often ask whether prospects should reply with a "thanks but no thanks" if they're not interested. Isn't it impolite not to? Well, it depends.

Whether you respond depends partly on your comfort level. Many people, for example, have trouble giving rejection — even for the right reasons. Not answering is the minimalist solution.

It also depends partly on the type of dating service you're using. If you're on an all-in-one service, you might know that the recipient has received your mail, opened it, read it, and saved or deleted it. On a service like match.com, you don't even know whether the recipient has received your mail because no feedback system is available.

You don't have to reply to an *initial* email query. Internet-dating etiquette is very different from table etiquette. So much so that we wrote an entire chapter on it (see Chapter 15).

At some point, you may be involved in two or more e-mail exchanges that seem promising, which, at times, can feel a bit scary. Why? Well, you may cross wires and screw them both up. Another reason is that you know you'll soon have to make up your mind — and you could easily be wrong. The best advice is to stay on e-mail as long as possible to get to know more about each prospect.

While on the subject of juggling e-mail exchanges with two (or more) prospects, for those of you who may be wondering whether putting one e-mail exchange on hold while pursuing another is okay, we have one more nugget of advice. We're not sure that approach works in the real world, but we know it almost never works in the online world. This exchange is pretty much how it goes:

He:

> I've enjoyed chatting with you for the last few days, but I've been simultaneously corresponding with another woman, and we've decided to meet. I don't know if it will go anywhere, because most of these things don't, but I want to be honest and not date two people at the same time. Would you mind if I contact you again, assuming you're also available, if my date doesn't work out?

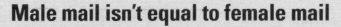

## Male mail isn't equal to female mail

Males get a tiny fraction of the mail. Even though most sites are within 10 percent of being equally balanced between male and female postings, you won't find any balance at all with respect to who writes most of the mail. Men write most of the e-mail, which is probably a cultural bias, but there you have it.

She:

> I don't think so. If she's more interesting to you than me, and if she doesn't work out, why would I? See ya.

Short of lying (such as "I need to break this exchange off because my grandmother is ill and needs my attention"), you probably won't find a way to make it work. People hate rejection so much that after they start an e-mail exchange and it finishes positively or negatively, they don't want to restart it

# Chapter 15

# Understanding E-mail and E-mail Etiquette

*In This Chapter*

▶ Looking at how e-mail is different from other forms of communication

▶ Dealing with intimacy and personal issues in e-mail exchanges

▶ Using good e-mail etiquette

*I*t's faster than a speeding bullet and more powerful than a loco-motive. It's e-mail, and you probably already know how different e-mail is from any other method of communication.

Unfortunately, some people let all that speed and power go to their head and use the Internet to get away with behavior that isn't accept-able in real life. Just like road rage, perfectly well mannered individ-uals become harsh, cruel, or make blatantly untruthful statements while hiding behind the anonymity of the computer screen. Lest this happen to you, this chapter sets you straight on the art and etiquette of e-mail communication.

## Understanding E-mail as a Unique Beast

The days of the engaging, handwritten letter went away with the 17th century. So if you think e-mail communication is merely a fast version of old-fashioned letters, you're in for a big wakeup call.

If you work in an office, you've probably had the pleasure of being on the receiving end of the electronic version of road rage — getting a nastygram from a coworker or even the boss. You've had a taste of why e-mail isn't like regular mail and *not* similar to spoken communication. What makes e-mail different is this:

- Unlike with spoken exchanges, with e-mail you get no chance to recover from a mistake by reading the recipient's facial expressions or body language.

- Unlike with snail-mail (written letters sent by post), with e-mail after you click the Send button, the letter is gone. You can't retrieve it if you have second thoughts. Even the U.S. Postal Service gives back mail that you dropped in a mailbox if you plead, but on the Internet, it's just *oops*.

E-mail isn't at all like spoken exchanges or snail-mail. It's a special beast, all its own.

## *Talking blindfolded with both hands tied behind your back*

Ever try to talk with someone blindfolded? Now you have a pretty good idea what talking is like during e-mail exchanges. Imagine having such exchanges with someone trying to initiate very personal contact with you.

Consider this:

- Without the usual restraints of complex physical and social cues, you can easily get carried away when writing e-mails. Keep in mind that e-mail can be stronger to the reader than the writer. Every exchange on the Internet is magnified because it takes place in a relative sensory vacuum with no immediate feedback.

- E-mail is so amazingly informal to the sender that it's almost like a daydream or conversation taking place in his or her head. And you know how crazy those conversations can get, especially after that second grande mocha. But on the flipside, e-mail is relatively formal for the recipient. Senders don't realize that recipients scrutinize a casual comment many times — especially in matters of the heart. The reader can devastatingly interpret an indiscrete choice of words, although the sender may have assumed that the comments would be taken lightly.

So our advice is to move no faster, and possibly a wee bit slower with intimacy issues in your e-mail exchanges, than you would in real life. Before clicking the Send button, make sure that what you wrote is something you'd say to a person face to face. If you'd feel embarrassed saying it in person, rethink the e-mail's content and consider the Delete button as your final rescue.

In addition, know that subtlety and certain innuendoes may not come across very well in e-mail because the recipient can't see the twinkle you had in your eye or that little bemused smirk you were wearing when writing your facetious comment.

A human being is on the receiving end of every e-mail you send. That human being, like you, is looking for a match to make his or her life more fulfilled. E-mail isn't the place to dip into the poison pen inkwell.

## *Imagining things*

Funny things can happen when you try hard to connect with someone without the benefit of nonverbal communication clues, such as body language, tone of voice, and so on. Your mind may supply all the nonverbal communication clues for you, even though they don't really exist. In other words, your heart may want to succeed so badly that your mind creates a fantasy world to fit your desires.

So if you find yourself experiencing any of the following, consider yourself in trouble:

✔ Imagining how your prospect looks in real life (beyond the two-inch photo you've been staring at for weeks), to the point where you're filling in the missing pieces in your mind.

✔ Thinking you know how your prospect's voice will sound even before you've ever heard it.

✔ Discussing intimate issues with your prospect via e-mail and feeling that you're engaging in cyber sex.

✔ Feeling sure that your prospect is just right for you based on his or her profile, phone conversations, and several weeks of heavy e-mail exchanges.

The chances are small that any of those experiences will hold up after you've met and dated your prospect for a while. But take heart. The chances aren't nonexistent. In fact, most people who succeed in Internet dating have probably experienced some or all the preceding feelings. Problem is, more often your mind is playing games with you. We suggest that you hold off planning the wedding until you've actually met and shared many happy life experiences together.

# *Questioning in the west and answering in the east*

Wanna know the No.1 way that e-mail differs from in-person communication? You can easily escape tough questions by simply not answering.

If you're doing your portion of e-mail exchanges correctly, you're inserting a few important questions innocuously into your e-mails. However, if you're finding that your correspondent routinely avoids core questions but otherwise answers many other questions, your alert system should be on overdrive.

Before launching into a tirade, simply restate the question standing by itself, without burying it in a host of other questions.

For example, say that your prospect didn't answer your questions about the age of his or her children and who has custody. Don't reapproach the subject like this:

> I really want to know more about your kids, but you seem to be avoiding my questions. You need to answer me. I have to know how old they are, who has custody, and why.

In e-mail, people sometimes perceive even slight anger as biting one's head off. So, instead, keep calm and just ask the question again in a gentle, nonoffensive, stand-alone way:

> I forget, did you ever reply to my question about the ages of your children and who has custody?

While on the subject of questioning and answering, we want to share one more factoid and e-mail uniqueness. First the factoid: Asking questions is always easier than answering them. Now the uniqueness: If a person begins as the one asking the questions, he or she ends up asking most of the questions.

In person-to-person communications, this tactic quickly becomes an interrogation, but in e-mail, because the exchanges aren't instant (this issue doesn't apply to those using an Instant Messaging feature), repeated questioning by one party to the other doesn't come off as so imposing. Interestingly, the recipient may not perceive the e-mail as an interrogation because after all, you're showing interest in the prospect's favorite subject: him/herself.

But even though you can ask all the questions, should you? Probably not. If you want to know more about your prospects, even their questions can give you hints as to what matters to them. Successful relationships require a balance. You may as well try to see whether you can find one earlier rather than later.

# Dealing with E-mail's Disarming Nature

If you choose to stay involved in e-mail exchanges for an extended period of time (days or weeks instead of a day or so) before meeting or phoning, you'll certainly encounter the phenomenon we call *e-mail's disarming nature*. We think the anonymous nature of e-mail is the root of it, but regardless, it's for real.

If you engage in lengthy e-mail exchanges with someone, you soon find that the intimacy of the exchanges far exceeds the intimacy you'd probably share on the phone and in person. (If you've had long-standing e-mail exchanges, go back and re-read those e-mails. Then ask yourself whether you could've said those things face to face.)

So is this disarming nature good? Well, on the plus side, you discover a great deal about your prospect. If your first meeting is successful, you probably will have several future dates. Regardless of that plus, though, you should move no faster than you would in real life (see the section "Talking blindfolded with both hands tied behind your back," earlier in this chapter, for the reasons).

However, the nature of the beast is very strong, and for better or worse, you may indeed find yourself involved in intimate e-mail exchanges with someone. Because you're down that road anyway, if certain issues are so important to you that they're deal breakers, you may find that asking about them is easier via e-mail than on a first date. Here are some intimate, deal-breaker issues people discuss via e-mail:

  ✔ **Attitudes about children.** This area is troublesome for just about anyone. For example, if you're a person with custody of younger children, you need to realize that many people lie about their true feelings on your arrangement (meaning, whether they're willing to deal with your children). Approach the issue indirectly instead of head-on. You're not likely to get a straight answer if you ask whether you having kids is a deal breaker. But asking a series of peripheral questions may get you to the same place. The luxury of being anonymous on e-mail is that you have the time to ask all your questions before making a decision about a face-to-face meeting.

Try these three examples of peripheral questions when discussing attitudes about children (which can lead to questions about whether having young children around is a problem):

- "What are some of your favorite memories of raising your children when they were young?"

- "Have you ever coached a kids' sports team or any kids' activity? What ages?"

- If applicable, "In hindsight, are you satisfied with your decision not to have children?"

✔ **Experiences in prior serious relationships.** You won't get a straight answer — via e-mail or otherwise — to a question about why a person divorced or ended a serious relationship because no straight answer exists. Relationships end due to circumstances between two people, neither of whom you know. So try a more roundabout approach with questions like these:

- "Who initiated the divorce or breakup?"

- "Are you still able to communicate with your ex in a civil manner?"

- "What are some important issues that you want to see in your next relationship?"

- "Has anyone ever asked you if you'd ever go back to the marriage/relationship?"

- "What do you wish you could have done differently?"

- "How has this experience changed your feelings about committed relationships?"

✔ **Nature of the commitment your prospect is seeking.** Almost all sites ask a basic question about whether you're looking for marriage, a long-term relationship, a date, or a pen pal. Most everyone answers with a long-term relationship, so obviously some people are lying. Therefore, exploring this question is important. A good place to start is to ask questions like these:

- "How long have you been online dating?" (Not "How long have you been signed up to *this* service?" We're talking *any* service.) The answer to watch out for is less than a month. Being on for years isn't a problem if the prospects have had some relationships in between. The newbies are the ones you need to know about because beginners need to get over the candy-store effect before they can get serious about relationships.

- "Have you had any success in online dating?" Note that this question is sometimes dangerous because you really don't want to hear about their prior conquests or failures. You just want to find out whether they're professional daters.

Some people are never happy with anything, and Internet dating gives them a chance to complain even more. Try a question like this to ferret out ultranegative types: "What is the worst thing that has happened as a result of online dating?" A great answer is something like "I haven't found the right person yet but am getting more skillful at discerning what's a good match." The worst answer is "I have met only frauds, crooks, criminals, and married men/women."

When people are negative about their online experience, run. Don't look back because you'll probably be their next negative experience. Sure, a small percentage of "bad" men and women are online, but you can easily brush them aside. The remainder should bring about a very hopeful, if not satisfying, experience.

# Examining E-mail Etiquette

Good manners. Protocol. Decorum. People expect them in real life but often overlook them online.

Trust us: Etiquette is just as important in e-mail as it is in person. Get to know the rules of e-mail etiquette as well as the guidelines for tracking prospects' data and answers so that you don't make a fatal online-dating faux pas.

## Knowing the rules of e-mail etiquette

You mean e-mailing actually has etiquette and rules like fine dining and job interviews? Yes. In fact, the following rules apply to e-mailing and are important to follow when dating online.

- ✔ **Ask open-ended questions.** In other words, ask questions that invite a broad range of responses and perhaps even a dialog. Judy here: I find this tip to be the most useful tool for Internet or any other kind of dating. People fill in the blanks with items that are relevant to the question, but you can also reflect on what the person's state of mind is. All information is useful, including choice of topic, content, phrasing, cadence, and grammar.

Bad start: "I see you were born in the UK. What year does your green card expire?"

Better start: "I see you were born in the UK. I used to work there, but I had to leave because everyone was driving in my lane. And in the opposite direction, too! So do you find life in Lake Wobegone to be much of a change?"

✔ **Ask top-priority questions first and, when they're personal questions, offer something personal first.** Note that this rule kind of contradicts the Keep It Light rule (later in this list), so you have to use it carefully. The point of asking your important questions early is that you may want to bail out if the recipient can't get past the deal breakers. And if you want to ask a tough question, you can't duck the issue when it comes back around, so you may as well just kick off the communication by volunteering first. It's a powerful technique.

Bad start: "Grown children are all I can handle. I can't bear the thought of raising any more teenagers."

Better start: "I'm fortunate to have grown children who are happily independent, pursuing their respective careers as a herpetologist and gaffer in San Diego. What about your kids?"

✔ **Avoid really hot topics at first and know that some are always too hot for e-mail.** For example, starting off with politics or religion isn't a good idea. Save those discussions until you have a better feel for the person you're communicating with. And some topics, such as past emotional problems, are so sensitive that you may not be able to convey your exact meaning in e-mail without having the benefit of in-person empathy and encouragement.

Bad start: "I see from your profile that you're a vegetarian. If we aren't supposed to eat animals, why are they made of meat?"

Better start: "I see from your profile that you are a vegetarian. How do you feel about dating a nonvegetarian?"

✔ **Keep it light, at least at first.** Don't shoot your opening e-mails like a series of machine-gun questions. You may be burning to ask it all, but take it slow and ask the softball questions first. (For example, skip the life and death issues early on.) You don't have to stay light too long. In fact, you may come off as uninteresting if you keep the inane questions flowing too long. Certainly matters that deal with necessary and unconditional features should come up fairly early, but try to maintain some restraint from pouncing on the big-ticket issues immediately.

Bad start: "Which of the two pictures you posted are most like you?"

Better start: "I hope you don't mind me saying, but your two photos, both attractive, are so different. Which do you like better?" (*Much* later, you can ask which one is a better representation, keeping in mind that he or she isn't at all objective about such a question.)

✔ **Never make your recipient feel uncomfortable.** If you have to pose a tough question, always provide a way out. Humor always does the trick.

Bad start: "How much of your essay is really true?"

Better start: "You certainly don't look 45. Maybe 40 but not more. Are you really 45? If you don't feel comfortable telling me, just give me the answer in Roman numerals."

✔ **Remain brief, at least in the beginning.** Nobody wants to hear your dissertation on the virtues of plastic duck birdcalls, at least not in the opening e-mail. Later, when you've established a rapport, you may well want to get back to ducks.

Bad start: "I really liked your profile. First, you have a great photo. I really think we're a perfect match. You look so great. You have great eyes, and a great body, too. Did I tell you that I've been online for years, and you're the first person that I know will be perfect for me? I've been on several online services, and everyone is a liar, cheater, or player. But I'm sure that doesn't apply to you. . . . [a few more shovels full of stuff here] I can't want to hear from you."

Better start: "Wow. Nice profile. Are you are writer?"

✔ **Stay honest and clear at all times.** Remember, you're writing to a real person. And this real person may be, if all goes well, the person you want to spend the rest of your life with. So clearly presenting your most pleasant and truthful self is important. Hostile and confrontational language has no place in your e-mail.

Note that the Internet is a bit freaky for everyone. The slightest strange move, and you'll be toast (we prefer to call it *poofed*). If you seem strange, even if your strangedom may work in person, it won't work online. Online people are very suspicious, at least until you establish trust. So take heed that even a few simple statements of opinion can come across as a psycho rant.

Bad start: I apologize for not posting my photo. My divorce isn't final and I don't want to antagonize my ex and the lawyers by having them discover that I'm dating. (**Note:** This insertion screams: "I HAVE PROBLEMS! Let's date!")

Better start in an essay: I haven't posted my photo yet, but I'll gladly send you one by e-mail. (**Note:** We think posting your photo is extremely important.)

## *Keeping track of prospects' answers*

Don't ask the same question twice. If you do, you appear not to be listening. You risk annoying, or even alienating, your prospect because all your conversations are recorded in your e-mail correspondence. (Don't act like you did when your parents talked to you and you said you didn't hear them.)

Unfortunately, however, most sites have such poor e-mail archiving and organizational tools that finding old information is difficult. The best solution is to maintain a paper (or word-processing) file for anyone you're communicating extensively with. Try these tips:

✔ Print the prospect's entire profile and photo. Doing so is critical because your e-mail exchange may outlive the prospect's subscription. (And if you get into a long-term relationship with this prospect, his or her profile will be an interesting keepsake.)

✔ Keep a running set of notes, abstracting the prospect's likes, dislikes, and such. You may think this idea seems obsessive. Remember, though, you're communicating with several people simultaneously. Trust us, you'll never keep the small details straight unless you write them down.

Regarding that second tip, we include the important tidbits you want to keep track of beyond what's in the prospect's profile:

✔ Children (names, ages, custody issues)

✔ Financial issues (job, spending habits, saving habits)

✔ Interests/leisure activities (sports, hobbies, level of commitment/involvement)

✔ Life events (foreign travel/study, career challenges/changes/ achievements, interesting life stories)

- Marital status (past relationships, causes of failure/ending, gory details)
- Other habits (alcohol, gambling, smoking, day/night personality)
- Politics (orientation, voting frequency)
- Sexual matters (values, beliefs, attitudes, birth control, safer-sex practices)

## Keeping track of your own answers

Don't dump your entire life history (and its baggage) on your prospect all at once. Yet, you may need to reveal some very significant things at the right time, and you need to remember whether or not you've done it yet. The only safe way to do so is to keep track of your answers, just as you do with info from your prospects.

Keep track of these examples of sensitive information that you may need to track — to remember whether you've conveyed it yet:

- Allergies to pets or environments
- A disability of yours or of a dependent family member
- For famous people, your true identity
- HIV or other medical/sexual status issues
- Multiple prior marriages/divorces
- Past (or ongoing) criminal history
- Significant debts

Don't take this advice the wrong way. We mean for you to reveal all this information truthfully and completely, but you can wait to share it at the right time.

## Keeping IM etiquette straight

Although e-mail etiquette is important to master, if you're going to participate in instant messaging (IM), you need to know some special rules.

An IM exchange is very much like walking up to a stranger at a party and starting a conversation. Treat it that way, but many people don't. Use the following tips when participating in IM:

- **Answer the questions.** IM exchanges are fast and furious. If someone asks you a question, but it was several lines ago, go back and answer the question. If you don't, you send a red flare saying: "I'm hiding something." The most common flare is: "Is this man/woman married?"

- **Be responsive.** If you can IM with 10 people at once and still seem interested in all ten, great. If not, your prospects quickly can figure you're only marginally interested.

- **Say goodbye.** This is the No.1 insult on IM. If you see no point in continuing, say so: I am afraid I have to go, I don't see that we have much in common, and so forth. Too many people think just disconnecting is okay. If you were at a party, would you just walk away from someone in mid-sentence? Don't do it on IM.

# Chapter 16

# Rejection!

*F*ear of rejection is such a powerful human emotion that it guides (and often misguides) our actions. Although we're rarely aware of it, nearly every action we take is subconsciously influenced by our inner fear of "losing face," as the Japanese would put it. And although this control mechanism is healthy, the problem is that our fear of rejection often overwhelms us and prevents us from making some sound decisions and taking reasonable risk.

In online dating, people tend to draw on fears they discovered from their first (and worst) teenage dating experiences. But you don't have to worry about that anymore. Not only are those teenage days long gone, but also Internet dating is so fundamentally different that you can't allow rejection to burden you. In this chapter, we aim to convince you to toss your fears out the window and give yourself a fresh start online.

## Understanding That Rejection Isn't Personal

The reasons for getting rejected in online dating aren't as obvious as you may think. Here are the biggies:

> ✔ **Your photo doesn't spark any chemical reaction.** Don't consider this reason to be an indictment of your photo. Aside from the fact that very few people are fundamentally beautiful to all, the rest of us are attractive to some but not to others. And thank goodness for that, or we'd all be trying to date the same person. Even men, who tend to be much more visual than

women, have a specific look that works for them, whether it's the girl next door, a tomboy, or something else. Just make sure that your photo says who you are and don't sweat it. (Turn to Chapter 12 for more about photos.)

✔ **Your profile has a deal breaker in it.** Some prospects can't live with or without certain things, such as anyone under 6-feet (190 cm) tall or with brown hair. The fact that you get rejected because of them is a *good* thing, not a bad one. That's why you list those attributes in your essay. Some easy ones include

  • Your physical characteristics and photo

  • Number/age/interest in children

  • Religious preference

  • Smoking/drinking habits

For example, if you're a wine connoisieur and don't plan to stop, but you write to a person who's a teetotaler, the person may blow you off (by not responding) for that reason alone. You'll never know exactly why, nor should you care.

If pretty much everyone is rejecting you, you probably put some zinger in your profile, and you need to get a zinger-ectomy. A common zinger is a profile that reads like a rule book. Check out Chapter 10 to know what to put in your profile and, most importantly, have a person of the opposite sex (a friend) look at your profile and give you some feedback.

✔ **You wrote to a person who's out of play.** A fair number of people online are (at best) looking for pen pals or (at worst) looking to play you like a video game. Many are charming and engaging writers, and they aren't trying to hurt you. Instead, they just love the entertainment of cyber dating. Some are married or lying about something that prevents them from being a serious date. And others are looking for a one-night stand (even though some sites specifically focus on sexual encounters).

✔ **You wrote to a commitment-phobe.** Some people think they want to find and date a mate, but they simply can't follow through for psychological reasons. They withdraw as you try to get closer. (You can read more on them in Chapter 19 on trouble dates.) If a commitment-phobe rejects you early enough, consider sending him or her flowers for saving you untold grief.

✔ **You wrote to someone who's overwhelmed.** Some people, mostly beautiful women, get so much mail that they simply can't cope with the flood. A few sites display *publicly*, how many perusals or hits a person got, and the information can be fascinating. For example, one woman with a movie star photo got 14,000 hits in about a month. The typical for a mere mortal woman was about 500 for that metro area. These popular people have a bigger problem than you think, having to sift through mounds of mail.

✔ **You wrote to someone who is intimidated by your photo/profile.** For whatever reason, the prospect you've contacted has decided that you're out of his or her league and may give you a pass based on insecurities or past experiences. You may never know the truth.

# Dealing with Rejection

We know of one sure way to never get rejected in online dating: Don't sign up. Beyond that, you *will* get rejected. Plan on it. Put it on your calendar.

Even if you never send a single e-mail to any prospect, eventually you'll receive some e-mails, and one of those people will then lose interest in you. You'll then have your first real rejection.

It'll get much worse. You'll be feverishly exchanging hot e-mails with a prospect, and suddenly he or she will disappear for no reason. You won't know his or her name or phone number, and you'll be blocked from sending him or her more e-mails. You'll be summarily rejected.

It happens more often on the Internet than in person. It hurts. *But it doesn't matter.*

## Just move on

What's the first cure for the rejection blues? Recognize that the fastest way out of the gloomy feeling is to go back to the hunt. Remember that glassy-eyed candy-store feeling you had when you first got on the Internet? Just get back online, and you'll get that feeling again.

Can't go back to the hunt because the local herd has been picked clean? Switch to a different geographic area, and you can find plenty of fresh faces. Many sites have overlapping communities, so you can switch geographic areas without taking the risk of a long-distance relationship (see Chapter 20 for that story). For example, Matchmaker.com has a Boston community, but it also has a New England community that includes Boston and surrounding areas. On Yahoo.com and others, you can accomplish the same thing by picking adjacent zip/postal codes or area codes. On Match.com and many other sites, you just have to expand your search radius a bit. The defaults are mostly 50 miles (80 km). Change them to 100 miles (160 km).

## Put the rejection in perspective

Most rejection occurs in the early stages of e-mail exchanges. One or two exchanges and then silence. Sometimes a simple "Bye." Instant messaging exchanges can end even more abruptly.

How much pain should the situation cause you? Practically none. Just remember how little time and emotion you have invested in the contact:

- ✔ You sent or received an e-mail.

- ✔ You exchanged a few more e-mails.

- ✔ The prospect figured it wasn't a match and ended the communication.

- ✔ You haven't exchanged names or phone numbers and either party can block further e-mails, so the deed is done.

A relationship isn't a relationship if even *one* party isn't interested. Thank your lucky stars if your prospect lets you know early on that it wasn't a match, even if you didn't see it coming.

Another thing to keep in mind is that Internet communications occur in a vacuum. You really don't know much about the prospect's life other than what the person has chosen to reveal. An apparent rejection may be due to some unrelated life event or crisis that you're not privy to. You may have done absolutely nothing wrong except communicate with someone at the wrong time.

Now for comparison, consider the price of in-person dating rejection:

- ✔ You made phone contact with your blind date, requiring the emotional investment of name and phone number exchanges, not to mention loss of anonymity.

- ✔ You made an appointment to meet.

- ✔ You drove to the appointed place.

- ✔ Your blind date was immediately or quickly disappointed, requiring you to spend the next hour in an uncomfortable situation knowing that rejection was at hand.

# Dishing Out Rejection

The Internet is a strange place, and what seems abnormal for in-person experiences is completely common on the Internet. Notice that we said *common,* not polite or considerate.

You need to know how to dish out rejection in an appropriate way. As with real life, we encourage you to do it quickly — and with a modicum of kindness, if possible. Granted, for some people, a more heavy-handed approach is necessary.

In general, give a rejection firmly. Polite is good, but if it doesn't work, try sterner and firmer. Anger doesn't help. If you need further coaching, go to your local electric company's customer service department and see how it handles you when you try to dispute a bill by saying, "I never used that electricity."

Many appropriate ways are available to encourage someone to move along. Each one requires its own special finesse. This section points out the major ways to do so in specific situations.

## After receiving the very first e-mail from someone

Say that you get an e-mail from someone, and you can tell immediately that you have no interest in communicating with that person. Here are the Internet-appropriate ways to say no:

- ✔ Don't reply at all, ever. Just delete the message. In Internet-speak, this tactic is completely understood to mean "Not interested at all, ever."

  Note that Internet dating sites vary in the sophistication of their features. On some sites, the person knows that you received his or her e-mail and read it. On some sites, the person also knows that you deleted it.

- ✔ Send a short reply saying, "Thanks for writing, but I'm not interested." Then delete the person's e-mail. If the person continues to write, don't answer. If the person persists, use the blocking feature on your e-mail system.

And for the record, the inappropriate ways to say no include

- ✔ Deleting without opening. Again if this e-mail is the first communication from a prospect, read it. The person spent the time to write it, so take the few seconds to read it. If your online system informs the user that their e-mail was deleted *unopened,* that is a big, and unnecessary, rebuff.

- ✔ Sending an e-mail saying "Not on your life, you loser."

- ✔ Using the block feature immediately. If the first inquiry was polite, you have no reason to take out the big guns so early.

Even if you don't want any further e-mails from that person, why slap him or her in the face because that is what it feels like to be blocked.

# In the middle of an IM exchange

Say that you're in the middle of an Instant Messaging (IM) exchange, and you realize that the prospect just isn't a match. The Internet-appropriate action to take is to simply say

> "I need to stop now. I've enjoyed chatting with you, but I don't think we're a match. I don't want to waste any more of your time. Best of luck in your search."

Wait for a reply. If it's an argument telling you why you *are* a match, simply sign off. Don't engage in further IMs. Block him or her if necessary.

And for the record, the inappropriate actions are

- Poofing — just breaking off the conversation in mid-stream and logging off. Would you hang up the phone in mid-conversation if you got bored?
- Saying "Gotta go" and logging off.
- Responding with anger or obscenities, even if some were directed at you.
- Sending a pornographic photo for shock value.

Regarding those first two actions, your prospect would probably think you had computer problems and keep trying to reach you, which isn't what you want. Regarding the third action, no stranger is worth any emotional investment on your part, especially negative ones. Don't go away mad. Just go away. And regarding the porno action, sending pornographic material can be construed as harassment and get you into a heap of legal trouble.

If someone has really incensed you, avoid further trouble even though you're anonymous. Resist the urge to "flame" people. They are unlikely to go postal on you, but some people are sufficiently sick to do some serious libel and slander. We've heard of people who flamed others by sending e-mails, warning people of a person's supposed bad character. ("Don't date this guy. He is [insert issue here].") Although you could sue them for defamation, who needs the grief? The best way to avoid this sort of thing is to kill people with kindness, even if they don't deserve it.

# In the midst of a phone call

Say that you're in the midst of a phone call with a prospect (after some e-mail exchanges), and you realize that he or she just isn't a match. The appropriate actions to take include

- End the phone conversation non-committally. Then send an e-mail saying that you have thought over the exchanges of the past weeks and don't think you're a match. This method has the advantage of moving your correspondent to e-mail and away from the phone, as a method of contact. Gradually, he/she will give up.

- Tell the truth and end the conversation, saying that you don't think you're a match and thanking the person for taking the time.

And for the record, avoid these inappropriate actions:

- Ending the conversation on a positive note, with no intention of continuing the exchanges.

- Hanging up the phone in mid-sentence. (Those darn squirrels. They chewed through the line again.) He or she will just call you back.

# When people are clueless

Occasionally, you'll run into people who just won't stop contacting you even after you've rejected them. Most often, people don't let go because they've developed fantasies from your photo and essay. When you start exchanging messages, the fantasies grow. If you're still anonymous, the situation probably isn't dangerous, but you may still feel pretty uncomfortable.

Spotting these people is tough because they seem so genuine and enthusiastic. So what's your No.1 warning sign? They express assumptions about the depth of your relationship with them long before it's appropriate.

### Avoid arguments

When your goal is to make a clean break from the person who won't let go (or any prospect, for that matter), never argue or defend yourself. You have to accept the bad guy or girl role unless you want to create an even angrier person out of your former prospect.

Realize that many people forget how little time they actually have invested in their exchanges and that they don't have a good perspective on their circumstances.

### If all else fails, let them down hard

When someone just won't quit bothering you and all else fails, you have to dispense with being polite. Just as dogs get only one bite (actually, they don't get any free bites), your discouraged suitor gets only one "apology" from you. Then it's over, babe.

The following line is pretty darn effective but only use it as a last resort:

> "You need to know that if you attempt to contact me again, I'll report your activities as an abuse to the dating site. The site will then begin to monitor all your e-mail messages and kick you off the system if it doesn't like what you're writing."

Afterward, break off the communication. From then on, no reply, no comment, no nothing.

We want to stress how important safety is at all times. If you think you have a problem prospect, even if you're anonymous, don't feel uncomfortable reporting the situation to the site operator (usually under *abuse* or *Webmaster*). The pay sites have a serious interest in protecting their customers and maintaining good public relations. If you do call for help, supply actual e-mails or other data giving the supporting facts.

Reporting abuse to the site is far more effective than just blocking a person's messages (a feature offered on most sites). However, if you're a drama king or queen, don't practice your art of "the sky is falling." If you fabricate e-mails and try to damage someone's reputation, you'll run afoul of several civil and criminal laws — maybe even antiterrorism federal law. Remember that nothing is ever completely erased on the Internet, so made-up abuse is pretty easy to expose. And if you report inappropriately, the site will monitor *your* mail.

If a former prospect is dogging you, but not seriously enough to report him or her as an abuse, on some sites, you can search in Invisible or Stealth mode. Doing so prevents you from being seen on the Who's Online feature. Note that at Match.com, you need to turn your invisible status on each time you log in.

# Chapter 17

# Going from Virtual to Real Contact

*I*f you're an experienced dater (or you can vaguely remember your last date 20 years ago), you may feel like falling back on your prior dating experiences to carry you into this next phase. We want to caution you to hold your fire until you read this chapter.

Just as the Internet has changed how you make first contact with people — *virtual* contact — the Internet has also changed what your first *real* contact is like. Remember, your first phone call and first face-to-face meeting after Internet contact is nothing like a blind date or even a second date. (You should have already spent the time on e-mail and on the phone getting to know your prospect.) Going from virtual to real contact is a hybrid experience somewhere between these two traditional scenarios. You need to take great care at this moment to prevent a budding relationship from doing a nose-dive because of misplaced expectations.

In this chapter, we tell you how to improve the chances to successfully transition a virtual date into a real date, and possibly into a mate.

# Getting Real at the Right Time

When to switch from e-mail/chat to the phone is a controversial topic. The precise answer is this:

Go to the phone when you reach a point where the written word no longer suffices to get your message across and you're consumed by curiosity.

The problem: For some people, the time occurs a few moments after the word *hello.* However, if you immediately jump to the phone, you're treating the Internet as a big phone book with names of potential dates and you're missing the power of Internet dating. And quite simply, the power of Internet dating is that it allows you to know a great deal about someone before you decide to make real contact. The amount you get to know depends on how long you're willing to stay virtual.

E-mail is amazingly disarming, and people write things about themselves that they'd rarely say in person — and never on a first date. So if you know what you're looking for in a person and you ask the right questions in e-mail or chat, you'll get far more info than you'd get during your first phone conversation or date. Strange but consistently true.

# Realizing the Benefits of E-mails before Phoning

Maybe something in the water causes some people to ignore the benefits of e-mail exchanges in Internet dating. More than likely, though, they're uncomfortable with the whole idea of writing versus speaking.

The Internet clearly favors people who know how to write, and if you're one of them, you have a powerful advantage over your competition. Writing allows the recipient to absorb your message at his or her rate and to re-read your words. And if you're an enchanting writer, you can deliver your message to the recipient better in words than merely over the phone. Writing also gives you a chance to deliberate.

## Many e-mails make for effective screening

In my experience, women tend to go to the phone much more quickly than I prefer. I know that you can't tell certain important characteristics about someone purely through e-mail, but for some reason, people are willing to open up on e-mail in ways they may not on the phone and certainly not in person.

After some experience, I effectively screened people through e-mail alone, to the point that the first phone call and meeting almost always went well — or even great. By the time I actually met someone, I had a pretty good idea that we had a lot in common, and I was rarely disappointed. So the percentage of women I met once and wanted to see again was high, and the feelings were almost always mutual. If I had jumped to the phone and met more women quickly, I probably would've had more frequent and disappointing encounters. Sure, I spent more time online, but it was far less intrusive to my life, and I had far fewer disappointments.

## In-person screening has its merits

I agree with Michael that e-mail is useful for gaining valuable insight into your prospect. I differ in degree. My personality style best fits in-person encounters.

I'm never comfortable giving personal information to total strangers. Although I was online dating, after I met the prospects, I then decided if they were worth further communication. Unlike e-mail, face-to-face meeting gives you a great deal of personality information that's unobtainable by any other means.

Although a great many of my first face-to-face meetings were also the last and those in-person meetings took more valuable time than e-mail would have, I was glad those people didn't know too much about me. I felt that the 30 to 45 minutes spent on a coffee date, even if unsuccessful, were still better than hours of online time with an unsuitable match. I was also okay with the knowledge that meeting early in the game meant that often the best part of the coffee date was the coffee.

# Use e-mail, not the phone, to discuss deal breakers

Even if you're not a great writer or your personality style best fits in-person encounters, you can still use e-mail to ferret out things about your prospect that matter to you. Deal-breaker issues are a must, for example:

✔ Handle issues about children (do you or your prospect have them? want them? and so on) before going to the phone. If kids are important to you but not your prospect, then the phone contact should never happen.

✔ Address issues about the accuracy of a prospect's profile in writing. Saying in person or on the phone, "Is everything in your profile true?" is difficult. But you can phrase one of your e-mail exchanges with tact, such as:

I see that we may have a lot in common, but I have one question that I must ask everyone I converse with: What on your profile isn't exactly correct? I think it's best to get past this earlier rather than later.

If you're going to ask this question, though, definitely have some tidbit to offer in exchange, like this:

Although I am listed in the 40 to 45 age band, I just celebrated my 46th birthday but felt entitled to maintain my age status, at least for a little while longer. Besides, I got an age waiver from the Webmaster.

Although we recommend staying online long enough to feel that you have a reasonable shot at a successful match, overstaying your e-welcome is also problematic. Some people may conclude that you're a cybernaut, unwilling and unable to join the real world if you can't get yourself to a phone. Even more important is that you can begin to create a completely false illusion about your prospect if you never connect to the real world. Your mind starts to fill in the missing blanks where data doesn't exist, which is particularly true of prospects who post fabulous photos. Remember, your mind is a busy factory. Give it some inspiration and add a bit of sexual intrigue, and you've got yourself a first-class fantasy.

# Going Live — the Risks and Rewards

Anybody who gets past your first barrier (e-mail) is worthy of a phone call. The phone is the halfway house of reality. You get some clues but not the whole enchilada.

## What you can discover on the phone

You can find out some fairly obvious traits on the phone. Phone contact gives you

- ✔ **Emotion.** An animated voice says tons. You find out plenty about your prospects, less by what they say than how they say it.

- ✔ **Feedback.** Most importantly, voice contact gives you some degree of instant feedback, and not just a responsive word but breathing (unless you're on a cheap analog cell phone, in which case you hear only a storm in the Baltic Sea in the background).

- ✔ **Humor.** Humor on e-mail is pretty flat unless you're a very good writer. The phone can release your inner comedian (but you had better have an inner comedian if you're going to try humor). If humor is something you want in a mate, you may as well see if your prospect is on the same humor frequency. (Several frequencies are out there, you know, and they don't cross over very well.) Go slow with humor because everybody on the phone line, especially early on, is a bit nervous.

- ✔ **Quick thinking.** E-mails give you a chance to think, compose, and polish. With Instant Messaging, you have even less time, but still some. Phone is instant. Dead air on the phone is as bad as dead air on the radio. A person who can't hold a conversation, well — is anyone home?

- ✔ **Social comfort.** In some ways, phone contact can be a bit more intimidating than in-person contact. Your most witty repartee, unaccompanied by a mischievous smile, may go lost or, worse, misinterpreted. For example, if you say, "I believe in saving the whales . . . for dessert," it may strike your listener with horror rather than the chuckle you intended. But on the flip side, if someone does well on the phone, the person has a better chance of doing well in person.

## What you can't discover on the phone

Phone contact is great but has its limitations, including the following:

- ✔ **The body doesn't fit the voice.** Have you ever listened to your favorite radio announcer/DJ for years and then one day seen him or her on TV? What a shock. How could such a great radio voice be trapped inside such an ordinary man or woman? You often assume just because he or she has such a fabulous voice that it's a package deal. The same thing can easily happen on the Internet. An engaging writer is like a great DJ with that trademark FM voice. The phone never gives you that.

- ✔ **The body language doesn't fit the voice.** You also can't get body language and social graces on the phone. A few people have told us that their prospects sailed through the e-mail exchanges and phone contact with an A+ but got an F on social graces after the in-person meeting. You won't find many of these types, but a few do exist, and they will get through your earlier screens.

- ✔ **The body isn't his or hers.** Body fraud (a.k.a. photo fraud) can pass completely undetected through the voice screen. Yes, you catch it when you meet, but by then, you're engaged and likewise crushed if the prospect isn't as advertised. We recommend asking for additional photos early, certainly before you meet but perhaps before you phone. Frauds pull the plug immediately if they don't have more photos ready.

- ✔ **The eyes have it.** Eyes say so much, which perhaps is the weakest link in phone contact. No amount of indirect communication can ever give you the physical nuances of in-person contact. And these personal touches are part of what generates the chemistry between two people. We can't explain it, but you'll know (and feel) the chemistry when you see it.

## What you gotta remember, above all else

Most online daters go to the phone to hear a prospect's voice. However, more often than not, the voice is a disappointment. E-mail lets you take a photo and conjure up what the person will sound like. Problem is, your prospects never have the decency to own the voice your fantasy created. So the first rule of phone contact is

Completely ignore the voice's tonal quality and regional accent because it probably doesn't matter at all.

The first voice contact is almost always shocking. Don't let this jolt throw you off the phone call's prime directive: finding out who this person is. We promise that if you like your prospect, after a few minutes of spirited conversation you'll barely even remember that you were shocked by his or her voice. Okay, if the person has an exotic accent or foreign dialect, give it a few extra minutes. The point is, don't get rattled. Unless the voice sounds like Donald Duck or, worse, Richard Nixon, it just doesn't matter.

# Your Personal Guide for Making the Call

Are you hesitant about what to do when you make phone contact? Well, we're here to help. In this section, we give you your very own alphabetized prep list and guide for making that first call to your prospect. Read the entire list first before jumping to phone contact.

- ✔ **Agree on a time to call, usually decided in your last e-mail exchange.** If you're using Instant Messaging (chat), you (or the prospect) can call immediately. If you're on e-mail, you can give the person a cell phone number and ask him or her to call (or vice versa). Check your e-mail regularly to see whether your prospect plans to do so.

- ✔ **Decide who's going to call whom during your e-mail exchanges.** Typically, the woman calls the man for safety reasons (see Chapter 18 for details about safety).

- ✔ **End the call on a positive note.** How you end the call may determine whether you have a second call, even if everything has gone splendidly. A positive note needs to be fairly direct. Even if you're not sure you want a second call, remain positive, or at least cordial. Your mama raised you to be polite, and the modicum of human contact on the phone requires a well-mannered exchange.

If you're absolutely positively sure you don't have a match, say so in the call. Doing so really isn't that hard, and people appreciate directness at this point (little risk, little loss). Try this:

"Look, I have to stop talking at this point because I've run out of time as I mentioned earlier. You seem like a really nice [guy/woman/alien], but I don't feel like I'm your match. I'm sure that you'll do fine in your search." Wait for an answer. If the person doesn't agree, insist that it takes two people to go forward, and you don't have a match. (See Chapter 16 for other ideas.)

If you're terminating a conversation and ending any further contact, don't agree to receive any follow-up messages from your prospect, even to be polite. Opening yourself to more messages from this person may seem like the nice thing to do, but don't do it. Tell your prospect that he or she is truly wasting time that could be better used for new prospects.

✔ **Identify yourself properly when you make the call.** Announce yourself as follows:

I'm (insert first name here). You know me as Man1234 on Quarkdate.com.

Don't identify yourself by first name only — by just John or Mary, for example — because your prospect may well have contact with others named John or Mary and you want your prospect to know it's you. Identify the online-dating site as well. (By the way, if you think you should be the only person your prospect is expecting a phone call from — for example, exclusivity — and you're on your first phone call, you need to check the dictionary under the word *delusional.*)

✔ **Keep the first call relatively short.** Keeping the call short is very difficult to do if the call goes well, but it's still a good idea because it makes for more desire to have a second call, which could be later that day. Maintaining a short call isn't coy; it just gives you time to digest this next big step.

Because you never know whether the first phone call is going to go well, you may want to start the call like this:

Hey, I'm glad we finally connected, but I need to warn you that my daughter (make sure you have a daughter) is expecting a call, so I hope you'll forgive me if I have to go abruptly.

This way, you've offered an excuse to retreat, just in case.

We don't believe in any of the various advice out there for being coy. Yes, plenty of current books tell women especially how to withdraw from men to snare them. Good advice for making publishing royalties but terrible advice for finding a mate. Coyness just doesn't work in Internet dating. It makes you seem weird. With total anonymity, coyness clearly shows up as a game — a game you'll lose to the next prospect online.

✔ **Look for signs to ferret out frauds during your e-mail exchanges.** Don't expect to see a warning label declaring "I'm a fraud!" on your prospect's profile, but you can look for other mixed messages. For example, if you can't call your prospect any evening *ever*, that's a bad sign, which may mean that the husband/wife/warden is present. (Note that figuring out who isn't what they say they are is actually a multistep process. This is just one step.)

✔ **Make notes of questions you want answers to.** Starting with lighter subjects is always best. Then progress to more weighty matters as the conversation evolves.

✔ **Protect your anonymity.** Even if you give your phone number, don't give your last name. And give only a cell phone number to protect yourself from being looked up in a reverse phone directory. If possible, use caller ID blocking (not always an option on cell phones, by the way). Again, Chapter 18 has the details on all this safety stuff.

✔ **Review some of your previous e-mails so that you can build on those points in your conversation.** Doing so shows that you're attentive and interested.

✔ **Send an all-important follow-up thank-you note.** Man or woman, you need to do this. If you liked the phone call, send an e-mail to your prospect shortly after, saying this:

Hi (insert name here). I really enjoyed our phone conversation. Sorry I had to cut it short, but I would've liked to keep going. Let's do it again soon.

If you want to keep your e-mail link alive after that first phone call (and you should), stay proactive to make it happen. Otherwise, you'll almost certainly lose the option. Sometimes people feel strange using e-mail after they've moved to the phone, but they shouldn't and won't if you make it okay. E-mail gives you the chance to ask difficult questions and communicate at odd hours. (We still write to each other for several reasons, one of which being work schedules.) When you write the follow-up thank-you e-mail, add

By the way, the phone contact was great, but I don't want to stop our e-mail exchanges just because the phone is available. E-mails are fun, too, and sometimes connecting by phone may be impossible with our busy schedules. Is that okay with you?

✔ **Take notes during the call.** The moment you hang up, you'll forget much of what was said (because you'll have been in a big fluffy cumulonimbus cloud and not listening well). So if you're smart, take notes. Otherwise, you'll feel pretty foolish during Call No.2 when you can't remember the names and ages of your prospect's kids.

# Making the First (In-Person) Meeting Memorable

Okay, you survived — no, you *thrived* — on the phone, and you can't wait to meet. Unlike going from e-mail to phone, where waiting makes sense, going from phone to in-person need not be delayed other than to ensure your safety.

If you're heading into a long-distance relationship (LDR), the preceding paragraph doesn't apply to you. Please read Chapter 20, where we go through the special steps required for an LDR. You need to do much more research before you get on a plane.

When you finally meet, you'll fill in those critical missing pieces — body language, dress, posture, and so on. Even the voice will be different because no phone can capture the quality of stereophonic ears.

Take heart, though, that if you've done your homework, the first date won't be a first date at all:

✔ You have a very detailed profile of your prospect, which you've looked at many times.

✔ If your prospect was a heavy user of "I'll tell you later" in his or her profile, you've gotten answers in your e-mail exchanges. They've revealed an amazing amount of personal information about your date.

✔ You've filled in the voice and humor part by phone, and you feel a chemical reaction getting close to critical.

✔ You took notes on the phone, so you know all kinds of tidbits that you can use in person (kids' names, your prospect's birthdate, and such).

## Setting up the meeting

If you read Chapter 18 on safety, you may think that the meeting is an exchange of spies across the North Korean border, but that's only the planning part. You need some time to get everything figured out (if you're meeting for the first time), so don't plan your meeting while on your first phone conversation.

Many people like to have at least two phone calls before meeting, especially when the first one is short. The constraints are mostly time and distance. Sometimes meetings are difficult to set up.

The choice of time can be important. Consider these options when to meet:

✔ **After rush hour (after work).** If you choose to meet at rush hour, you may be late, which can be annoying and thus start the date on a bad note.

✔ **Way after rush hour (evening, after dinner).** This time is good because you don't have tons of traffic, and you don't have to decide whether it's a dinner or coffee/wine/beer/water date. The only problem may be childcare for your kids (and that's one more reason why going too quickly to meeting people is an impractical idea).

✔ **Lunch.** This option is fine, but it guarantees 1 to 1½ hours together, for better or for worse.

✔ **Coffee break (morning or afternoon).** This option is great because the time is relatively short. You really need 30 minutes at a minimum if it goes well and 15 if not.

✔ **Weekend (anytime).** This option is really good, especially in the afternoon because a great coffee date can turn into a second rendezvous in the evening if all goes (better than) well.

The choice of location is even more critical. Consider safety issues, such as choosing a well-lighted public place. (If you haven't already read Chapter 18 on safety, skip over there for the scoop.)

In addition, you have convenience considerations, which boil down to who can get to whom. Hopefully, you're both flexible, but you may be meeting in a part of the city that neither of you knows. Having the woman select the location so she knows the terrain (for safety reasons) is reasonable. And, finally, both of you have level-of-expectation issues. Your level of expectation (what you want to happen as a result of this meeting) should be the primary dictator of the kind of place you meet at. Here are the options:

✔ A public place, like a well attended park

✔ A coffee shop (If you choose Starbucks, be sure to have Scotty beam you down to the exact coordinates because all Starbucks establishments look alike — and sometimes they're only a few feet/meters apart. Been there, done that.)

✔ A lunch or dinner place

✔ An expensive lunch or dinner place

✔ A (noisy, smoky) bar

If you've had little contact with the prospect before the meeting, your level of expectation should be pretty low. So meeting at places to have a meal, especially an expensive or prolonged meal, is inherently a bad idea. Meeting at those kinds of places raises expectations too much and tends to be self-defeating.

Our vote for the best place to meet? Coffee shop. Almost always. Starbucks probably didn't realize how perfect its place would be for first-date meetings (coffee dates).

Coffee shops are

- ✔ Convenient (everywhere)
- ✔ Inexpensive (although on a per-gram basis, cappuccino is almost as expensive as platinum)
- ✔ Well lit with plenty of people (safety issue)
- ✔ Not intended for two-hour dates (which makes it logical to bail when your coffee is finished)

## Preventing a meltdown while en route

Things do go wrong. Traffic jams, snow, lost addresses. We can think of a million reasons why you may not meet up at the appointed time. Many people who have a computer also have a cell phone. If you're going to Internet date for a while, get a cell phone. You need to exchange cell numbers so you can contact each other if you're late or have to cancel. Miss a first date in the Internet world, and you're exiled to Cyberia in a flash.

## Planning what to wear ("Will my tiara be too much for Starbucks?")

If you have to decide whether you should wear the crown jewels (or run out and get some) or your 60's love beads, you're making everything way too difficult.

While most first meetings are in casual locations, some people like to dress up, just to seem more professional. It all depends on what makes you look good, without making you look foolish and out of place. Just don't show up after a tennis game, sweating like a race-horse. Even Seabiscuit tidied up for public appearances.

## Planning how to ID each other

As ridiculous as this comment sounds, you may not recognize your date on arrival, especially at a coffee shop. Even if you've taken our advice and exchanged more photos in advance, you probably have a 50/50 chance that you'll ask various people if they're your date. In fact, you'll be tapping several other people on the shoulders who are also on Internet coffee dates. (Several people even reported that they were very frustrated about not being able to date that *other* one who was waiting for his or her date.)

Because smoke signals are impossible to decipher in a smoky bar, I have used radio signals — a cell phone — in a bar. (Yeah, I know: Why was I meeting there?) Those cheesy signs chauffeurs use at airports are, well, cheesy. So what do you do? The best plan is to tell your prospect what you'll wear.

Women, if you have no idea what you're going to wear, just tell him you'll be wearing black (because after trying on ten different outfits, that's what always looks best, right?).

## Getting ready for picture shock

If you think voice shock is bad, wait until you experience photo shock. Almost no one looks like his or her pictures. If you've gotten a look at several photos in advance, and they were taken under different lighting conditions (indoor and out), you probably have a decent idea of what your date looks like. But even if your site offers a short video to watch, you'll still be surprised.

Realize that if you've made it this far through e-mail and phone, and you liked what you read and heard, and the photos weren't fraudulent, don't sweat the differences between the three-dimensional person and the two-dimensional photos.

## Preparing a course of action in case of extreme disappointment

If the person standing before you is *very* different from his or her photos (especially if you had several of them), then you have a decision to make. Fortunately, unlike a first meeting in a long-distance relationship (see Chapter 20), you have little invested, especially if you're on a coffee date. So what will it be — fight or flight?

## Should you go for up$cale offers from generou$ prospects?

What do you do if someone offers an upscale restaurant as your first meeting place? Actually, the more important question is should you have dinner or even lunch as a first meeting, regardless of how upscale it is?

We think having dinner or lunch as a first meeting is a bad idea generally, but there may be exceptions. The primary problem is the potential waste of your time. Unless you have spent plenty of time online and on the phone and have exchanged many additional photos, you never know what you're stepping into. If you start a lunch or dinner, you've gotta finish it even if you know it's a dead end.

Furthermore, the more expensive the commitment, the greater the pressure on the non-paying party (often the woman). And if you don't want to be in that bind, do you want to split the cost of a meal you may not want to be at in the first place?

We can think of nothing worse than looking at your prospect and realizing you're in for a long and tedious meal — imprisoned in the equivalent of a 90-minute infomercial — especially when you've worked all day. If you've put yourself in that situation, then resistance is futile. Just hope that your date is a fast eater or ask for your dinner to go. (We don't recommend feigning an epileptic seizure. People frequently overdo this method, which can elicit a brief but extraordinarily pricey escorted conveyance to the local ER.)

The point is, who needs the headache? Go for coffee in the late afternoon on a weekend. If it goes great, you can discretely propose reconvening at a different establishment.

### Fight: Stay awhile and see where it goes

So he or she is five years older, 25 pounds (11kg) heavier, and 4 inches (10cm) shorter than expected, and your date smells really bad to boot. Are you gonna bail? You certainly have the right to, especially if you've gone to some lengths to avoid this very fraud.

If any of those frauds are deal breakers for you, then by all means, tell your prospect that the time to reveal those inaccuracies is long gone. If you have the guts, tell him or her not to make any further attempts to contact you and that if the person does, you'll turn him or her in to the Web site for abuse.

On the other hand, if the person still looks attractive and none of the frauds would've stopped you from meeting him or her, then you only have to deal with the fact that the relationship was built on a serious and deliberate deception. Generally speaking, we think you should consider switching to the flight decision, but each case has its extenuating circumstances.

### Flight: Stop the show and get out

You're totally within your rights to stop mid-sentence and walk out. Don't be embarrassed about it, either. More than likely, your prospect has cooked up a good story to explain the deception. And the reality is that he or she has probably used that story before.

Unless you can see a basis for clemency, don't bother. If you followed this book's suggestion to ask early on whether the person had any inconsistencies in his or her profile, and the person insisted that no inconsistencies existed, then he or she deserves to get dumped. Furthermore, you're helping others by giving him or her a good shellacking right there. Perhaps he or she might finally get a clue!

Besides the choices of fight and flight, you have a third option: interrogation and then flight. If you can't bear to be abrupt, you may as well get your money's worth out of a bad situation. Ask him or her the W questions: who, what, when, where, and why. If you get insight into why people lie and deceive, then you may improve your fraud-identifier and see the warning signs the next time around.

# Making not-so-small talk

By the time you show up for the first meeting, you're not on a blind date, or at least you shouldn't be. Granted, if you rushed toward meeting, you may be more blind about your prospect than if you'd spent more time online or on the phone. However, you're still ahead of a true blind date. After all, you'll at least have carefully read the prospect's profile (right?) and have notes from your phone calls (right?).

Before the meeting, look those items over once more. (Don't bring them with you.) If have high enough hopes for this meeting, you'll remember the important stuff and have plenty to discuss beyond small talk.

If you aren't too affected by photo shock and your prospect is "pretty" close to what you expected, you have a reasonable chance of having a nice time. Perhaps a *very* nice time, which you don't want to end quickly. (The test: If your coffee is very cold but you don't want to break the conversation to get a fresh cup, you're having a good time!)

## Ending the date on a high note

Plan to end the meeting before you run out of emotional gas. Follow the same plan you used with the first phone call: Start the meeting with an apology that you can't stay long because (insert excuse here). Even if you're having a smashing time, you'll be on sensory overload at some point, so end the first date at that time and plan for the second.

And just as with ending the first phone call, end the first meeting on a positive note. If the date was good, being too positive is better than being noncommittal. Your prospect will at least get the right message, at the risk of being a bit too strong.

Note, though, that if the date was a flop and you both know it, you may as well admit it if your prospect doesn't and spare yourself the trouble of doing it later.

If you're not sure, then end positively and think it over after your head clears.

# Post Datem

You survived the first meeting. You're either ecstatic, relieved, or unsure.

## Following up the date with an e-mail

If the date went well, send a thank-you e-mail as soon as you get back to your computer. If you send yours before your prospect sends his or hers, you look a whole lot sweeter — and sweetness counts even for Arnold Schwarzenegger bad-boy types.

If you're not sure what you think about your date, then wait awhile before e-mailing.

If you're certain that the date has zero chance of a future, don't waste any time. Write that e-mail now. We always recommend being courteous but firm. Don't prolong the explanation or make excuses. And please, no further communications, no matter how tempting.

## Giving yourself time to unwind

One thing is certain: You'll be somewhat addled, especially if the date went well. Give yourself a few hours to unwind and collect your thoughts. And while you're collecting your thoughts (and you're going to hate hearing this), write them down on the same papers that house your other notes. Trust us, doing so will really help you later, and if you've actually found the love of your life, you'll be fascinated years later when you read what you wrote down.

## Getting ready for cyber jealousy

Jealousy isn't new, but add a cyber twist and it can burn. So what's the cyber twist? Anyone can tell when you're online. It varies by the site, but they all report, in some form, when their subscribers log on. Many sites actually time and date stamp when you were last online, even if you set your mode to invisible.

Now as you know from regular dating, people can be very possessive and very unreasonable. Add the extra ingredient that your cyber movements may be traceable, and you've got a nasty formula for people who are overly possessive.

## Knowing when to put out the SOLD sign

So when should you stop looking at prospects online after meeting someone you like?

- ✔ When *you* feel like stopping, whether your prospect does so or not. You may not feel good about further prospecting, but if he or she doesn't share that view, don't press your position. Allow everything to take its course. Set ground rules when you're both ready.

- ✔ When you both agree to stop. This requires some solid communication skills, usually a sign of a fairly advanced relationship.

- ✔ When you obviously both need to stop looking that doing otherwise would insult the other. For many people, that's when you start being intimate (yes, we mean having sex). Keep in mind, however, that people have very different standards for the significance of intimacy. Resolve this issue with effective communication.

Even if you both agree to stop looking, should you resign your membership immediately? If you do and your budding relationship falls through, you can't reinstate it. If you don't, you send a poor message to your potential mate about your expectations. Our advice? When you stop looking because you think your prospect is worth getting to know that well, then send the strongest sign you can and quit your membership. (Be sure to tell him or her!)

## Getting back on the horse if things don't work out

You know the story. If you get thrown from a horse, try to get back on as soon as possible so that you don't spook yourself. The same goes if your prospect/date didn't work out. Fortunately, the Internet horse is way easier to get back on than the hoofed kind. After coming back from a bad dating experience, nothing is better than spotting a new prospect and exchanging a few e-mails.

Remember, to the next person, you're fresh goods with no sign of damage from your last encounter. Actually, you're much better for the experience, although you don't know it and certainly don't feel it. We're all a sum of our prior experiences. Most of the time, more experience is a good thing.

# Part V
# Skirting the Hazards
# of Online Dating

The 5th Wave          By Rich Tennant

"My suggestion? I think we should list you as a 'man of many facets', rather than a 'man of many body parts'."

## In this part . . .

*I*nternet dating is like all other forms of dating; there are no rewards to those who take no risks. In this part, we want to assure you that the risks are small and indeed, more manageable than in other forms of dating because of your ability to remain anonymous. Beyond safety, have fun and hopefully find what you want. To do so depends, in part, on avoiding common pitfalls of beginners.

In this part, we give you a heads-up for trouble signs and techniques for sniffing out trouble spots so you never even get close to any. We also help you navigate the tricky waters of dating where there are too many prospects or too few, and we offer advice on how to cultivate a long-distance relationship.

# Chapter 18

# Safety First

A few years ago, online-dating stories were great fodder for those sensational TV news/magazine shows. Those TV tabloids desperately wanted to find something new and horrible to report.

Nowadays, the stories are far less frequent because online dating has become more mainstream. The stories just aren't as sensational anymore. But has online dating gotten safer? Or more dangerous? We doubt that online dating has changed much at all.

In some ways, the Internet is the most uncontrolled meeting place. Anyone with computer access and a few minutes time can assume any identity. Fortunately, some barriers to entry exist, eliminating a good part of the "riff raff" and leaving you with a much smaller job of segregating out the rest. In this chapter, we give you some of the tools you need to do just that job. No, you can't always avoid the bad seeds, but you can weed them out. And you'll be better prepared when you find one.

 This chapter focuses on safety for men and women. Yes, even though women in North America may have more to fear than men, men run into similar frauds. Just because you're male, don't ignore this advice. Our guidance may take many detours out of your online experience.

# "Is Online Dating Really Dangerous?"

Online dating can be dangerous, but if you're a smart dater, online dating isn't any more dangerous than dating someone in person that you don't know well.

The danger in dating comes from not knowing the person. Unless a true, mutual friend introduces you, you know very little about the people you meet. And if you first meet people in a public place, like a bar, library, restaurant, subway station, supermarket, or bookstore (where a lot of people meet), then you know even less.

Most people find some security in the fact that they first meet others in a place of apparent affinity, like a bookstore. ("Surely he's educated!") But because those kinds of establishments are public places, anyone can assume the apparent affinity. So meeting people in uncontrolled circumstances has its hazards.

All dating has its hazards. Most risks are emotional, not physical. Don't get discouraged because some people are capable of ruining your day. Just minimize the damages and move on. Otherwise, your own fear will trap you, and you're letting the bad guys win.

# Jealously Guarding Your Anonymity

The No.1 advantage you have over the bad guys (which we mean to include both men and women) online is that you're completely anonymous until you decide to give up that advantage. Too many people cast that shield away much too quickly and easily. Yet it's like virginity: After you lose it, you never get it back (at least with that person). Furthermore, anonymity is very helpful online.

You need to realize that you can

- ✔ **E-mail anonymously.** All professional dating sites maintain some sort of double-blind protection of your identity over e-mail.

- ✔ **Phone anonymously.** Through cell phones, caller ID blocking, and even public phones, you can keep your name and number secret.

✔ **Meet anonymously.** With a little planning, you really have no reason why someone needs to know more than your first name at the first meeting.

# Using a Big, Sturdy Safety Net

In the world of online dating, the smartest thing you can do is to create a big safety net to prevent all sorts of bad situations from happening. And this advice doesn't apply just to women. Men have safety issues, too, although they tend to be less physical. Still, if you're a man, consider whether you'd want to have a safety net in place if something bad *were* to happen (and consider that the bad something could actually involve someone who's stronger than you).

## Tell others what's going on

Never go to a meeting without telling someone you trust all the Ws — who, what, when, where, and why. Include enough detail so that the person you trust can locate the prospect online, too. This precaution may appear unimportant, but it can make a world of difference.

We say this point a couple times in this chapter, but it bears repeating. You must meet in a public, well-lit place like a coffee shop. Tell a good friend where you are, when you're meeting, and approximately when you're coming home. If you have a cell phone, bring it along.

This task of telling a friend is much easier for women than men, who often don't want to admit their fears to anyone. But men, take heed: Admitting your fears and staying safe is far better than the alternative outcomes that are possible.

If you're uncomfortable telling a friend in person where you're going and with whom, just send the details in an e-mail. Include where you're going, with whom, the prospect's profile name, and which dating site you're using. Tell your friend why you're e-mailing those details but not to worry.

## Use the phone wisely

The phone can hurt you or help you in online dating. For example, if you don't take precautions, you can lose your anonymity, putting your safety at risk. On the other hand, if you take a cell phone to your meeting place, you can get help if you feel threatened.

## Words to live by

When dating online, follow these two safety tips.

- ✔ **Never let your guard down.** After reading the safety recommendations we give in this chapter, select some or all of them as your code of conduct. Make sure you don't violate them. You don't know who will be your problem prospect, if you ever have one. Treat everyone with the utmost respect, but be firm about your standards.

- ✔ **Trust but verify.** In dealing with the Soviets on arms reduction treaties, President Ronald Reagan never wavered from his Trust But Verify position. Because previous administrations weren't so dogmatic, the Soviets, at first, didn't take him seriously. Reagan held true to his words and it worked. You'll also get resistance to your safety rules, but you don't have to bend. Don't worry if this prospect doesn't work out. You can find many more fish in the Internet sea. Besides, if your rules aren't ridiculous, those prospects who don't want to follow them send a disturbing message regarding their underlying attitudes about you.

### *Keeping phone calls anonymous*

Giving someone your phone number can lead to a complete loss of anonymity unless you're very careful. Remember these important facts:

- ✔ Home phone numbers are often traceable back to you through a mere Internet search. You can find out whether personal info about you is available online by running a search (through Google, Yahoo, or other search engines) for the words *reverse phone directory.* Dozens of such directories exist for the United States and Canada. (They each use different databases.) If you type in your home number, you may be shocked to find that your full name and address are listed. If you pay a few dollars more, you may be further surprised as to what else is publicly available about you. The lesson to remember is that by divulging a single phone number, you can give away the entire store.

- ✔ Most telephone systems in North America provide for caller ID and various ways to block your *outgoing* home phone number (a feature fittingly called *caller ID blocking.* If you don't know the codes, you can find them through a search engine online.

Some phone systems reveal your phone number *even* if you have the caller ID blocking feature. In particular, anyone with a toll-free number (800, 877, and so on) always has access to your phone number no matter what you do to block it. No gadget can help you overcome this access, despite what advertisements may say. Your phone company controls this situation, and Lord knows, we have no control over phone companies.

Sometimes you can find (or purchase) Caller ID blocking for cell phones. At present, each cell-phone company decides whether you can block your caller ID.

For the truly paranoid (or those who lack a cell phone), you can makes anonymous calls somewhat cheaply. The solution? Prepaid phone cards. Even for local calls, they don't transmit your home phone number because you dial through a toll-free (800) number to connect to the recipient's system. The call's recipient usually gets an out-of-state number on his or her caller ID. Explaining the number may be a little tricky, but otherwise it works.

### Calling for help with a cell phone

Taking a cell phone to your meeting place is a good idea. In addition to being able to call your prospect if you're running late, you can discretely call for help if you feel threatened.

In addition, a cell phone can get you out of nonthreatening but uncomfortable situations. If you're uncomfortable with your prospect and need an excuse to terminate the date, go to the restroom with your phone and call your best friend to make a surprise visit to your meeting site. Use his or her arrival as the excuse to terminate the meeting.

## Is it safer to just call from the office?

At least from the office, yours is just one of hundreds of phone lines, right? Not always. Granted, office phones are better than home phones, but you don't have much control over how they work. You rarely have Caller ID blocking as an option, for example.

On the other hand, the number that's transmitted to Caller ID isn't necessarily your extension number. To find out what shows up on Caller ID, dial your cell phone from the office and see what the readout shows. A readout that shows your extension number isn't good because a person can then call your extension and get your voicemail, which invariably includes your full name. Even if the readout doesn't include that info, the person can press # or 0 to reach the operator, who can then tell the person who owns that extension.

See how tricky this phone thing can get?

Want to plan ahead an escape route in case your meeting ends up miserable? Arrange to receive a "Gotta go!" call at a specific time (if your emoting/acting skills are reasonable). When the call comes, say either "I can't talk right now. I'm on a very nice date" or "Oh no! I'll be there right away!" If the situation requires you to say the latter, then leap from the table with a hasty apology and make your escape. (If this tactic sounds terribly devious, you're right. But sometimes, desperate times call for desperate measures.)

## Be car smart

Two points of danger exist with cars (aside from accidents):

✔ You don't want to ride anywhere with a stranger, so don't ever let your prospect pick you up at home or your job. You should always drive your own car there and back.

Granted, saying no is tougher if your prospect is taking you to a nice restaurant instead of to a coffee house, but you still need to resist. Just say that you need to drop off some dry cleaning on the way or give some other excuse. If all else fails, just say, "I'd feel more comfortable driving myself." Your prospect should understand, and is he or she doesn't, you may want to rethink your meeting.

✔ Your license plate is a source of easy access to your personal data. In most states and provinces, people can get the owner of a car (name and address) by either looking up the plate number on the Web or paying a small fee down at the Department of Motor Vehicles (DMV).

Don't let your prospect see your car. Use these suggestions:

✔ Arrive early, before your prospect (assuming that both of you aren't reading this book).

✔ Park your car away from the front door of the meeting place, preferably in a lighted place but not visible from the front windows. If you live in one of the 20 U.S. states that have only rear license plates, you should park facing the building.

✔ Leave last so that your prospect doesn't know which car is yours. A good excuse is to go to the restroom (where you can't be followed, unless you're on a same-sex date) and then to your car. You may also say that you want to call home and check on your kids before you take off. (Be sure to have kids if you use this tip.)

## Be mindful of drugs, alcohol, and guns

As in any dating situation, you need to keep an eye on your drink at all times to eliminate the possibility of your prospect slipping something in. The rule is never to let a drink out of your sight when you're with someone you don't know. If you have to leave (to the restroom), down your drink quickly, bring it with you, or spill it.

And, of course, the drink itself — alcohol — can cloud your judgement, so we suggest that you keep the number of drinks to an absolute minimum. You want to remain alert and sober for the duration of the date, as well as the drive home. The last thing you want is to be incapacitated and require the date to drive you home.

Guns are a growing problem — not particularly to Internet dating but to public places in general. Many U.S. states (no Canadian provinces) allow patrons to bring concealed guns into restaurants and other businesses *unless* the establishment posts a notice on every door. If you're concerned about being in a gun-free zone (or if you want to carry yours to the meeting place), check your state law and plan your meeting at a location that suits your style of armament.

## Bring enough money

Even if you're only going for coffee, plan ahead because you may go for dinner, too, if everything goes well. If you're not ready to reveal your entire identity, how will you use your credit card?

Okay, if your prospect pays for dinner, the problem is solved, but it may raise other issues or a sense of obligation that you don't want to add in. Bring enough cash to cover most situations.

# Staying Safe without Becoming Paranoid

Your prospect won't notice any of the precautions in this chapter if you handle them matter-of-factly. Whether parking your car in a safe place, giving out only a cell phone number, or whatever, no one is going to notice. And even if they do, they'd respect you for being smart.

If, however, you appear to be ridiculously cautious (read *paranoid*), your prospect may detect it. Find a happy balance that seems to work most of the time. If almost everyone else would consider your actions strange, they probably are overboard.

*WARNING!*

# Are you an Internet addict?

Internet (or cyber) addiction isn't a true diagnostic term, but that doesn't make it any less of a problem. Internet dependence may be a better term, but either way, it means you're spending excessive time on the computer — to the point where it messes up your life. Do you recognize any of these symptoms:

✔ Lying or trying to conceal how much time you spend online

✔ Noticing a decrease in physical activities, even to the point of disregarding your health

✔ Staying online a lot longer than intending to, to the detriment of time needed for work, family, friends, or even sleep

✔ Craving or even feeling withdrawn when away from the computer

✔ Feeling angry or irritable when challenged about the amount of time you spend online — or just plain denying that you have a problem

✔ Not being able to stop

Internet-dating addiction is a special form of general Internet addiction. When people first start Internet dating, they typically can't believe what they see — an endless list of small photos showing hundreds of prospects, many of whom look immediately attractive. At that moment, the fear of not being able to find enough potential dates evaporates. For the first time, people feel that they have a real possibility of demanding exactly what they want in a date/mate, and they feel that they have the luxury of rejecting potential dates for the most trivial reasons because the supply and availability seem endless. The danger in this abundance is not knowing when to stop. In addition, e-mail interactions, which become mini e-relationships, can become completely intoxicating. Sometimes the pleasure of e-mail exchanges themselves becomes addicting and replaces the original objective of meeting one person.

Here are some suggestions for people who realize that they may have a problem and are ready to make some changes:

✔ Move the computer to a *less* private place in your home, or out of your home altogether if that's the only thing that will help you resist temptation.

✔ Install time-blocking software if possible. Decide in advance how much time you'll spend on your computer per day or per week, and when you reach that limit, the software will cut you off.

✔ Try to co-mingle the real and the virtual world. Don't stop dating through conventional methods, which provides a good source of balance.

✔ Get a cyber-buddy — someone you trust, from the real world whom you can enlist to monitor your online activity. Having a friend call you on the phone when temptation strikes may help so he or she can talk you out of turning on the computer for any use besides business or other legitimate need.

✔ Keep the computer off when not in use. Make Internet surfing as inconvenient as possible when the urge strikes you.

The site most notable for helping people is www.Netaddiction.com. It offers comprehensive information and materials to help individuals, couples, and families who've been affected by cyber-related problems, such as online sexual addiction, virtual adultery, and compulsive behaviors, such as gaming, gambling, stock trading, and e-auctions.

# Chapter 19

# Unmasking and Avoiding Frauds and Players

---

## In This Chapter

▶ Looking at the most common frauds in online dating

▶ Finding out what a *player* is so you know who to watch out for

▶ Exposing and getting rid of frauds and players

---

*1*n most Disney cartoons it's easy to tell the good guys from the bad guys. With online dating, everyone is invisible (until they decide to reveal themselves), and there's no telling who you're dealing with. But fret not. In this chapter, we identify the most common online bad guys (a generic term that includes gals, too, by the way) and tell you how to sniff them out.

## Keeping Your Guard Up

On the Internet, just as in any public place, you probably know very little about the people around you. Furthermore, after having some really great encounters with nice people online, forgetting that the next person could be a real creep is easy.

Even though your chance of running into one of those creeps is, say, 1 in 100 (a reasonable assumption), you could run into three in a row. So every time you meet someone, look for clues that something isn't right.

Check out these primary reasons why online dating is so attractive to a few antisocial characters:

> ✔ **Anonymity easily allows for perverse behavior.** One of the great advantages of Internet dating is that you can remain anonymous as long as you want. Strange people recognize that, until exposed, they're completely safe doing antisocial things.

✔ **Masquerading is too easy.** No verification system exists, so people can easily pose as something they're not.

✔ **People tend to let their guard down on the Internet.** Just as the oddballs are safe behind their computer screens, so are you in a way. However, after a few hours of exchanging pleasant e-mails and eyeing great-looking prospects, online dating seems more like watching TV than walking on the streets of a big city at night.

This chapter is about safety against frauds and players — and keeping your guard up against them — but the risk of being on guard is that you may lose your ability to trust anyone, and worst of all, it'll show in your e-mails. Being on guard can sabotage your ability to meet really great and honest people. So, in using the techniques for exposing and avoiding the bad types, remember that the vast majority of people online aren't frauds and players, and even those who are, aren't dangerous. Mostly, they're just wasting your time. With that in mind, remain aware of problems but otherwise keep it light.

# Knowing Who the Frauds Are

A good defense includes knowing your enemy. This section lists the most common problem types. (The section "Avoiding Frauds and Players" tells you how to avoid or unmask them.)

Just like in real life, the best overall advice is to be aware of your surroundings and look for clues. They're usually right in front of your face. We also know that one person's nightmare may not be so bad for someone else. So, if we've defamed your favorite species of problem, we apologize in advance.

## The married

Presently married people are by far the largest problem group in online dating. And just so we're clear, by *presently married,* we mean currently married, intending to remain so, and not always revealing that fact. This category includes men as well as women, although men clearly outnumber the women.

Married prospects come in many flavors:

✔ **People who are openly married.** In other words, they tell you flat out that they're married. You've gotta give 'em credit for being open. But even among the open ones, you find two types:

- **Those looking for a discrete relationship on the side.**
  These people want you to know upfront that if you're
  going to mess with them, you're there for only one purpose: clandestine sex. This type is pretty rare on mainstream dating sites, like Match.com and Yahoo.com but
  common on more risqué sites. If that is your thing, a
  quick search on Google.com will find them.

- **Those in open marriages.** These people aren't trying to
  hide their extramarital relationships from the spouse.
  The spouse is into the same extramarital thing. You
  won't find this type often on mainstream sites because
  of the availability of the alternate communities that
  sanction these activities.

✔ **People who lie about being married.** These people say they're
divorced, single, or, the most audacious, widowed, when nothing could be further from the truth. These people are dangerous — not physically but emotionally — and they're tough to
spot, too. (But later in this chapter, in the section "Avoiding
Frauds and Players," we give you the toolkit.)

✔ **People who exaggerate their *separated* status.** These delusional types only *think* they're separated. Yeah, they're separated sometimes, like when the spouse is at work and can't
see them on the Internet. Many people don't date separated
prospects because these people are generally not ready for a
serious relationship. (The divorce process is at least distracting,
if not mentally debilitating.) These prospects are usually in total
denial of the situation and often make very convincing claims of
their positive mental health. If you buy these claims, you may
put yourself at risk, but this group is fairly easy to ferret out.

## *The men posing as women and women posing as men*

We figure this element is pretty small, but it can be annoying if you
meet people who are lying about their gender.

The most probable group of offenders? Teenagers (a double problem — see the following section) who are trying to prove that they
can entice a man or woman into feeling stupid. You may get tricked
by such a person and never find out because these pranksters
rarely want to meet or talk on the phone.

## *The older posing as younger*

We don't mean the usual 5-year grace-period adjustment. We mean a 20-year age-ectomy coupled with an ancient photo. We hear a fair number of stories about this situation.

These people (both men and women) aren't hard to detect, but you have to look for small clues. The posted photo may have subtle clues, such as outdated hairstyle or clothing.

We recommend that you keep up an active exchange of photos with a prospect who seems to have high potential. Ask for a photo of a recent event that you discussed online. ("Hey, why don't you send me a photo of you on your recent trip to the Blackout Gulch coal mines!")

## *The criminal element*

Generally, real criminals are only interested in your money (for example, your credit card). So, in general, the longer you keep from meeting a prospect, the less interesting you'll be as criminal prey.

If your e-mail or phone discussions move quickly to personal financial issues, be cautious. Even if you have been asked to prove your identity (perhaps a valid request at some point), don't ever provide social security or financial account numbers.

## *The porn site purveyors*

These people are really common on the more risqué sites. If a woman (rarely a man) suggests that you see her private photo collection at her Web address, well, that's what you'll be seeing — for $4.95.

If you're a newbie male online dater, don't get swept away by your first e-mail from an incredibly attractive woman. Often, the porn purveyors troll for you guys and send you a heart stopping e-mail. Most guys just laugh it off, but the freshmen are apparently going for it (otherwise, the porno babes would quit).

You can find sites full of women (and men) who just want casual sex. Here's the rule: The more explicit the posted photo, the less likely you're ever going to meet her for a real date. Most of these postings are from "professionals" of various kinds. The ads with no photos are the place to start, but even then you must accept that a percentage aren't genuine.

# Identifying the Players

We identify players as people who are using online dating sites for entertainment purposes, at your expense. These people are not true prospective mates seeking a long term, loving relationship. Their profiles are listed on legitimate dating sites and they appear to seek contact, e-mails and interaction, as if they are sincerely interested, then fade into the mist when there is a possibility of a real encounter or commitment.

Almost everyone online:

- ✔ Hates players
- ✔ Isn't one
- ✔ Has no real idea what a player is

Neither do we, but we do know the types of people that online daters tend to include when using the word *player:*

- ✔ People looking for a one-night stand
- ✔ People looking for intrigue/entertainment by exchanging e-mails/instant messages
- ✔ People seeking your money
- ✔ People using online dating as a form of therapy

Technically, we don't consider the first two types to be players. People looking for casual sex tend to go to the sites where they have a better chance. If they started on a mainstream site, they'd have a long search, especially because the essay police prohibit a lot of colorful language, which flows so freely on the risqué sites.

One type of player is not truly dangerous but rather insulting: prison inmates. Yup, some institutes of higher lockup have Internet access. We hope that someone's monitoring them, but who knows. This situation is very rare, but ask enough questions about location to get rid of these guys/girls. As far as we know, cell phones aren't allowed in prison, so a phone call generally ends that exchange. Just asking for a phone number is enough.

# Avoiding Frauds and Players

We know of no surefire answers for avoiding all the frauds and players out there. Fortunately, the really dangerous ones (psychos and stalkers) are extremely rare. Your true risk of running into one is probably greater than being hit by a tornado but less than being struck by lightning. (Does that help?) The other types are far less dangerous and easier to detect, although they're also far more common.

This section covers some techniques that, like broad-spectrum insect repellant, will either expose them (and like cockroaches, make them scurry for cover) or make you seem so unappealing that they'll seek a different victim.

## Unearthing the deceitful

The most effective technique for unearthing deceitful prospects is to scrutinize the info that's available and then slip in questions to probe sensitive issues.

### Scrutinizing the data

Carefully check the available information on your prospects. If you answer "yes" to any of the following questions, consider it a big red flag:

- Are they paid subscribers or just freeloaders? Paid subscribers normally pay by credit card. (The credit card leaves a paper trail for a wife or husband.) Granted, some can manage the deception because the spouse doesn't see the credit card statements.

- Have they been on the service for a long time? Longer subscribers are more likely to be serious.

- Do they claim to have a clandestine job and can't give you details?

- Do they have strict rules about availability (weekdays, not weekends, and so on)?

- Can they provide only one phone number (work or cell) after the relationship has progressed to an in-person stage?

- Are they living lavishly but short on cash? Do they ask to borrow from you or use your credit card?

- Do they always turn off their cell phone when with you so they don't get other calls?

- Did they give you expensive or inappropriate gifts early on in your meeting?

### Asking plenty of questions

In addition to scrutinizing the information, ask questions. Try to sprinkle them throughout your conversations. If they're softball (innocuous) questions, you can lob them and your prospect won't even notice them. Eventually, you have to use the hardball (direct) questions, but hold them until later because they may be unnecessary.

For example, if prospects indicate that they're separated, you need to ask follow-up questions. Here are the softball questions:

✔ When did you move into separate homes? How far apart?

✔ Who has custody? How do the kids manage two school districts? (Questions like these will be simple for someone truly separated but perplexing for someone who has never thought of it.)

Later, you can ask the hardball questions, like in what court are the divorce documents filed? (They may in fact not be filed, but the mere question may create a level of fear that you'll dig deeper). Here's an example of how to phrase the question: "My divorce was filed in the 5th district [it doesn't exist], and boy were they slow! Where is yours filed?"

Also ask for phone numbers and work information. You can't get this information immediately, but if you're keeping notes (and you should be), you can use this data later.

At the appropriate time in your interaction with a prospect, ask whether calling this evening is okay, and if you get a *"no"* several times in a row, ask why.

### Letting your fingers do the walking

The home phone number is the key to a mother lode of information. If you have good reason to believe that something is amiss, proceed cautiously and probe more to get the truth (and calm your nerves). Try one of these tactics:

✔ Use a reverse phone directory (see Chapter 17). Very often, you can get the person's full name and address.

✔ Call the home phone during the day. You'll often get an answering machine. If it answers with "Hi. The Johnsons aren't home," it may be Mr. and Mrs., but on the flip side, it could also be the children. This example brings up a related point: If your prospect says he or she has no children and you call at 3:30 p.m. and a child answers the phone, then you know something is wrong. Then you have to ask yourself whether is the issue is worth investigating.

A work phone number is also a powerful piece of information. If you call the number and get his or her voicemail, the voice should match the person you've already talked to by phone.

Also powerful is the prospect's occupation or even his or her company's name. If the company is small, for example, call the receptionist and ask for George or Clara. Even if you don't get any further, you can reassure yourself knowing that you don't have a complete fraud on your hands. You may want to leave a message with his or her secretary — give your first name and say that you want to talk about getting together tonight. If your prospect is married, you'll never hear another word. You've suddenly become a risk to him or her.

By becoming a risk to exposing the secret, you're now an undesirable prospect. But if you're not careful, you'll also become a nuisance for otherwise forthright people who don't want their personal lives invaded so quickly. (You don't want to come across as a stalker or freak — exactly what you're trying to avoid.) Therefore, stick with softball inquiries until you have reason to suspect a problem.

Use a laser-guided weapon against the married ones. Put a clear warning in your essay: "I'm really a sweet woman, but I have no patience for married men. If you don't want me to expose you to your wife, stay clear of me." Don't go overboard. A brief warning does the job without any collateral damage.

If you choose not to put a precision-guided warning in your essay, try being direct but matter-of-fact very early on in your e-mail exchanges:

> Oh, one more thing, just before we sign off for the night. I ask this of all the men I converse with, so I want you to know that I'm not suspicious, but here goes: If you're married (or insert other undesirable characteristic you're worried about), let's break it off right now. I don't want you to tell me. Just don't respond to my e-mail next time. I'm just not interested.

## Defrauding the lesser frauds

Other issues like height, weight, age, and so on are best addressed with an offer for up-front honesty. Try this:

> I like our e-mail banter, and I wouldn't like it to go into a tailspin when we meet. I ask this of everyone I hope to meet, so don't take it personally. If your profile contains anything that isn't exactly true, please tell me now so that we can get past it.

Once you meet and realize that you've been seriously duped (for instance, a sixty eight year old posing as fifty) walk out immediately. Then report the fraud and block them from future correspondence. Don't send them a nasty e-mail. They could be psycho, and inflaming them may be downright dangerous. Just cut them off.

## Checking out the seemingly good ones, too

If you find a prospect who may be a keeper, remember that you need to know about this person's past — things he or she may try to keep secret (like being divorced — but for the third time). Our advice isn't just applicable to online dating but *any* dating. Being emotionally involved means that your defenses may be at their weakest, so it takes determination to bring yourself to investigate.

In addition to investigating your prospect's past, don't forget to check these items out also:

- ✔ **The friends and family:** Meet them. And soon. Friends are easier to meet early. If he or she doesn't introduce you to any and they're local, why not??

- ✔ **The lifestyle:** Does his or her lifestyle correspond to his or her likely income? The car, the house, the job — they need to make some sense together.

## Digging deep with your own e-shovel

You can glean a lot about someone by just spending a few hours on the Internet. Granted, most people aren't famous enough to be listed on Google, but checking is so easy to do, you may as well give it a try.

If you're going to do serious snooping, be prepared to get caught red-handed. That's probably okay if you're prepared to voluntarily divulge similar information about yourself. Still, think about snooping before jumping in because it's a risky strategy.

Try these ways to look up information about your questionable prospect:

- ✔ **Check out your prospect in his or her home town and in his or her last place of residence, especially if the residence was out of state.** The person may have moved to get away from his or her past. You can use local newspapers' online archive systems as well as local government Web sites.

✔ **Look up public records about professional complaints if you're dating someone who's professionally licensed.** Doctors, lawyers, and accountants (among others) have public records about the complaints that people may have filed against them. Many are online. Feel free to look them up or call the licensing agency who handles that field. And don't forget that electricians, plumbers, notaries, and plenty of other professionals are licensed. You won't find out as much about them, but you could hit the jackpot (and that usually means bad news).

✔ **Run a name search on all phone directories that you can find on the Internet.** Make sure the data is consistent with the prospect's current address. If not, try to figure out why. Often, the prospect's ex lives at the original homestead, and your prospect's name is still on it. If you find the ex-homestead (and your prospect may have confirmed the general location anyway), you can look at the transfer deed at the county court house to confirm that your prospect is divorced because it'll appear on the chain of title.

Sometimes real estate records are easier to check than finding divorce records.

✔ **See whether your state or county keeps a record of divorces and criminal convictions online.** If you go to the trouble of getting a prospect's divorce records, you'll be astonished at how much private information is actually public. Some divorce records are embarrassingly detailed.

# Nightmare on Med Street

I'm a very trusting person, but just for the heck of it, I tried a simple background check on a guy I was e-mailing online. He was a doctor, so I knew he had to be licensed, and I knew he had recently moved from another state. On a whim, and with no real reason to suspect a problem, I logged on the licensing database of doctors for the last state he worked in. I expected him to have a pristine record and that would be that.

But that wasn't what I found. He'd been suspended three times in the prior state for prescribing narcotics to himself. Then when he moved to the other state, he was admitted on probation (because of his prior activities in the old state).

I found more. The new state had discovered more problematic activities, but it didn't post what they were online. A quick call to the licensing office, and I received free of charge, the entire transcript of various disciplinary proceedings he underwent in the new state! Needless to say, I broke off all further communications.

# Getting help with background checking

If you really want to know something about your prospect's past and you're not lucky enough to find it through your own Internet search, you may need to engage some help. Two kinds of help are available:

- Commercial Internet search services
- Professional searchers, which can be either background check companies or private investigators

After having your prospect checked out, should you tell your prospect what you did? Probably not, but be prepared in case you get caught. Your reasons are legitimate, and the fact that you went to the trouble may be impressive. If you didn't consider the prospect to be worthy of your attention and time, you never would've checked him or her out in the first place.

### Using commercial Internet search services

Internet search services are highly unpredictable in their level of quality. In general, don't expect much value for the money. Typically, these services don't have access to "on the ground" resources, so all they can do is a better version of what you've already tried in terms of fact checking and background searches you can do online yourself.

Having an Internet search service run a credit check on your prospect may be useful because a credit history is now considered a good predictor of a person's reliability for employment. Keep in mind, however, that such searches are generally illegal without the prospect's permission. If you're getting this info from the Internet, be sure that it comes from a reliable source and isn't fabricated. The only reliable sources are major credit check agencies, like Equifax, Experian, and TransUnion, and they won't give out this data without a release or a legitimate credit-related purpose (like applying for a credit card).

The cost of commercial Internet searches is typically $25 to $75. Only use a service that guarantees some minimum results before it debits your credit card.

## Using the pros

Two types of pros arc in the search business:

- **Background check companies:** Background check companies normally check the history of potential employees. School districts use these companies to ensure that their bus drivers don't have criminal records, for example. One such nationwide company is PRS in Minneapolis, but you can find others in your area. Check the Internet under background checks. Be sure to hook up with a company with a phone number and call to find how it conducts its searches.

  Another way to find a fairly reliable source is to call the human resources departments of several large companies and ask for referrals. If the company uses one service for its top executives and another for midlevel managers, use the top-level referral. Companies often skimp on this service for lower-level employees. If you're going to do this investigation, you're probably pretty serious about a long-term partner. Clearly, don't skimp.

  Good background checkers have correspondents on the ground throughout North America and can locate many facts no one else can uncover — most significantly, criminal convictions. To make their efforts pay off, you must provide them with a fair amount of data, such as social security number and address. They tell you what they want, and your job is to give them enough data to do a valuable search. The cost of this service is highly variable. Assuming that your prospect isn't a fugitive from justice in several jurisdictions, expect to pay $150 to $300 for a decent check.

- **Gumshoe investigators or private eyes:** The real foot soldiers of investigations are private investigators (PIs). Think of TV's Magnum, Rockford, and Perry Mason's PI, Paul Drake. A PI follows your prospect and finds out what his or her current lifestyle really is. You shouldn't need to use such a person if you've, say, met the parents, siblings, friends, and such. But if you're a very high-income person and want to be sure that you're not dealing with a con artist, a PI is the only way to go.

  The cost is high (thousands of dollars), depending on what you're looking for and how long it takes to find it.

# Chapter 20

# Special Circumstances: Big Cities, Small Towns, and Long-Distance Relationships

## In This Chapter

▶ Dealing with the competition and intimidation that come with living in a big city

▶ Getting around the ruts in the road when living in a small town

▶ Knowing about the hurdles of a long-distance relationship

*T*his chapter covers three distinct subjects with special online-dating circumstances:

✔ Living in a big city poses the problem of being lost in the crowd of a big Web site with thousands of competitors, which is no different from entering a bar packed with people and an impossibly high noise level. You have to do something special to get noticed.

✔ On the other end of the spectrum is living in a small town, which poses the problem of simply not having enough choices online to take full advantage of Internet dating. Furthermore, your posted profile may expose you to town gossip.

✔ And potentially linked to either living situation is the long-distance relationship, dating outside your local area, which is a hard road to travel and certainly not for everyone. (We've been in a long-distance relationship for two years now, so we understand.)

Fortunately, several workarounds are available for the problems that come with these special circumstances. In this chapter, we tell you what you need to know.

# Big City, Stiff Competition

Can you ever have too many great prospects? Not really, but remember that you're a prospect, too, and if you don't get on the radar, you don't exist. The problem of living in a big city — dealing with the competition — can be quite intimidating.

## Surviving the intimidation factor

If you take the time to look at your competition, you may begin to think, "Why would anyone contact or reply to me?" Here's what you need to remember:

- Everyone thinks that the competition is stiff.

- Fortunately, not everyone is looking for the same person, so in fact, you may have little competition.

- If you ask prospects what they think about the availability of great prospects, they almost always say slim pickins! So what may look like an infinite number of competitors may not matter to someone seeking a certain combination of traits in a best match.

- Internet dating is new, and very few people have mastered it. You're reading this book, however, and have the advantage! Even if you only do the few things we recommend about essay writing and e-mail exchanges, you'll be far ahead of the pack.

The preceding advice is all fine and dandy, but in the end, there's really only one reliable way to avoid the intimidation factor: After you study the lay of the land and get your essay written, *never* look at your competition again. Period.

If you still find it challenging to dive into online dating in a big city, remember that the bigger the city, the less distance most people are willing to travel for a date. For example, geographically, New York City is relatively small compared to sprawling cities like Dallas and Ft. Worth. Yet many New Yorkers think twice before engaging with a prospect any distance beyond a few miles, let alone outside their borough. So in effect, you're dealing with a relatively small community. Using that line of thinking, you can always try some of the workarounds for people living in small towns.

## Getting noticed in the crowd

There are several easy ways to give your profile the best chance of being viewed and perused. In various chapters of this book, we go into detail about them, but the following list is the quick scoop on how to stand out:

- ✔ Find out how your dating site ranks profiles in a search. Every system does it differently. (Take a gander at Chapter 6 for more information.) Note, though, that some sites consider this information a heavily guarded state secret and use complex formulas that even we can't decipher. In addition, sites change their formulas from time to time.

  In general, look at where you fall in the search list to know whether you're rising to the top and try to note what action on your part changes your rank. For example, see whether frequently logging on makes a difference or whether changing any aspect of your profile — however small — does.

- ✔ Post an interesting photo (see Chapter 12 for specific ideas). And if you have multiple photos posted, change the first one every few months to freshen up your posting. A viewer may find your alternative photo more appealing and would've passed you over if you hadn't changed your photos.

- ✔ Choose an interesting but not obnoxious screen name and create a memorable tag line (see Chapter 8).

- ✔ Figure out how to make the site think you're a new or updated posting. (We provide this information for several sites in Chapter 6.)

# Small Town, Mighty Slim Pickin's

The first thing we need to do is roughly define *small town* and *slim pickins* for online dating, because we're not just talking about *Petticoat Junction:*

- ✔ A small town for online dating may be as large as 250,000! But remember, a town of 50,000 on the East Coast isn't the same as a town of the same size in the Midwest. On the U.S. coasts and in parts of Canada, the population density is so high that towns and big cities tend to run together.

✔ We use the term, "slim pickins" in a subjective manner, but consider this: If you're 40 years old in a town of 50,000, figure that you may have 2,000 singles in your area who are age appropriate (say, within five years of your age, plus or minus). Of those, half are of the opposite sex. Of those, only 10 percent are online, and they're spread out over five national dating services. Now *that's* slim pickins. But hold on a minute: If you're 22 years old in the same town, and it has a college or university, the story is completely different.

Keep in mind that your town's size isn't a true indicator of the number of available online daters. You need to consider many more factors. Nevertheless, if you live more than 50 miles (80 km) from the Top 20 population centers of the United States (or Toronto, Montreal, or Vancouver in Canada), you may have to reach out farther to find a sufficient pool of online dates. The goods news, however, is that no matter how small the pool may be online, it's usually much smaller through traditional means (say, meeting someone at a local bar). But if you live in such a town, you already know that!

Another factor you need to consider about small towns is that they tend to be much closer-knit communities. One of the cornerstones of online dating — anonymity — is more difficult to maintain when so many people know each other. Consequently, many people in small towns don't post their photos. (And if you don't know how we feel about *that,* turn to Chapter 12.)

So, yes, if you live in a small town, you're up against some challenges. Try these suggestions:

✔ **If you won't post your photo, be proactive and send your photo with your messages.** Or you can post your photo on a third-party site, like Yahoo.com (at http://photos.yahoo. com/) Doing so keeps you somewhat more anonymous but not invisible.

✔ **Make your essay less revealing.** We don't mean that you should dumb it down, but you can remove some of the giveaway identifiers. For example, instead of writing "I'm a teacher at the local high school," try "I'm in education."

Or you can try this suggestion if you want to reveal little: Instead of putting your actual postal (zip) code into the system, select a postal code from a town that's relatively close — just a few miles away — so that it appears online as your hometown. Once you establish communications with someone, you can discuss your reasons for giving a less than accurate zip code and reveal the correct one.

✔ **Use multiple Internet dating sites simultaneously.** Although we're not big fans of this approach, you may have to use several sites to get access to a bigger audience. You may, however, find that in your locale, more people gravitate to one particular dating site.

✔ **Go online frequently to see whether new prospects show up.** People get discouraged pretty quickly if they don't get mail right away. Be ready to strike before you lose a good prospect.

✔ **Be patient.** People come and go online all the time. Particular slow times are around Christmas, and hot times are around Valentine's Day.

✔ **Broaden your horizons.** If you're willing to travel to the next biggest city, Internet dating gives you the best chance you've ever had to break into a new town without years of getting to know the lay of the land.

# Long-Distance Relationships (LDR): Growing Roots on a Slippery Slope

In the olden days (before the Internet became mainstream in the 1990s), the only way people got involved in long-distance relationships was purely by accident. Meeting someone at an out-of-town wedding — a favorite of movie scripts — is a very good example. Still, such situations are pretty rare.

The Internet not only makes long-distance relationships (LDRs for short) much more likely to occur, but also it encourages them by the ease with which people can become exposed to others in different parts of the country and, frankly, the entire world. By its nature, online dating draws you beyond your immediate borders. Most Internet dating sites are national, if not international, in scope.

Granted, some sites break up their communities according to metro areas so that cross-border searching is somewhat confined, but almost all other dating sites consider location to be just another choice, like eye color and height. For example, at Date.com, the search screen lets you choose by city, state, or province. Personals.yahoo.com is one of the few that actually discourages LDRs by limiting your search to a limited radius around your zip/postal code. Dating sites want you to peruse their entire database, so they tend to encourage you to look at people outside your home area.

But is dating people outside your home area a good thing? Well, we certainly think so, or we never would've found each other. But LDRs take root on a very slippery slope, and we can tell you from personal experience that getting those roots to grow and flourish is one of the most difficult of challenges. We can also tell you that when you've found the right person, you don't mind the distance (so much).

With such an endorsement, why would anyone engage in such a difficult journey? Remember that you don't have to settle just because no suitable matches are in your area.

## Making life easier

If you decide to take the LDR route, consider these options:

- Search for prospects in a city you'd like to move to.
- Search for prospects in a city with a big airport — preferably a hub city and a non-stop flight.
- Search for prospects in a city that supports the line of work.

---

### Einstein's theory of online-dating relativity

If Albert Einstein had focused his energy on online dating instead of nuclear physics, he surely would've concluded this:

> The distance between prospective dates is inversely proportional to the square of the traffic jams to get to the prospects.

For example, a long-distance relationship to a person in Greenwich Village may be someone 10 miles away in New Jersey (and many New Yorkers told us exactly that), whereas in Minneapolis, which has a metropolitan area almost 100 miles wide, traffic is sufficiently fluid that all prospects are in reach.

So *long distance* may be better explained in terms of how long it takes to travel to see someone in person rather than how far away the person lives. And even that line of thinking may not be quite accurate. We live two flying hours away from each other. Someone living in San Diego may live four driving hours from his or her prospect in Los Angeles, depending on the traffic.

So what's the point? We've found that people have very firm ideas of what they consider too far to travel, but if they get hooked on someone, even far away, their rigid ideas seem to melt.

---

One thing you can't count on in an LDR is that your family and friends will be supportive (if you're the one moving away). Like anything in life, it's a balancing act and your happiness is ultimately what you need to consider.

## Broadening your reach

If you live in a city that's not within the Top 20 metro areas and you're looking for a very specific match that severely limits your available pool, you have two options:

- ✔ Give up on your must-haves
- ✔ Broaden your reach

Many people seem to find themselves in this predicament due to some of the following common reasons:

- ✔ Religious preference
- ✔ Sexual orientation
- ✔ Ethnic preference
- ✔ Educational-level preference
- ✔ Other must-haves (like a 6'11" blonde, blue-eyed PhD specializing in Egyptian hieroglyphics who likes to jet ski and has a sensitive side — and owns a small country)
- ✔ Small town (not a must-have but a lack of local prospects)

You'll find that several special-interest communities cater to specific preferences, but they're inherently LDR territory. For example, Jdate.com for the Jewish community is structured for easy national and international searching.

## Bowing out if LDRs aren't for you

Know that even if you're resolute and never want to see what's on the other side of the mountain, tempters and temptresses will seek you out because online dating has attracted people from all around the world. If you're determined *not* to get involved in a long-distance relationship, take one of the following steps:

- ✔ Just say no. Politely advise the prospect that you're unwilling to endure the pain of an LDR and you refuse to even get started.
- ✔ Ask the prospect to call if/when he or she moves to your town.

> ✔ Ask the prospect upfront whether he or she is willing to relocate if things work out. (You'll still be heading into an LDR, but most of the heavy lifting will fall on your partner.)
>
> ✔ Consider the possibility of moving the mountain (you) for the prospect who might be the love of your life. We know its tough, but finding a perfect mate is even tougher.

Whether a person is willing to relocate is a mighty important question to ask before you pursue any ongoing communications with an out-of-towner. So why don't all dating sites offer that as a routine question? We don't know, but we wish they did. Fortunately, we know of two sites that do. Jdate.com and AmericanSingles.com, every user is asked the question, and the answer (Yes/No) is mandatory.

# A Hitchhiker's Guide to a Successful LDR

Okay, your mind is made up. You are fully prepared for an LDR. Here's what you need to know:

> ✔ Can you leave your job? If your job requires licensing (such as law and medicine), are you prepared to study for and take the licensing exam?
>
> ✔ Can you bring your kids or leave them behind (assuming they're in college or on their own)?
>
> ✔ Do you have aging parents or other relatives whom you'll be leaving behind? Who will help them?
>
> ✔ If your LDR falls apart, would you remain in the new town or move on again? Can you handle that possibility?
>
> ✔ Can you get enough face time with your LDR prospect *well* before you relocate, to really know whether you know each other?

## Planning the first meeting

Ok, you find yourself having a wonderful e-mail and phone exchange with a long distance prospect. You can't wait to meet. You need to do more than pack your bags and fly off.

### Who comes to whom?

It's not an obvious question, but it might make a big difference in how the future unfolds. If you already know who is relocatable, then the person who's likely to move (should all work out) should be the one to travel. Some people insist that a woman should never travel, but we can't see why that's so. Consider the options:

- ✔ **Going to his or her city.** You have to do the traveling, which costs money, but you get to see how he or she lives — a major plus for you. And you get to run if things don't go well.

- ✔ **He or she comes to you.** You control the turf, but if things don't go well, you can't leave your own city.

### Who pays for the travel?

Maybe this is a no-brainer, but not everyone is of equal means. You may want to split the costs with him or her. That option not only shows involvement but also takes away some of the economic pressure of being beholden to someone for footing the bill.

### Where should you both sleep?

For this discussion, we're going to assume that the prospect is coming to you. This same advice would apply, though, if it were the other way around:

Should you invite him or her to your house? Well, in the end, it's your call. But first consider what you'll do if things don't go as planned. Kick him or her out of the guestroom? Out of the house? We think the hotel is safer in many ways for both of you.

LDR meetings are never first dates in the traditional sense. So much communication occurs prior to the first visit that a higher degree of expectation and certainty exists (or you wouldn't bother to meet). As a result, LDR first meetings can be very intense and, consequently, very sexual. If this setup doesn't appeal to you, you need to make it clear (*very* clear) to your prospect that this is a first date like any other first date and you want to keep it that way. LDRs are not at all like ordinary relationships. They're more like a relationship on a Saturn V rocket.

### What about the kids?

Definitely don't forget about them. If you're visiting someone who has children, it's best that they don't see you for a while — and vice versa if the prospect is visiting you and your kids. Even if the kids are teenagers, a parade of dates — especially from out of town — sends the wrong message.

### Meeting on neutral territory (a third city)?

If you book a hotel room, should you each book one? The practical side of each of you might say, "Why waste the money?"

> ## "So if the prospect is willing to relocate, am I technically still in an LDR?"
>
> Yes! Unless you're dating in the 24th century and Scotty can beam your mate over every night after work, relocation is a really big life event — and a time-consuming one. Very few people have jobs that are completely portable, family and relatives are almost never portable, and friends are hard to leave. If your LDR partner is willing to move to you, you'll still endure a long transition. Figure at least a year to make most moves happen. Got time?

Our suggestion is to book separate rooms. You need a safe harbor to retreat to, unless you have very understanding friends or family in town willing to take on a last-minute houseguest if things don't work out.

### What about safety issues?

This is a big one. We've devoted a whole chapter to safety, but special warnings apply here. You need to check out your prospect much more carefully because the stakes are higher. A flim flammer, or worse, could wind up being your houseguest (or, alternatively, you could be sleeping over at a wacko's place). But don't get overly paranoid about it, either, because LDRs can be the best experience of your life. Here are some tips for safety:

✔ Explain to your prospect that you need to verify his or her identify because of the special circumstances. Ask for a home and work number. Call the phone numbers and verify that the person lives/works there.

✔ Go online and use a reverse phone directory to see if the phone number leads you back to the information the prospect gave you.

See Chapter 18 for the full scoop on staying safe.

## Deciding how long the first visit should be

Start with this rule: Make the first visit short enough that you will be sorry that it was so short if things go well. Assuming you aren't flying from another continent, you can always arrange a much longer visit quickly. If you stay a half weekend, there is always the option of paying the airline penalty and extending for a full weekend.

If you end your time together wishing you could stay longer, consider the meeting a great success . . . and get back on the plane without regrets.

 If you fly to meet your prospect, you might want to use your frequent flyer miles instead of a Saturday night stay ticket. Frequent flyer mile tickets can often be rebooked for longer stays without penalties. This way, if the meeting is a total flop, you won't feel so doggoned upset spending a lot of real money.

## What to do if you get bamboozled

Imagine this scenario: You meet, breathless with anticipation, and there, greeting you is a complete stranger. They don't look like their photo with respect to height, weight, age, or whatever. And this deception was obviously intentional. What to do? Try one of these options:

- ✔ Walk away in disgust and go to an all-night cinema so that you can hop the red-eye out of there.

- ✔ Have a cup of coffee and learn what you can to avoid having this happen again.

## Returning home and sorting it all out

The two ends of the spectrum are that the first meeting was a disaster or it was a great success. Regardless of the outcome, you've got to come to terms with it.

### What to do if the meeting was a disaster

If your date was a disaster, do the following immediately on your arrival home:

- ✔ Get back on the horse as soon as possible (meaning, go back online immediately). Doing so will boost your ego and let you know that there are still good prospects out there.

- ✔ Evaluate what went wrong. Find out what happened with your dating radar. Why didn't you see it coming? Two possible answers exist:

    You never could've seen it coming. Such is life sometimes.

You refused to see it coming. Such is the problem of fantasy dating. You need to re-calibrate your personal sensors to report to central command (your left brain) that something was wrong that your right brain didn't detect. (And now you know why having half a brain is so dangerous.)

✔ Next time, ask better questions online about those hot button issues that you let get by you this time.

## "Tell me the truth: Is it worth all the trouble?"

Flat out, an LDR that works is worth every bit of the effort it takes. In fact, when it's working well, you don't sweat the distance, the cost, or the hassle. You only sweat the time apart.

Unlike so-called easy local relationships, in an LDR, you recognize immediately how precious your time together is. That lesson doesn't go away when you finally live together, and it may be the most important lesson of a long-term relationship.

Bottom line? The Internet gives you the entire world to date. You may find the person of your dreams if you only open your horizons.

# Part VI
# The Part of Tens

SUDDENLY LINDA FOUND HERSELF MYSTERIOUSLY DRAWN TO THE STRANGER ON HER TRAIN THAT DAY.

## In this part . . .

We know we give you a lot of important stuff in the preceding chapters. You won't remember it all, so we want to give you a quick refresher on some of the key points to know about how to succeed at Internet dating.

# Chapter 21

# Ten Ways to Screw Up Online Dating

*Y*ou need to have the right attitude whenever you embark on a new venture. Remember that success isn't instantaneous, and that we all make mistakes. We, the authors, as well as countless people we've interviewed, have made a fair number of them with online dating and in life's daily activities. But we want to save you the time and trouble (with your online-dating activities).

Online dating is fast and fairly painless but some of it isn't at all intuitive. This chapter discusses some mistakes, especially common to newcomers, that you should be aware of so you don't shoot yourself in the mouse before you get the hang of it.

## Failing to Initiate E-mail

Failing to initiate e-mail is the mother of all Internet dating mistakes. Face it, guys. Women initiate only about one tenth the amount of e-mail that men write, so if you're hanging back and not writing, your competition is going to get the woman first. Women: if you want to have more control over whom you meet, you have to make the first contact. Otherwise, you waste your time (and subscription money) hoping that men will write to you. If you see what you want, be proactive and contact the guy yourself or you'll be stuck with interacting only with the ones who contact you. And why give up all that freedom of choice?

Finally, many dating sites are full of people who can't write to you (because they haven't paid the subscription fee), so waiting for them to write is a true exercise in futility.

# Lying in Your Profile

Falsifications in your profile are the No.1 complaint of online daters. A few sites have started to ask subscribers to take an oath of honesty (it remains to be seen if it helps), or publish what percentage of their profile is true.

So you think, why not fudge a bit on your weak points? A little younger, a little taller, a little lighter. How can it hurt? Because your "little fib" will always be discovered as a lie. You're just hoping that by then, your prospect will have seen what a great person you are and your lie won't matter. But it will. You'll have started your relationship on a foundation of dishonesty. If you must lie about age, weight, height, and so on, please explain the lie and the reasons for it right in your essay or in your initial contacts so that it stops right there.

# Posting an Old Photo or a Photo That Doesn't Resemble You

Though posting a photo of yourself that is no longer accurate isn't a lie per se, you're deceiving a potential prospect, and your prospect will be extremely disappointed. If you really like one particular photo, but your friends don't think it's an accurate depiction, at least post a second one that is accurate.

# Mentioning Overtly Sexual Topics in Your Initial E-mails

Unless you're on a sexually oriented site, your initial e-mails need to be rated T (tame) or PT (pretty tame). If you touch on sex topics too quickly, your prospect may think sex is your primary and maybe only objective. Remember that your prospects don't know anything about you and the slightest indications that your intentions are inappropriate will make them run for cover. Give it some time and start slow. When the e-relationship progresses to a suitable level that it is appropriate to approach sexual topics, you can both agree on what words are comfortable and what are offensive.

# Mentioning Past Failed Relations Often

We're sure your stories of relationships gone bad would make great daytime drama, so save them for that. As far as getting to know someone new, remember that your first e-mail exchanges tend to amplify what you say. Even a hint of negativism can be a tremendous put off. When your prospect asks about your sordid past, dish it out slowly.

# Insisting on Meeting in Person Right Away

If you think of Internet dating as an electronic telephone book of available singles and nothing more, you're missing the point. On the Internet, you can find out tons about your prospects before you meet them, so that you only meet the ones who are worth the effort. This screening process involves reading profiles carefully, exchanging a series of e-mails, which can run from days to weeks, and having at least one and perhaps two phone conversations. If your prospect gets through these steps, then your chances of having a successful meeting are substantially greater. Furthermore, you don't have to worry about your personal safety as much if you know more about someone before you give up your anonymity, which usually occurs when you first meet.

# Sending the Wrong E-mail to the Wrong Person

Oops! I meant to write Jane123 not Jane345. Internet dating starts out with a flurry of e-mails that are fast and frenzied and to many prospects at the same time. A bit like direct mail advertising, you never know who will respond. Getting mixed up with several parallel e-mail exchanges is very easy unless you keep good records (and it's not 3 a.m. after a few drinks from an unsuccessful date). Unfortunately, we know of virtually no recovery from a misdirected message. Even though no one should be offended at this early stage, they usually are. Fortunately, you have more fish to choose from in the sea. Just don't screw up with "the one."

# Mentioning That You Want to Marry in Your First E-mail

Need we say more? Okay, could you hold off until the second e-mail? This faux pas applies not only to offers of marriage but also to vows of eternal love, declarations that they're the perfect mate, or even offers to date exclusively. You get the idea.

# Shying Away from Asking Your Prospect Important Questions

If you lob only easy questions in your e-mail exchanges, you'll end up meeting a lot of people who

✔ You know nothing about

✔ You wouldn't be meeting in the first place had you screened better early on

Remember that Internet dating gives you the advantage of finding out information about your prospect before you even commit to meeting him or her in person and giving up your anonymity. If you waste the advantage, you are on a semi-blind date.

# Never Being Satisfied with Anybody

Internet dating exposes you to a never-ending supply of fresh prospects. In your former life (before Internet dating), you had limits, but now those limits appear gone. Many people have trouble pausing long enough with one prospect to find out if they have a potential keeper. Try to remember that if you believe you have infinite choices, you need an infinite time to check them all. Better to work on defining what you're looking for in a partner and when one seems to meet those criteria, stay off line and focus on that prospect.

# Chapter 22

# Ten Ways to Succeed at Online Dating

**In This Chapter**

▶ Meeting the person of your dreams from the comfort of home

▶ Putting online dating in perspective

*A*ny activity that has at least 20 million participants must be a mainstream activity if not a social movement, right? So although many people have tried Internet dating, not all are getting its full benefit. In this chapter, we give you ten key elements on how to get the best online-dating experience.

## Starting with a Positive Attitude

Although Internet dating may have started with computer nerds in chat rooms way back when Al Gore invented the Internet, those days are long gone. If you're still stuck with perceptions of those bygone days, give yourself a slap (or ask a bystander to do so) and snap out of it. The best way to meeting people is passing you by. Special note to those people who didn't grow up with a computer mouse in one hand and a baby rattle in the other: Be grateful that you're single in a time when Internet dating came of age.

## Beginning Slow and Gaining Momentum

Face it. You're probably a novice with online dating just as much as you were with every other new experience. Give yourself time to figure it out. Specifically, if you fall in love in the first week or first month of online dating, you are either darn lucky or deluding yourself.

# Avoiding Discussion of Your Previous Relationship Woes

When you talk about past troubles, you come across as a negative person. When you have the same discussion on e-mail, rather than in person, you come across even more negative, and you don't have the eye contact to know when you've gone overboard. Save these discussions for a more advanced stage of your relationship.

# Writing an Essay That Reflects You

Remember that you're trying to attract an *appropriate* match. If you write something that describes what you want to be rather than who you really are, you're sure to disappoint your prospective match, sooner or later. If you have someone help you write your essays, use them only to critique your work and encourage you. If someone else writes your essay, you may as well send him or her on your dates.

# Remembering the Number of Psychos on the Internet Reflects Real Life

The Internet is a microcosm of society, not a separate branch. Just as you may meet at a bar, Laundromat, or hardware store, "crazy" people lurk on the Internet, too. But certainly, no more and no less. Most of the horror stories about online dating are media hype looking for something titillating to fill the space between ads. The fact is that the power of anonymity unique to online dating gives you increased security over face-to-face dating, if you take care to guard that special power.

# Not Taking Each Internet Contact Too Seriously

You're going to get rejected from time to time, but remember what little emotional investment you have while you're still in the e-mail exchange phase. On the other extreme, take care not to become too enamored with a prospect's photo and initial e-mail exchanges. Hold you emotional fire until you have some face time.

# Resting from Time to Time

Even if you bought a six-month's subscription, don't plan to become a dating demon by being online without a break in the action. Having too many choices or too many unsuccessful contacts can make your brain glaze over, and you may lose your will to date. The reason you bought the six-month subscription is that the lower price allowed you to take several pauses ever few weeks.

# Reconsidering Your Non-Negotiable Criteria

Online dating is unique because it immediately allows you to select made-to-order prospects with the exact height, weight, and eye color you desire. If you're finding that prospects with these perfect match physical standards are less than perfect personality matches, reconsider your *must-have* criteria.

# Posting a Photo Immediately

Your profile is just a bunch of words without a photo, and most people only respond or search for those profiles with photos. So in the end, if you're serious about online dating, post a photo. Don't let opportunities (great prospects) pass you by. Post your photo as soon as you sign up to a dating service.

# Knowing When to Hold 'em and When to Fold 'em

In the e-mail exchange part of online dating, you may find yourself having superb banter, when suddenly you come across a roadblock, such as a discovery about your prospect that makes him/her an inappropriate match (like allergies to pets or small children). Trust your instincts; stop wasting time.

# Index

# Notes

# date.com
# FREE Trial Membership!

# Get a **FREE** month on JDate®.com

## *The #1 Jewish Dating Website*

To take advantage of this special offer, register at www.jdate.com
and buy a three-month subscription, then mail in this completed
coupon and you'll get a fourth month of JDate Free!

JDate member #: _____

Email address: _____

Clip & Mail this Coupon to **JDate Special Offers**
**8383 Wilshire Blvd., Suite 800**
**Beverly Hills, CA 90211**

No photocopies of this coupon accepted; one offer per customer. Expires June 30, 2005

---

## Get a **FREE** Month on

# AmericanSingles®.com

To take advantage of this special offer, register at
www.americansingles.com and buy a one-month
subscription, then mail in this completed coupon
and you'll get a second month FREE!

AmericanSingles member #: _____

Email address: _____

Clip & Mail this Coupon to **AmericanSingles.com**
**8383 Wilshire Blvd., Suite 800**
**Beverly Hills, CA 90211**

No photocopies of this coupon accepted; one offer per customer. Expires June 30, 2005

# ALWAYS TALK TO STRANGERS.

**Visit lavalife.com or call 1-866-242-LAVA to meet thousands of other singles.**

# Get in the game.

## Try Match.com for 10 days. FREE!

Ready to put your learning to the test? Check out all of the great singles on Match.com, then send email and instant messages to them FREE for 10 days.

Go to www.match.com/getstarted and take advantage of this free trial!

## match.com

Save 25% and things happen.

Fold on line "A", then fold back lines "B" and "C".     B     A     C

Made in the USA
Lexington, KY
05 December 2017